KENNETH, THIRD LORD DUFFUS

THE TARTANS

of the

CLANS AND FAMILIES
OF SCOTLAND

By

Sir THOMAS INNES OF LEARNEY

LORD LYON KING OF ARMS
K.C.V.O., ADVOCATE

FIFTH EDITION

1950
W. & A. K. JOHNSTON LIMITED
EDINBURGH AND LONDON

First Published December 1938
Second Edition 1945
Third Edition 1947
Fourth Edition 1948
Reprinted 1949
Fifth Edition 1950

PRINTED IN GREAT BRITAIN BY W. & A. K. JOHNSTON LIMITED, EDINBURGH

CONTENTS

iii

Contents

The above " District " tartans are examples of tartans worn by those connected with territories, but not associated with any clan. The " Jacobite" tartan formerly borne by adherents of the House of Stuart is now appropriate to any of the lieges of our reigning Sovereign, who is the Heir by Tanistry of the ancestral dynasties of our unbroken line of Kings of the Picts and Scots, emerging as High Chiefs from the romantic mists of primeval Caledonian annals.

A full list of Septs and Dependent s will be found in W. & A. K. Johnston's pocket-tartan-books, *Scottish Clans and Their Tartans*, and *The Scottish Tartans*, so it has seemed unnecessary to repeat the list in this volume.

THE SCOTTISH CLAN SYSTEM.

HERE are few Scottish institutions which remain subjects of such unfailing interest as the Clan System which has projected into the twentieth-century world the simple but impressive tribal ideals of primitive civilisation. In no other country have these survived as they have in Scotland, or so powerfully influenced the development of the social system of a kingdom. Whilst, however, armorial bearings and heraldry have, during centuries, received the attentive investigation of experts and accredited government departments, clanship and what has for the past two centuries become the popular outward evidence thereof, the tartan, have been relegated to a relatively trifling section of serious heraldic literature, and largely left to amateur exposition. The subject has accordingly been the victim of an amazing amount of loose thinking, ignorance of contemporary law and custom, and haphazard imagination, which is not only at variance with historical and legal facts and scientific research, but has indeed made the subject of clans and tartans, however interesting, one on which the serious genealogist and historian has latterly become almost apologetic, and the whole subject has been regarded as pertaining rather to the souvenir-shop than to the scientist. This attitude has been fostered from our institutional law writers, and the almost complete neglect of our native Picto-Celtic laws, though prior to the eighteenth-century clanship was treated seriously by the Scottish Parliament as it always has been by the Court of the Lord Lyon, and in the administration of the Scottish Law of Arms.

Since the Lord Lyon's jurisdiction comprehends "all badges and cognisances whatsoever borne and used," and his duties in particular have reference to (a) Family and community genealogies,[1] (b) The

---

[1] The Law Officers of the Crown have expressed the opinion that " the heralds " (i.e. the College of Arms in Chapter) have an original jurisdiction in matters of pedigree (A. C. Fox-Davies, Right to Bear Arms, p. 108), and the Lord Lyon King of Arms' earliest official declaration upon the duties of his office asserts that preservation and record of genealogies was the original inherent and pre-armorial duty of his office (Innes of that Ilk birthbrief, 1698, Familie of Innes, 46), and his certificates " were conclusive."

armorial insignia of the leaders holding high military or civil jurisdiction throughout the realm,[1] the clan and its leaders were amongst
the communities and persons with whom the Lord Lyon *inter alia*
was specially concerned.   Indeed, much of the business which renders
the Lyon Office such a popular Department of State, and most of the
recent Lyon Court litigations, have been directly or indirectly concerned with aspects of the clan system which, for example, could hardly
have arisen in the College of Arms in England ; indeed, *Scottish heraldry
has been considered and treated as inseparable from the subject of clanship.*[2]
It is a point of striking constitutional importance since Scotland
possesses a *Court of the Law of Arms,* and a Government Department,
under statutory as well as Customary Law regulation, operating the
Law of Arms, that this, from the earliest stage in which we can trace
its functions, has been concerned not merely with a narrow noble
caste, but with phases of the clan system, and this fact has given the
department of the Lord Lyon King of Arms a national importance and
immediate interest to the whole people, not only in Scotland but of
Scottish descent throughout the world.[3]

When and how far our picturesque and peculiarly Scottish clan and
family tartans came to have their present significance, as badges of
racial identity, is a matter of controversy, but they are *now* unquestion-
ably definite " cognisances " of that character, and have been regarded
as such for approximately two centuries.   They are the complement
of armorial bearings, badges, and standards of chiefs and leaders,
and it is proper that the subject of tartans and of clanship should be
treated seriously as the broad basis of the Scottish system of tribal
cognisance, of which badges and heraldry are the higher and more
specialised sphere, and the Royal Arms the pyramidal apex.   W. F.
Skene, the Historiographer Royal, dealt, as a pioneer, with the polity
of Celtic Scotland.   Miss I. F. Grant has recently done much to explain
its economic features.   Dr J. Cameron has recently treated of early
Celtic Law.   It accordingly seems desirable, in presenting—at the
desire of Messrs W. & A. K. Johnston—a somewhat larger collection
of Scottish tartans, to give a practical survey of clanship, and the
clan as a social and legal entity in modern Scotland.   The historical

[1] Nisbet's *Heraldry,* i. 6 ; Fox-Davies, *Art of Heraldry,* 10 ; T. Innes of Learney, *Scots
Heraldry,* p. 14.
[2] Sir Æneas Macpherson, Advocate, *Loyall Dissuasive,* 49, 63, 72 ; Nisbet, I. 268, 425 ;
II. iv. 22 ; Sir Geo. Mackenzie, *Works,* II. 618, line 17 ; 633, line 12 ; G. Seton, *Law and
Practice of Heraldry,* 1863, p. 9 ; J. H. Stevenson, *Heraldry in Scotland,* 207, 218, 323 ;
J. Dallaway, *Heraldic Enquiries,* p. 197.
[3] In the Lord Lyon's jurisdiction over *Change of Name* (Lyon Court Act, 1867, Sch. B. ;
Forlong, 7 Rettie, 910; *Clan Gregor Act,* 1775, cap. 29 ; *Statutes at Large,* XII. 299), the
Lyon Court yearly entertains far more numerous petitions regarding Change of Name from
all ranks than it does petitions regarding Genealogies and Armorial Bearings, which are
confined to the chiefs and *duine-uasail,* though of course under the Scottish social system
the latter and their honours are a matter of immediate interest to every member of the clan
or name (Innes of Learney, *Scots Heraldry,* p. 2).

accounts of the clans and families, although based on those of Messrs W. & A. K. Johnston's previous works, have been, so far as circumstances admit, revised, and include matter of fresh interest; whilst, as is usual in the Peerages and Baronetages, the arms of the chief or chieftain (where registered) appear at the top of each article,[1] as befits the close connection between heraldry, tartan, and clanship, and the list is not confined to Highland tartans, but includes those which now distinguish the great Lowland [2] surnames.[3]

Even if a number of these tartans are no older than the Royal Visit of George IV., they are nowadays definite racial cognisances, and it would be mere snobbery to neglect them because all of them are not old.[4] The relationship of clanship to feudalism, which has been much misunderstood, is also one which, if clanship is to take its proper share in the Scotland of the future, requires to be more clearly appreciated. Indeed, but for Feudalism, we should have had no Clans to-day, probably no " clans " at all, as we Scotsmen understand the term.

" The Clan was a hybrid institution, a mixture of tribal tradition clustering about the *ipso facto* landholder of the soil, whether he held possession by feudal charter, lease or feu, or mere sword-right[5] and the chiefs, largely because of the inefficiency of the central authorities, continued to fulfil the functions of the tribal leader." [6]

Central authorities are often more than "inefficient"—their influence becomes disastrous to local life and custom. It was just because the Feudo-Celtic system proved the ideal machinery for perpetuating the "functions of the tribal leader" and the *spirit of the tribe*, that " clanship " developed in Scotland instead of tribalism being destroyed as in most other lands.

It has been suggested that there was this fundamental distinction between clanship and feudalism, that under clanship possession of land and influence depended upon pedigree, whilst under feudalism possession of influence depended upon the possession of land. What is overlooked is, that under the Feudal System possession of the land, to which power and influence were annexed, depended upon pedigree, just as much as under the pre-Feudal Celtic régime. The real distinction was, that the pedigree, or alteration of pedigree, depended, under feudalism,[7] on a charter from the " immediate lawful

---

[1] A number of these arms are reproduced by courtesy of *Burke's Peerage and Baronetage*, *Debrett's Peerage and Baronetage*, and *Burke's Landed Gentry*. Clansmen should appreciate that these publications are often of immediate interest to themselves as containing, at considerable length, the lineage of their chiefs and chieftains, whereas the present book supplies a brief sketch history of the clan or name as a community.

[2] I am of course not suggesting that " Borderers " went about in the kilt. On the West march and in Galloway they may have done so, but not in, *e.g.*, the Merse.

[3] The families of the Lowlands and the Border and also " Highland Clans " (*Privy Seal*, II. No. 790) were often designated by the term " Name " or " Surname." *Cf. Chef du nom et d'armes*, of heraldic law.   [4] *Cf.* Fox-Davies, *Heraldry Explained*, p. 17.

[5] If Miss Grant means without written title, I should define this as allodial *duthus*-tenure for *servitium Scoticana* to the *Ard Righ*.   [6] I. F. Grant, *Lordship of the Isles*, 327.

[7] Each feudal lord was *chef de famille* over his fief, or " house " *cf. tigh-airn*, thus " feudalism "—the " development of the family "—*was* organised clanship.

superior," and ultimately the Crown; whereas, under the clan system, the pedigree depended on vague and frequently differing systems of tribal custom, and, apart from occasional intervention by the *Ard Righ*, who thus already exercised as chief the functions of a feudal superior, there was no definite body of law or hierarchy of power with an obligation—let alone means of enforcing it—to secure the continuity and organisation necessary for developing civilisation.[1] In the Anglo-Saxon polity of England there was not even the binding sentimental tie of Celtic tribalism, nor any sense of Celto-Pictish heredity or permanence.[2] In Scotland feudalism provided the framework upon which the clan system was built into a permanent structure in the realm, which has enabled it to survive down to the present, and which for long prevented the pure commercialisation of land. The full value of land cannot be enjoyed by those who merely look to it bestially as a means of subsistence. The aspect in which it provides the highest enjoyment is that in which it represents the ancestral home of the race. That involves concentration of interest more intensely upon a smaller area—the sacred home of a tribe or branch.

It is this intensity of tribe-affection for even a poor and barren inheritance, which is immediately evident on entering Scotland. This is of the essence of Clanship—the tribe and *its* soil—but with the subdivision into still more individual but equally sacred holdings. Not only in secular, but likewise in sacred affairs, the intense appreciation of continuance and heredity is evinced in the hereditary character of the Celtic Church, with its married priesthood and lines of hereditary Abbots.[3] It is this all-pervading sense of racial continuity, running through all our institutions, which gives the key to Scottish civilisation. Moreover, it is the subsistence of that continuity as a still vital force that strikes an appeal to the deepest instincts of human nature, and gives our institutions their unfailing interest, charm, or, if you will, "romance"—not only to Scots themselves, but to all who pause to consider what "Scotland" stands for in the story of the Nations.

There is sometimes a tendency to emphasise an idea of cleavage between the Highlands and the Lowlands of Scotland. Distinguished critics, such as the Hon. Lord Mackay, Sir John Lorne Macleod, G.B.E., and the late Professor Sayce, amongst others, have protested against this relegation of Celtic influence to a small section of the country, which some would whittle down even further, whilst Sassenachs endeavour to devitalise the "Garb of Old Gaul" by eliminating its native gaiety and ornaments.[4] That a distinction existed between

---

[1] Jas. Hogan, *The Irish Law of Kingship*, Proceedings of Royal Irish Academy, 1932.
[2] A. E. F. Jolliffe, *Constitutional History of England*, pp. 1–100.
[3] They were not "lay" Abbots, as uninformed persons think, *v. Highland Papers*, I., 85.
[4] Comment in *Scots Heraldry*, p. 132; *Scotland before 1700*, pp. 43 54 166.

the Highlands and the Lowlands has long been recognised, but according to the records of an American statistician [1] and as one of our most painstaking modern Scottish historians [2] has pointed out, the division falls considerably beyond the "Highland line" as supposed by nineteenth-century writers. It was by no accident that the Firth of Forth was called "The Scottish Sea" and that Northern Scots in early times referred to Fife and Lothian as distinct from "Caledonia." The distinction of race and customs, as well as social characteristics, runs in a diagonal line through the Ochils rather than along the Grampians, and includes Renfrew and Galloway, both distinctly "Highland" [3] as compared with Lothian and the Merse; whilst in 1385 when the King of Scots was at Stirling, Edinburgh people referred to him as being "in the Highlands." [4]

I pointed out in *The Clan Divisions of North-Eastern Scotland* [5]

Achievement of Skene of Skene, from the sundial at Skene House, 1736.

that the North-East of Scotland, [6] comprehending the ancient Celtic Mormaerships of Mar, Moray and Buchan, [7] is the area from which much of our information regarding Highland garb and customs has been drawn, including the evidence which refutes the wretched story that the *feile-beag* or kilt was invented by an Anglo-Saxon engineer, "Major Rawlinson" [8]; and it would have been unnecessary for the Burgesses of Aberdeen to issue prohibitions against the wearing of

---

[1] *Scientific American*, May 1931, p. 312 :—" Cephalic Index of the Breadth of Heads of living Europeans."   [2] I. F. Grant, *Social and Economic Development of Scotland*, 483.

[3] *Romantic Story of Highland Garb and Tartan*, p. 36.

[4] Hume Brown, *Early Travellers*, p. 10.

[5] *Scottish Notes and Queries*, Sept. 1931 ; *Braemar Gathering Year-Book*, 1933.

[6] The prominent part taken by this area both in the *War of Independence* (Evan M. Barron), and in the Jacobite Risings (A. and H. Tayler, *Jacobites of Aberdeenshire and Banffshire*), has never been appreciated by Southern historians.

[7] This district, though hereditarily Gaelic (*e.g. Book of Deer*), for dynastic reasons only was in opposition to the Bruce.

[8] *E.g.*, the armorial bearings of Skene of Skene, J. G. Mackay, *The Romantic Story of the Highland Garb and Tartan*, 69. Rawlinson was a *Quaker*, not a Major ! and engaged in iron-smelting at Invergarry, 1727–31.

tartan and plaids by citizens of Bon Accord,[1] had there not been a strong tendency for both men and women to adopt Highland garb,[2] and had these not been the accustomed wear in the neighbourhood. Perhaps the earliest post-mediæval representation of the *feile-beag* [3] is, indeed, that in Gordon of Rothiemay's map of the City of Aberdeen, 1661,[4] and his evidence is not confined to his illustration, for he describes the garment as "folded all round the body about the region of the belt,"[5] whilst both James Brome, 1669, and Captain Slezer, 1693, regarded Elgin as a Highland city.[6] Similarly, Sir William Wallace wore an Ersche mantill,[7] that is, a tartan plaid, at Dundee.

During recent years a subject which has been hotly debated [8] is, whether clan tartans as such are an ancient institution, or an invention of Stewart of Garth and Sir Walter Scott.[9]   The late J. G. Mackay, like Lord Archibald Campbell, claimed that clan tartans were not only deliberately arranged, but formed an elaborate system of identification by dress, as technical as armorial bearings,[10] whilst Col. Haldane, following the late Campbell of Islay, deduces that they "date at the earliest from the raising of the clan regiments, and that the great bulk of them is not more than 150 years old."   The truth appears to lie between those extreme statements, for tartans were never intended to, and did not, have the precise distinctions and ready recognisability of armorial bearings.[11]   Mr Mackay gives much interesting information regarding the manufacture of tartan, and the manner in which the changes were rung upon the basic sett of a Highland Chief; he does not, however, succeed in adducing evidence that there was a scientific system of arrangement, and circumstances are against the existence of a *science*. Equally, Col. Haldane fails to show that the absence of such a system is inconsistent with the existence both of clan and district designs.   I am afraid his article falls under the scope of those, stigmatised by

[1] Haldane suggests that this merely shows that tartan "had no special significance as the cognisance of the Highlanders." The whole North of Scotland was, however, essentially "Highland,"—even Fife, *vide* the "Law Clan Macduff."

[2] *Extracts of the Council Register of Aberdeen*, II., 27, 373. By a Council statute of 1576, burgesses and deacons were forbidden to wear plaids, which if worn were to be forfeited to the City Hospital. Again, in 1621, the Council dealt with the "Uncivil form of behaviour" of a great many women in the burgh, "of gude qualitie, quha resorts both to kirk and market with their plaids about their heads and by their example the meaner sort of women uses the same form of uncivility."

[3] For early examples of kilts, see the figures on the Shrine of St Machan.

[4] *Romantic Story of the Highland Garb and Tartan*, 77.

[5] *History of Scots Affairs*, App. p. xliii. It is also described as a "petticoat," and by 1639 likened to the "bases" (16th century military skirt worn with armour) shaped just like a kilt, *see* H. Norris, *Costume and Fashion*, iii, 36.

[6] *Scottish Notes and Queries*, Feb. 1931, p. 25.   [7] Blind Harry's *Wallace*.

[8] The best summary of the History of Tartan is the Introduction to D. W. Stewart's *Old Rare and Scottish Tartans*.

[9] Lieut.-Col. M. M. Haldane, "The Great Clan Tartan Myth," *Scots Magazine*, Sept., Oct., Nov., 1931.   [10] *Romantic Story of the Highland Garb and Tartan*.

[11] No more can one believe that floral badges would be of any value as cognisances in battle. They are probably symbolic flowers, as the *Thistle* is of Scotland, or tribal charm-plants (*Antiquity*, XX., 42). Some of the alleged badge-plants do not even grow in Scotland. As *cognisances* the conventionalised plant-badge is well known to heraldic law.

Mr Mackay as assertions that "the Highland dress as now worn is of modern design," and that "tartans, as distinctive clan patterns, are of recent date," which appeared in *The Scots Magazine*, 1785.[1] An attempt was at that time, as on several occasions since, being made to have the wearing of the dress by Highland regiments discontinued, and the 1785 article was written "with the intention of discrediting the dress as a national garb."

Much of Col. Haldane's argument is based upon the Black Watch tartan, and its supposed similarity to, or distinction from, those of Campbell, Forbes, Gordon, Sutherland, etc. There is little doubt that the Black Watch tartan was a deliberately invented one, variations of which were subsequently adopted by certain clans in place of, or in addition to, earlier (usually bright) tartans associated with their clans or districts.[2] The "Royal Stewart" tartan is described by Haldane as "Garth's second dilemma," for he says that either this tartan was not connected with the House of Stewart, or else its use by the pipers of a Hanoverian regiment was impossible. It is significant that what Garth really said was, that the pipers always wore *Royal,* or Stewart tartan, and if this tartan, which King George V recently described as "My personal tartan," was in origin "The Royal" tartan, and only incidentally "Stewart" tartan, there was no inconsistency in its use by the pipers of a Hanoverian regiment. It may well be the "hieland tartan" of which 3 ells were required in August 1538, to make "The King's Grace's trews," and with which it is interesting to note that His Grace wore a coloured velvet "hieland coat" lined with green. If, then, this be the *Royal tartan,* Haldane's comments are disposed of, and it becomes obvious why George II. used it for his pipers, instead of equipping them in the regimental Black Watch sett. With these reasonable explanations, Garth's statements upon the subjects of tartans in general appear to be thoroughly vindicated. Haldane's comment is :—

"They only prove the prevalence of favoured setts in certain districts; the prevalence of peculiar fashions is common enough in many districts, in many lands. The only special characteristic of the Highlands in this respect is that the districts in question seem to have been generally very restricted."

What strikes him as trivial is precisely the aspect in which the Scottish system of civilisation has differed from that of other lands,

---

[1] *Romantic Story of the Highland Garb and Tartan,* p. 27. The writer may observe that it was his grandfather, Col. Innes of Learney, C.V.O., who, overcoming War Office opposition, secured the kilt for the Royal Aberdeenshire Highlanders (now 3rd Battalion Gordons).

[2] The old Campbell ("dress") tartan was evidently red (*Memoirs of a Highland Lady,* p. 257, Records of Argyle, p. 437). Forbeses and Gordons wore the Huntly district tartan. There is what appears to be a red Mackenzie plaid at Messrs Anderson & Sons, 16 George Street, Edinburgh, and the Sutherland tartan worn by Lord Duffus was also fairly bright-coloured. The old *Gordon* tartan, a bright sett in red and green, with overchecks of yellow and black, is preserved in the portrait at Abergeldie Castle of the chieftainess, Rachel Gordon of Abergeldie.

and one which goes to the root of our national character and social evolution.[1] In his ninth head he observes :—

> " It is clear that tartans of well-recognised sett were woven in every district of the Highlands, and probably varied not only from island to island, but from clan to clan. In some places there might be only one sett in common use ; in another several. It might thus be easy to distinguish a Kintail man from one of Glenmoriston or Glenelg, but it would not necessarily follow that the sett or setts prevalent in Kintail would be the same as those in Gairloch or Strathconan, although all three were Mackenzie lands. Mackenzies, Maclennans and Macraes might use indifferently the setts prevalent in Kintail, whereas about Ullapool, Mackenzies and Macleods might equally indifferently be using quite other setts that happened for the time being to be in fashion in that district. Some setts such as Lennox, Atholl, and Huntly, have retained their district names, even until this day, but there is no doubt that there must have been many now known by clan names, that were formerly thus associated . . . It no doubt began to be assumed that the district tartans were used by the clan that lived in them."

There is something to be said for parts of this, but a great deal to be said for his last sentence, for Fraser of Reelig observes : [2]—

> " By the sixteenth century clan territories occupied by the different clans had become more or less defined and it is reasonable to suppose that some of the patterns originally common to these territories had become accepted as one of the distinguishing marks of the clan then in possession,[3] but, most important, he says ' that district and clan setts continued side by side ' and that ' such patterns of tartan as were recognised could shew great variation in detail ' but this ' does not necessarily prove that distinctive tartans were rare.'"

The clans clung tenaciously to both their native districts [4] and their patriarchal customs, and the weavers of one clan were unlikely to be the weavers of another even where the population was mixed, but a clan or sept would often take its favourite pattern along with it. Most Highland wives made their own and their husband's plaids.[5] Whilst a clan might be hereditary in theory, it was, as often as not, at any rate in part, synthetically created in a district,[6] and whilst one influence would be to encourage the use of a single tartan, there would be a strong tendency for the original clan or district setts to be perpetuated, when these would be represented as " sept setts." We can hardly doubt that the Chiefs of " Bow o' Meal Gordons," [7] Grants in Strathspey and Frasers in Inverness-shire, must have found that to cover their clansmen with a garb of roughly similar design was as useful in clan-founding as to unite them under a common surname, though the tendency was rather to insist upon a similarity of general hue than on similarity of detail.[8] On the other hand, " septs " could be " absorbed," and a " clan surname " imposed, but there would often be those who would say : " This is no' my plaid, bonnie though the

[1] *Juridical Review*, March 1933, p. 14.   [2] *Some Notes on Highland Tartans.*
[3] Miss I. F. Grant points out that *Clan Maps* are not to be regarded as " watertight " divisions : there was much superimposition of clan upon clan.
[4] *Social and Economic Development*, p. 524.   [5] *Memoirs of a Highland Lady*, p. 27.
[6] *Social and Economic Development of Scotland*, 479.
[7] Alexr. Smith, *New History of Aberdeenshire*, p. 307.
[8] Haldane admits this at p. 141. People seem unaware that, even with modern weaving machinery, precision of pattern is seldom more than approximate, owing to variation of thread-thickness.

colours be"; and there old district or "sept" setts may survive as relics of the absorbed race. Both Reelig and Haldane agree as to the concurrent use of *Clan* and *District* setts, but a remarkable feature of eighteenth-century illustrations is that they so frequently depict the doublet, plaid, or upper garment as a different tartan from the trews or *feile-beag*. Indeed, it appears to have been the practice to wear the plaid of personal or "clan" tartan, and trews or other lower garment of the "district" tartan, though precisely "which was what" would no doubt be a very involved question ; the point is that the variety of the dress enabled the inhabitants of each locality to conform to the predominant local (district) or (synthetic) clan sett without abandoning their personal (patriarchal) clan or (sept) sett. Even in modern Highland dress such combination can be most effective, and a variety of the custom, based no doubt on the tradition of wearing two tartans still prevalent in some parts of the Highlands, is to have a plaid of the mother's tartan.

No doubt it was not until about the eighteenth century that the clan tartans became *conscious* and *acknowledged* badges of identification. But that is not to say that they had not actually *been* badges of identification for a period, nay, it implies that they *must* necessarily have been so ; for we do not recognise institutions while they are growing, but only realise them when they are, or have become, an accomplished fact. We may be sure that neither clan nor district tartans were originally invented as such. No one in the Middle Ages "patented the clan tartan idea" ; it arose naturally, and developed gradually, and was no doubt only consciously realised a generation before its proscription. This identity-conception revived with renewed energy when that proscription was withdrawn.

In certain cases, however, the tribal significance of tartan was appreciated as early as the commencement of the seventeenth century, as illustrated by a letter from Sir Robert Gordon of Gordonstoun, then Tutor of Sutherland, to Murray of Pulrossie [1] in 1618,

" requesting him to furl his pennon when the Earl of Sutherland's banner was displayed and *to remove the red and white lines from the plaides of his men so as to bring their dress into harmony with that of the other septs.*"

This not only illustrates the close relation of heraldry to clanship [2] but that the tartan had by then a clan-significance. It would seem

---

[1] Letter by D. Murray Rose in *Northern Chronicle,* quoted by J. H. Stevenson, K.C., in *Macrae v. Macrae,* 1909, Lyon Court, typs. p. 167.

[2] The " pennon " would be the standard or rallying-flag displayed by Pulrossie as Chief of the Sutherlandshire Murrays. Pulrossie, as a " branch Chief," thus " challenged forth " a pennon. According to the ordinary Law of Arms, there was nothing to prevent him displaying a pennon, if he had been " allowed " it by Lyon. The Tutor, however, apparently thought, as high-commander in the field, that he had such a power. Very likely he was endeavouring to suppress chiefly and chieftainly insignia in general, owing to Sutherland being bound by Huntly to remain a Gordon cadet. He similarly advised the young Earl to endeavour to suppress Mackay's " pincell " and the highland dress.

that the Gordon Earls of Sutherland [1] had already adopted the "modern" dark tartan, and designed to obliterate the bright stripes of the older tartans, and also, no doubt, to eliminate so far as possible traces of the older tribal divisions, and to bring all their followers under the immediate sway of the Earls. [2]

The matter, however, has an even greater significance, for the Murrays and Sutherlands were of similar origin, and if they were (as it appears) both wearing a dark-based tartan with red-and-white overcheck—and Pulrossie's tartan was evidently very like what is known as "Sutherland-ancient"—then the parent check must have dated back to the twelfth or thirteenth century. This indeed may seem indicated from the sett termed "Murray of Atholl," which has a similar hue of background with a red overstripe while the Northern Murrays evidently had red and white. It looks as if Murray, Murray-of-Atholl and Sutherland-ancient had a common origin in a sett basically used in the *de Moravia* tribe from the twelfth century. It was no doubt " the Murrays' tartan " without being consciously " *The* Murray tartan," but—as the illusion to that other " cognisaunce "—the pennon—shows us—it had a definite significance by 1618.

There has been speculation as to what tartan the Gordons wore prior to the institution of the Regimental sett. There is fortunately evidence of this, hitherto unnoticed, in the portrait of Rachel Gordon of Abergeldie. [3] Her plaid is of bright red-and-green tartan with narrow yellow and black stripes, with what seems a pale purple between these. It is not " Huntly," but has a similar bright character, which one would expect in the tartan of a powerful clan such as the Gordons of the North-East.

Whilst much scorn has been hurled at " Lowland tartans," and, in so far as the *Vestiarium* is concerned, rightly so, we have to recollect that (1) As already pointed out, the term " Lowland " meant little more than Merse and Lothian. (2) Sir Walter Scott, who has been charged with " tartanising " the Lowlands, stated what is no doubt accurate :—

" The general proposition that Lowlanders ever wore plaids is difficult to swallow . . . I have been told, and believed until now, that the use of tartans was never general in Scotland (Lowland), *until the Union*, with the detestation of that measure, led it to be adopted as *the national colour*, and the ladies all affected tartan screens."

No doubt the " Jacobite " (political) tartan and a number of older Lowland tartans were invented at this time, and it is noticeable that the Royal Company of Archers (a " National " body) adopted tartan in

---

[1] Who on account of not taking the *name* were not regarded as Chiefs of the Sutherlands (*Loyall Dissuasive*, 35).

[2] For Gordonstoun's policy, see Sir W. Fraser, *The Sutherland Book*, II., 351, 358, 359.

[3] The Laird of Abergeldie has kindly allowed me to examine the detail of this, illustrated (J. Stirton, *Crathie and Braemar*, 98).

1713–15—long before any of the " Highland " Regiments were raised.[1] At the time of the Union, patriotic Scots regarded tartan as the *National garb.*

The circumstances and the patriotism, which moved Scotsmen and, perhaps even more, Scotswomen[2] to extend the Celtic garb even to some of the older and better known of the Lowland " surnames," appear to deserve the benefit of Col. Haldane's admission that :—

" The present attribution of setts to Highland clans and families is, however, old enough by now to deserve all respect, since," he adds, " it grew out of a deep-seated desire to preserve the separate identity of the Highlanders."

According to Sir Walter, the use of tartan, even in the Lowlands (and by the Royal Archers and the ladies of the capital), arose out of a " deep-seated desire to preserve the identity of " Scotland and its characteristics. That is a desire which would be acknowledged by most to be one " deserving of all respect," and if Garth and Scott were, as Haldane would have it, " dreamers of dreams who out of a (*not* so fabulous !) story fashion a nation's glory," we recognise to-day that, but for those visionaries who could see both the Scotland of the past and a Scotland of the future— but at all events Scotland as a national entity—Scotland to-day would have been as shadowy a name as *Mercia, Bernicia,* or the other lost kingdoms of the Heptarchy.

Archery Medal of Alexander Macleod of Muiravonside, 1735.

Whilst Edinburgh is the administrative capital, the *Moot Hill of Scone* is the constitutional centre of Scotland, and the Court *in* Edinburgh is after all but the Court *from* Scone. Our Scottish Monarchy is a Celtic one, and whilst the old district garb in the provinces of Fife and Lothian was (with some exceptions) no doubt the hodden grey, blue bonnet,[3] and Shepherd check, the tartan holds sway as the characteristic *national garb* of the greatest area, the most ancient, sovereign portion, and the most distinctive part of the Kingdom, and

[1] It was not until towards the middle of the nineteenth century that the Royal Archers, whose ancient and historic garb had been the tartan, succumbed to the notion that tartan was inappropriate to the " Lowlands," and substituted uniforms based on Lincoln Green and the English Gentlemen-at-Arms. The historic portraits on the walls of Archers' Hall, and Raeburn's celebrated " Nathaniel Spens " remain as evidence of the older Scottish attitude.

[2] It has been remarked that Scottish women have shown themselves throughout the ages more intensely patriotic than the men.

[3] The Scottish national headgear both in Highlands and Lowlands, *e.g.*, matriculation of Arms, *Highland and Agricultural Society*, Lyon Register, XXIX., 71.

therefore properly holds its own in the administrative capital. When Garth and Sir Walter brought the tartan to Holyroodhouse in 1822, they therefore instinctively did what was proper to be done, and had alike principle and precedent for its warrant.

The gallant tartan array of the Royal Archers in 1713, the tartan-sashed ladies of the capital in 1707-15, those like Miss Jean Rollo who wore her tartan gown in the Canongate, even after the proscription of 1746, and was consequently arrested,[1] and the verses of Allan Ramsay, all proclaim that, then as now, " the first of garbs . . . of such an antique date " [2] is the proper national garb of Scotland.[3]

In these circumstances I have not hesitated, at the public desire, to include a selection of Lowland tartans, and those which have for the past couple of centuries been associated with the Border clans. It is merely snobbery to jeer at certain tartans because they cannot be proved to be old. The only ground for derision would be if in any case it were attempted to suggest they are older than they can be proved to be. Since the national consciousness at the dawn of the eighteenth century recognised tartan as the national garb of Scotland, and as fulfilling a practical and outward visible badge of the spirit of kinship, found alike in Highland clan and Border name, such tartans are not to be ignored, though in South-Eastern Scotland it is in trews and plaid, rather than in the *philabeg*, that we should expect to find their owners using them.

In the development of Scotland, as Professor G. G. Coulton observed in delivering the Rhind lectures, 1931, the two most important features have been Tribality and Inheritance. Through every branch of Scottish administration or activity these can be traced. They have been the fundamental basis of the Clan system in the Highlands and the Surname system of the Lowlands ; they modified the system of Church government ; they formed the basis of the Parliament and Peerage of Scotland ; and the pinnacle beneath which they are united is the Crown.[4] Well did Sir Walter, in his panegyric upon the Royal Visit of 1822, exclaim of George IV. :—

" He is our kinsman. It is not too much to say that there is scarcely a gentleman of any of the old Scottish families who cannot ' count kin ' with the Royal House from

---

[1] *Scots Peerage*, VII., 203.

[2] Ramsay evidently did not regard tartans as a recent innovation, or inappropriate to the capital.

[3] The tartan was worn equally by men and women. The men's garb has evolved naturally with each century, but misunderstanding appears *now* to exist regarding women's Highland dress. At Highland Gatherings, little girls dressed in travesties of Highland male attire offend the eye and bring the National Garb into disrepute. The olden dress of Highland women was beautiful, so also were the tartan frocks of the eighteenth century (some of which were exhibited at the Inverness Highland Exhibition, 1930) ; but the tartan kirtle (light silken pleated skirt) worn with a simple corsage and Celtic embroidery, and with light silk *arisaid* fastened by a brooch, is again being worn in a suitably modified style, both for dancing and for social evening wear. This is pre-eminently the National dress for the women of Scotland, as historically correct as it is artistically charming.   [4] *Juridical Review*, XLIV., 122.

which our Sovereign is descended. In this small country blood has so intermingled that far the greater part of our burgesses and yeomen are entitled to entertain similar pretentions. In short, we are *the clan* and our King is *the Chief*. Let us remember that it is so ; and not only look towards him as a father but to each other as if we were, in the words of the old song, ' Ae man's bairns.' " [1]

Hardly is there a Scot to-day who cannot in some line of ancestry connect himself with the Royal line of Fergus Mor McEarc, and claim as a kinsman [2] Our Sovereign Lord, King George VI. This sense of kinship, the bond between the *Ard Righ Albann* and the great Peers and Chiefs, between these and the *duine-uasail*, and between the latter and the clan, has had the most far-reaching effect upon our Scottish civilisation ; for between the Peerage, the Houses of Chiefs and Chieftains, the Baronage, the Gudemen or lesser Lairds, and Tacksmen, it has been calculated that at the time of the Union there were (in a population of about a million) over ten thousand titled houses, each as proud and as nobly descended as any of the great Continental *noblesses*. Allowing for the expansion of even the near circle of these houses and lines of Chieftains, it follows that about 1 in each 45 people were actually members of a " titled or Chiefly house, and that about one-half of the Scottish nation consciously regarded themselves as members of the aristocracy." [3] Such a proportion is unknown in any other nation,[4] and the moral and social effect upon the Scottish nation has been incalculable. Under the clan system, the lines of Chiefs and Chieftains were regarded as pegs upon which hung the glory of the whole race or sept, and their pedigree, preserved by the clan bards and historians, was treasured as the common pride of all the descendants of their line. But in this system no attempt was made to found a noble-caste, public-school class, or snobbery of that description, and the younger members were expected by degrees to subside in an ever-extending pyramid into the *duine-uasail* and body of the clan, carrying with them through all ranks of the nation the pride and glory of lineage and achievement, and the sense of acknowledged blood-brotherhood upon either side, stretching throughout the whole gamut of the Caledonian social system.[5]

There are attributes which can only be perfected when inheritance is coupled with a favourable environment, and these highest social assets are not perfectly preserved beyond three or four generations, when separated from the conditions in which they flourish : hence the national importance of a steadily continuing but non-caste aristocracy which

---

[1] *Hints to the Inhabitants of Edinburgh*, 1822, p. 15.
[2] Erasmus observed of the Scots, that " Their habit is to make great boast of their birth, and to claim kindred with the Royal Family."
[3] Innes of Learney, *Scots Heraldry*, pp. 6, 148.
[4] An analogous condition did arise amongst the *noblesse* of Quebec Province (A. C. Despres, *Noblesses de France, et du Canada*, cap. II., III.).
[5] *Scots Heraldry*, pp. 6, 67, 139 ; *Scotland before 1700*, XII. ; *Social and Economic Development*, 19, 52, 81, 476, 516 559 ; Stewart of Garth, *Highlanders of Scotland*, 25, 50.

B

sets the style and character of a nation. Through the Celtic system, in whose lines of Chiefs, Chieftains, and Peers these attributes were developed, these benefits were, as by a refreshing stream, spread throughout the ranks of each clan and house. Thus it is that in Scotland no servile yokels of the rural English or Continental type are found in the Highland glens; and the clansmen reared in the crofts and cottages bore, and in most parts still carry with them, the old pride of race and of a glorious past. So it is that the clansman has so often risen, when chance or circumstance favoured,[1] from herding the kine in some peaceful Highland glen to take his place as an equal, and not as a *parvenu*, amongst the princes and the statesmen of the Continent, or has with calm and graceful confidence assumed the direction of vast enterprises throughout the Empire.

A recent critic [2] observes that :—

" It was only for a short time that there was a really strong and definite divergement between the Highlands and the Lowlands. It did not appear until fairly late, it was noticeable by the sixteenth century, and it began to die out even before the '45. It was a difference due merely to social and political conditions, for the various racial strains from which the Scottish people are drawn, are mingled in nearly equal quantities in both divisions of the country."

There is some truth in this, though it is overstated ; but as a comment on Professor Coulton's second Scottish national characteristic, viz., *Inheritance*, there is *much* truth in Dr Ramsay's other observation that " the ownership of land appeared to be their dominant passion." The extent of that passion and its primary attachment to a specific locality, rather than to the Realm as a whole, has not been realised by many recent authors.[3] Some have led themselves to imagine a fundamental cleavage between clanship and feudalism.[4] That is far from being the case. Feudalism was never imposed on Scotland. Scotland adopted the process of feudalism. Both Skene and Miss Grant suggest that there was something not far removed from it in existence shortly before the final feudalisation, but what we have to grasp is that a Celtic Scotland leapt at feudalism *because that feudalism appealed to the clamant passion of the nation to secure the principle of Inheritance and a Fixity of Tenure in their possessions and traditions.* Actually, the feudal system is, in

[1] *Memoirs of a Highland Lady*, p. 353 ; W. Wood, *Secret of Spey*, p. 176.
[2] A. W. Ramsay, *A Challenge to the Highlanders.*   [3] *Juridical Review*, XLV., p. 1.
[4] Miss Audrey Cunningham commences *The Loyal Clans* with these words, " The clan system in Scotland was an unusual combination of patriarchal and feudal institutions," but from this she proceeds to elaborate a theory that the two elements were incompatible. Writing in Cambridge and confessing neither local nor ancestral connection with the Highlands, her book is really an interesting example of the characteristic English antipathy to everything " feudal." She appears to suppose that, had " feudalism " been abolished in Scotland, as it was by Edward I. in England, the clan-system would have survived under a Napoleo-Tudoresque régime (p. 436), in practice administered through *Intendants* and Lieutenants. Obviously it could not : the Bruce himself well realised that in Scotland monarchy was bound up with feudo-clanship. For some reason Miss Cunningham describes the Royal lieutenants as " feudal," whereas they were machinery of the bureaucratic system she desiderates, which Richelieu set up in France after destroying the self-governing Feudalism of Henri IV.'s France.

fact, the development and organisation of "the Family"; so the Clan System was *necessarily* "feudal in the strict historical sense," as our modern historians recognise,[1] for feudalism, with its graciousness, is simply *the organisation of the Family*, and as a happy rural community. Clanship and the Scots instinct of Tribality, the maintenance of sub-infeudation, which the Plantagenets abolished in England, and the incorporation of many older Celtic customary provisions, made Scottish feudalism the means of perpetuating the hundreds of tiny Celtic provincial states or clan territories, which together form the Realm of Scotland.[2] These little "countries," each of which originally formed an allodial or *duthus* unit, were gradually resigned to the *Ard Righ Alban* (who thus became a feudal overlord), to be held on a tenure which it was fondly believed would give a *greater security* to those who had, in the words of one of the old clan historians, "first raised fire or boiled water upon these lands,"[3] a tenure too which would (in the language of a celebrated charter granted by Macdonald to one of the vassals of the Isles) endure "so long as the waves should beat upon the rock."[4]

No doubt the feudal system did not achieve all that was hoped by the *duthus* Chiefs, who during the eleventh and twelfth centuries exchanged the Celtic tenure of their "countries" for a feudal vassalage; yet in most cases the Kings of Scots did loyally carry out the principles of the Celtic bargain.[5] Throughout the ages schemers (both Celtic and non-Celtic!) naturally strove to work the feudal machinery (or a "judicious mixture of feudal law and Celtic practice")[6] in opposition to their neighbours' interests and with a view to extending their individual power; but this goes on happening whatever system may be in force, and will probably go on doing so under different forms of "political activity." What is now realised is that, had Scotland remained un-feudalised, the "Celtic social system" would have collapsed entirely, for the Normans in their feudal system did invent a practical business means of Government, and *a means of Government which was more adaptable to Celtic and to patriarchal conditions than any other form of Government which I can imagine.* Miss Grant has expressed the same opinion :—

"It was *by means of feudal institutions* that the rising clans made good their position, and especially by means of feu-farm." In the case of several clans she points out :— "The *original source* of the connection was the holding of land, in other words it *was a feudal connection* that gradually developed into one that was partly clannish, whilst the institution of the feudal custom of landholding by charter, and the subsequent develop-

---

[1] A. Mure Mackenzie, *History of Scotland in Modern Times*, 41; F. F. Brentano, *Old Regime in France*, 5, 7, 11.
[2] The Scottish Parliament, *Juridical Review*, March 1933, p. 3.
[3] D. Stewart of Garth, *Sketches of the Characters of the Highlanders of Scotland*, 26.
[4] *Scottish National Manuscripts*, II., p. xiv.
[5] The murder of James I. was an instance of Celtic revenge, for infringement of the implicit compact on which the Kingdom had been built up.   [6] *Loyal Clans*, p. 35.

ment of feu-farm tenure, though it placed those Chiefs whose title to their lands was precarious in a position of great disadvantage, seems to have tended on the whole to the *stabilisation of the clan system.*" [1]

Even Miss Cunningham admits :—

" The connection with land gave a permanence and stability to feudal institutions which the corresponding Celtic customs and assemblies did not display," [2] and on account of practical needs, feudalism " became an *integral part* of the clan system " and " contributed largely to saving the Highlanders from the disintegration and anarchy which overwhelmed the tribal organisation in Ireland." [3]

Had it not been for the forms and binding obligations of that early but peculiarly Scottish brand of feudalism, the continuity of the patriarchal grandeur of the clan countries could never have been maintained throughout the changing centuries. It was when the " chains of feudalism " (so called) were struck off by a " liberating " Anglo-Hanoverian Government, that the clan system was (for the moment) destroyed, and the Highlands of Scotland were made a silent and a smoking desert.

It is fashionable to praise the Heritable Jurisdiction Act of 1748 as a stupendous constitutional revolution. So it was—but not quite in the sense popularly supposed.[4] By that statute, which for most *practical* purposes devitalised the local Baron Courts, that (along with the Clan Councils) functioned in the Highlands as well as in the Lowlands, Scottish landed properties were converted from little constitutional states into unfettered autocracies, which too often passed, in consequence of financial exactions, into the power of Southern profiteers, or whose management devolved upon the " factors " of Chiefs and Chieftains who had been educated in the South of England. Before that statute was passed, Lairds and Chiefs had to reckon with the views and wishes of the inhabitants of their estates.[5] Evictions, deer afforestation, etc., could never have been carried out as they were, had the old Baron Courts remained a living force. Economic re-distribution would have taken place,[6] but it would at least have done so with the consent of the

---

[1] *Social and Economic Development of Scotland*, pp. 502, 516.
[2] *The Loyal Clans*, 43.   [3] Ib. 17.
[4] The Act abolished neither " feudalism " nor " superiorities " as suggested in *The Loyal Clans*, p. 355. It merely struck at the clannish and local-government aspects, and the Regalities which were no essential part of the Scottish feudal system and had long been criticised by Parliament (Erskine's *Principles*, I., IV., 5). The Clan Council and the Baron Court really worked synonymously, and both Chief and Baron had to rule " in fact, if not in name, by the consent of the governed " (*The Loyal Clans*, 24). For the Scottish baronial power, like that of the feudal Chief, depended on the loyalty and approbation of the members of his Baron Court (*Social and Economic Development of Scotland*, 52, 81, 95, 198; *Juridical Review*, Vol. 45, pp. 12, 19, 22; W. C. Dickinson, *Baron Court Book of Carnwath*). Baron Courts still exist in law, and since the abolition of Parish Councils, 1929, are the only remaining form of really local democratic self-government in Scotland.
[5] The Scottish Parliament, *Juridical Review*, March 1933, pp. 20, 22.
[6] As Mr Adam points out, *Clans, Septs, etc.*, p. 345, the " clearances " were actually attributed to adverse and ill-considered economic legislation, but one has to realise that the *whole policy* of the Government was to arrange the de-Celticisation of the Highlands. The Poor Law, the Heritable Jurisdiction Act, Dress Proscription Act, the encouragement of

inhabitants. It has been a striking but hitherto unnoticed circumstance, that " clearances " were possible only in the " tack system " districts of the West. In those portions of the country where a high degree of sub-infeudation had taken place, *the feu system did provide the requisite protection* against clearance or depopulation. Indeed, as Miss Grant points out :—

" Such a form of social organisation accorded very well with the natural pugnacity and clannishness of the Scots. It is this natural affinity between the national characteristics of the people and the form of government and social organisation, that made the feudal system in a strange sense a truly popular one.[1] . . . Feudalism survived in Scotland, when it had become a worn-out institution in all neighbouring countries. It would be interesting to know how largely it did so because in Scotland, more than elsewhere, into the purely feudal relationship had crept something of the greater warmth and fervour of the simpler and more ancient bond of union of the clan." [2]

The old clan lands have in too many cases now passed from the race to which, or to whose Chiefs and Chieftains, they of right belonged,[3] or only some ruined keep, moot hill, or deserted burying ground remains to testify to the former grandeur of the clans. But Scotland to-day is clamouring that its deserted straths shall be re-peopled. This will never be achieved by unloading upon the land a spiritless " peasantry." The clansmen were not peasant yokels, as patronising demagogues imagine. However poor their circumstances, they were fired with pride of race and magnanimity of character, glorying in their land and in those traditions which crowd one upon another in the stillness of the mountains or in the restless soughing of the wind and sea.[4] Vast tracts of old clan lands are, however, in the market to-day, and in several cases the suggestion has already been made (first, by Mr Seton Gordon—let us trust it will materialise) that the clan as a body should take steps to recover at least some part of their ancient " clan country," and re-people the vacant straths with well-selected descendants of the old races. Here is indeed a magnificent social prospect and a vision of the future, which ought to inspire our clan Societies and the successful children of the Highlands who have attained wealth and power in all quarters of the Globe. Business or other ties may now

sheep farming, and moral discouragement of those Chiefs and Lairds who retained " Scotch habits " and " barbaric " ideas about clanship " followings," and the favours held out to those who adopted Sassenach standards, all contributed to effect the tragedy.

[1] *Social and Economic Development of Scotland*, 198.

[2] Ib. 52, *cf.* Bell's *Lectures on Conveyancing*, 3rd Ed., p. 576.

[3] The land of course did *not* belong to the "Tribe" or Clan ; it belonged to the Chief or Chieftain (*Soc. and Economic Development*, pp. 79, 487), but the Clan or family Council had a right to prevent him from ruining the race by " prodigous and misguided " dissipating of the patrimonial inheritance (*Social and Economic Development*, p. 522). The " Family Council " still holds an important place in continental social life. It is only in England that the family organisation is almost entirely ignored.

[4] Those who compare the relative habits, mental outlook, traditions, and folklore of the continental peasant with those of the Scottish clansman, or of the crofters and the farm servants of the Lowlands, quickly realise there is *nothing in common between the clansman and the peasant*, and the Scottish ploughman or cottar is inspired by loftier thoughts and traditions, in fact by the spirit of clanship.

too often prevent these successful scions of Highland blood from personally returning to settle in the old lands, but the Companies Act has
placed within the hands of the Highlander machinery by which the
spirit and purpose of clanship could be renewed to-day.   There can
be little doubt that Clan Societies (Incorporated, Limited) [1] might
supply an outlet for both the funds and the energies of the children of
the Gael, and that these could restore the vigour of life to the empty
Highlands with greater celerity and success than the circumlocutory
measures of some Government Department necessarily lacking racial
and Celtic enthusiasm.

Corporate tribal ownership on this or a Trust basis has indeed
been started by several clans, and the development of the Highlands
on a tribal basis promises one of the most important sociological
movements of modern Scotland, each clan providing by such a Company
or Trust the combination of a real-property Investment Trust with the
amenities of a " Country Club " for its members, and, where desired,
residential quarters for an hereditary chief as hereditary Representer
and embodiment of the race.   If such institutions are to be realised,
it becomes essential that the structure of the clan, the succession to
the chiefship thereof, and its branches and their legal status, should be
clearly understood.

THE NATURE OF THE CLAN.

The word " clan " or *clanna* simply means children, *i.e.* the descendants of the actual or mythical ancestor from whom the community claims descent,[2] in so far as these remain within a tribal group
which, as a social, legal, and economic entity, is treated as a unit.
In the Middle Ages, law and custom did not treat of individuals, but
of groups.[3]   The earliest groups were personal and pastoral, but as
soon as a group settled, the territorial influence of the land which it
had occupied affected its structure.[4]   Both the group and the land
were called after the chief, who in theory was actually owner of the
whole group and of the land of the group, with absolute power over
every member.[5]   In some forms of tribality, the land belonged to
the tribe as a unit, but in Scotland, as Miss Grant points out,[6] there

---

[1] There is no reason why clanship should not seize the machinery of the Companies
Acts just as it seized on feudalism.   The Clan *Trust* is the more popular type.

[2] Skene, *Celtic Scotland*, 1880, III. 331 ; J. Cameron, *Celtic Law*, 1937, p .79; *Macrae v.
Macrae,* 1909 ; Lyon Court, typed Report, p. 17.

[3] Misapprehension on this point perplexed witnesses in *Macrae*, p. 85, regarding the
band for the " haill remnant gentles and others of the said name of Ra " (A. Macrae,
The Clan Macrae, 1899, p. 341).   Such terminology was normal, *e.g.* in " Letters of Slaines "
(*cf.* Barclay of Towie, *Familie of Innes*, 1864, p. 161).

[4] Sir Henry Maine, *Early History of Institutions*, 64 ,72.

[5] Maine and Pollock, *Ancient Law*, p. 211.

[6] *Social and Economic Development of Scotland*, 79 , 487.

was never communal, or in that sense "tribal" ownership. The Celto-Pictish principle emphasised the patriarchal chiefly element in which the chief was the parent, ruler, landowner, and proprietor on behalf of his *clanna* or children. This parental aspect is implicit in the very term *clanna*, which strikes at the root of the modern *canard* of " elected chiefs." The clan was in fact a " mixture of tribal tradition clustering round the *ipso facto* landholder of the soil "—the chief " fulfilling the functions of the tribal leader."

The clan, however, was actually a tribal organisation in the transitional stage where it is modified by territorial settlement, and before the influence of property in a commercial sense has destroyed the tribal element.[1] The perfect feudalisation of Scotland provided exactly the legal background which made possible the relatively perfect balance of racial and territorial tradition, in process of steady growth until the fifteenth to sixteenth century, and enabled this not only to develop during several centuries, but also to be projected, with all its grandeur of conception and practical social value, into the modern world. This combination of *pride of race with pride of soil* comes to form in clanship perhaps the most exalted and powerful relationship of people to soil and chief to people which has ever been evolved as a social system.

Like other tribal bodies, a clan was capable of recruitment by adoption,[2] which is also a recognised feature of heraldic law [3] and of the nobiliary and feudal law on the Continent, though not found in the Common Law of Scotland. This has led to a confusion of ideas, when the clan has come before the courts of Scotland, whose jurisprudence is so largely established upon Lord Stair that our older native jurisprudence is "discarded or ignored."[4] He nevertheless clearly lays down the principle and order of succession to our old Scottish dignities, and observes that, with us, heirs male only take where the grant or investiture specially so provides.[5] Sir George Mackenzie of Rosehaugh, a native Highlander, who treated of our Laws of Arms and precedence, is necessarily a useful guide in any points which our more conventional jurists have ignored or touched with hesitation. During the past century the clan as an institution has been thrice discussed in the Court of Session, where in 1862 [6] Lord Ardmillan in the Outer House delivered himself of a peroration upon clanship and feudalism, disfigured by really glaring errors in elementary legal history. He concluded that "clans are not corporations which

[1] Maine, *Early History of Institutions*, pp. 72, 85, 96, 112, 120.
[2] Sir Henry Maine and Sir Frederick Pollock, *Ancient Law*, 146 ; Sir Henry Maine, *Early History of Inst.* 69 ; J. Cameron, *Celtic Law*, 220.
[3] Nisbet, *Heraldry*, II. iii. 58.
[4] *Sources and Literature of the Law of Scotland*, p. 77, per Rt. Hon. T. M. Cooper, K.C.
[5] Stair, III–5–8 III–5–11.   [6] *MacGillivray v. Souter*, 25 Dunlop, 772.

law sustains, nor societies which law recognises or acknowledges."[1] The Inner House, Lord Colonsay presiding, confined themselves to holding that they did not find any such distinct statement of any practical qualification for membership of the clan as to exclude the heir-at-law. They were thus cautious, and far less dogmatic than the Lord Ordinary had been. Lord Curriehill observed :—

" It is perfectly competent to make it a condition that an heir be a member of a known and legal association, *e.g.* the Highland Society, and if the Clan Chattan were a body of that kind, I am not prepared to say that it might not be a lawful condition. Two and a half centuries ago, bodies under the denomination of clans were distinctly recognised by the legislature," and he adds, after referring to the Clan Acts, that "these changes are such as made the continued subsistence of the clan scarcely consistent with law." "I do not say that they are expressly abolished, but that subsequent legislation was of a kind with which the existence of the clans was inconsistent."

His Lordship, it appears, formed the impression that clanship was of a purely " military character." Lord Deas merely considered the condition insufficiently defined :—

" I am still left in the dark as to what constitutes membership of the clan. Is it regulated by law ? If so, by what law ? By charter or statute ? If so, what charter or what statute ? By agreement ? If so, by what deed ? By immemorial custom ? and if so, what is the precise nature and effect of the custom alleged ? "

Accordingly, the Court left the matter open, merely holding that nothing had been shown to overrule the ordinary descent of heritage in a claim to an estate restricted to members of Clan Chattan. Strange to say, neither in *MacGillivray v. Souter* nor in the preliminary pleas in *Maclean of Ardgour v. Maclean* (1937)[2] did the Court consider a proof requisite on the nature of a clan[3] and its chiefship, before pronouncing upon these subjects. In the latter case, however, the Court of Session made the important advance (the House of Lords had already gone much further in 1922) of what amounts to answering Lord Deas's question : " Is it regulated by Law ? If so, by what law ? " in conceding that the chiefship of a clan is at any rate cognisable in " law " for one purpose, a right to *armorial supporters*.[4] To Lord Deas's

[1] For an acid comment on this by the late Sheriff Macphail, see typed Report, *Macrae v Macrae*, Lyon Court, 1909, p. 352.
[2] *Scots Law Times*, 1938, 49. The Ardgour Petition (1936) did not raise the subject of " clans " directly, it dealt with the " stem family." *Clan* was introduced, and a judgment pronounced on the subject solely on the assumption that (*a*) the French word " Chieftain " necessarily related to " clans "—whereas it may apply to any territorial family ; (*b*) the term " branch " referred to " clans "—whereas it is equally applicable to families (11 Dunlop 1139). The writer, moreover, is perfectly clear (*infra*) what Chiefs and Chieftains *are*, but (*re* S.L.T. p. 65) can find no legal or definable character " *highland* chief." Any chief or chieftain anywhere is just a chief or chieftain (*i.e.* representer) of the group concerned. If highland domicile were the criterion, many Sassenachs would be " highland chiefs," and if ancestry, what ancestry ? Jane Porter's term " *Scottish* Chiefs " seems the only " quality " cognisable in Scottish Law—and the Law of Arms in Scotland.
[3] In *MacGillivray v. Souter*, remit for report on this was recalled, to regret of historians.
[4] Prior to the nineteenth century supporters, however, were never assigned to, or re-

question, " What Law ? " therefore the only possible answer is " a right, of course, regulated by the *Law of Arms*." [1] In administering this law—including " Visitation " under 1592, c. 125, as interpreted by the Court of Session in 1926 [2]—the Kings of Arms as judges " enquire into all matters concerning . . . titles or designations . . . degrading interlopers and upstarts." [3] This necessarily covers titles relating to any legal community, and titles indicated by arms, and the clan as a community was *expressly recognised by the Imperial Parliament in 1775* [4] when the proscription of the surname " Macgregor " was rescinded in favour of members of the Clan Gregor—

> " so far as respects the clan Gregour or MacGregors shall be and stand repealed "

are the *actual words* of the statute—thus disposing of Lord Curriehill. Here the subject (*Name*), as in " supporters," is one within the Law of Arms and Lyon's jurisdiction.[5]

The clan and chief are thus subjects necessarily cognisable in Lyon Court and involving rights under the branch of Nobiliary Law (*i.e.* the law of dignities and insignia), denominated the " Law of Arms," which is excluded from ordinary courts of law and cognisable only in Courts of Chivalry.[6] Lord Mackay's surmise proves in fact well founded :—

> (Supposing the Clan and Disarming Acts) " had as it were eliminated clanship from ordinary civil or statutory law, I am unable to think that can be true of the Law of Honours." [7]

The House of Lords had indeed in 1922, already conclusively related clan-chiefship to holding the undifferenced arms.[8]

ferred to, as of right pertaining to Chief *of Clans* as such. Nisbet and Mackenzie both say " Chief of *Families*," and it is *qua* Chiefs of " Families " and " Names " that supporters were awarded—as Stevenson points out, *Heraldry in Scotland*, p. 323. Indeed, the term " Clan " does not even occur on the page cited as authority at S.L.T. p. 67 (viz. Stevenson, pp. 87–89), and the Macnaughton award, 1819 (Lyon Reg., II. 172), seems the earliest example. The reason is that the mediæval attitude was, to paraphrase a well-known phrase, " Show me the Chief of the stem-family, and I will show you the Chief of the Clan "—or " Name."

[1] Since their lordships agree that a " right " exists—moreover, a heritable right—it is an axiom of law that such right must be justiciable somewhere. Lord Dunedin immediately pointed out that their lordships' further conclusion—that clan chiefship is not determinable in a court of law—must from the very terms of their own opinion necessarily be wrong. The " right " being one existent only in " the law of arms," must moreover necessarily be justiciable in a court of the " law of arms " (*see below*). This right to supporters being a " dignity " (1938, S.L.T. pp. 67, 70) such right is excluded from the jurisdiction of the Court of Session (*Lauderdale v. Scrymgeour Wedderburn*, 1910, S.C. (H.L.), 44.

[2] *Macrae's Trustees v. Lord Lyon*, 1927, S.L.T., p. 292.   [3] See p. 54 (footnote.)

[4] 15 George III. cap. 29, *Statutes at Large*, XII., 299.

[5] *Forlong*, 1880, 7 Rettie, 910. In view of the terms of the statute, if anyone applies to Lyon for official recognition of assumption of the name *Macgregor*, obviously Lyon must require proof that the petitioner is a *member of the Clan Gregor*—and does so.

[6] *Scots Law Times*, 17th July 1937, p. 156 ; *Herald and Genealogist*, II., 13 (*Grey v. Hastings*) ; *Report on title of* " *Rt. Hon.*" *of Lord Provost of Edinburgh* (1938) ; *Lawson*, 1863, Lyon Reg., VI., 71, and judgment.

[7] *Maclean of Ardgour v. Maclean*, 1938, *Scots Law Times*, 65.

[8] See p. 28 n. 2 : *Maclachlan of Maclachlan* (Lyon Court), 2nd May 1946 (L.R. 35,72).

Effigy of Maclean of Ross of
Mull, showing *leine croich*,
or saffron shirt; early use
by "highland chieftain"
of an armorial shield.
(*Soc. of Ant. of Scot.*)

What Lord Dunedin saw is that Lyon Court, unlike our other courts, is a Court of Chivalry, which exists precisely for trying these matters cognisable " *by* the Law of Arms," and which are, from their nature, outwith the jurisdiction of other Courts.[1] That is the point in the existence of Lyon Court.

The matter academically referred to in *Maclean of Ardgour* [2] was expressly considered in *Seaforth v. Allangrange*, where the Lords of Appeal unanimously held the Chief of a clan synonymous with the person entitled to the undifferenced ancestral arms.[3] This settles that Lyon Court in determining, as by law it must, right to such " incorporeal *heritage*," determines also the chiefship of the clan, the arms of whose *eponymus* are being rematriculated.

" Arms," says Nisbet, " are hereditary marks of *honour* regularly composed of certain tinctures and figures granted or authorised by sovereigns for distinguishing, differencing, and illustrating persons, families, and *communities*," and the first of their uses is the distinction of the nobility.[4]

" The family," in its wider and heraldic sense, is a statutory [5] group including all persons actually affiliated, or even adopted, to a central " stem " deriving from the founder of the race. Two such family groups, of even wider scope, the *Clan* and the *Name*, are recognised features of Scottish heraldic law and are grouped in mediæval Scottish statutes.[6] *Both these groups consist of aggregates of families, comprising not only determinate but also indeterminate or presumed cadet branches of the central stem.*[7] In the Lowlands and on

[1] W. Cruise, *On Dignities*, 251 : A. C. Fox-Davies, *Right to Bear Arms*, 147.

[2] Jurists will have little respect for the 1937 Ardgour opinions, throughout which (as Lord Dunedin, present to hear their delivery, noticed) runs the inexcusable inconsistency of treating clan and chief as " unknown to law " yet at the same time recognised in law in relation to hereditary insignia—supporters, and indeed arms ! Chiefship of a clan was not even before the court, which duly reaffirmed Lyon's well-recognised jurisdiction in chiefship of a family (crave 11, 1938, S.L.T., p. 80, which he " has jurisdiction to consider," p. 80, *cf.* 11 Dunlop) and the 1938 proof establishing " clan and family mean exactly the same thing " stultified the irrelevant *obiter dicta* made in 1937. In the Interlocutor of 18th July 1941 much of the 1937 one was abandoned.

[3] For the Lords' precise words in 1922 S.C. (H.L.), 39, *see* p. 28, n. 2, below.

[4] Nisbet, *Heraldry*, II., pp. 1 and 2.   [5] 1672, cap. 47; *Acts Parl. Scot.*, VIII., p. 95.

[6] 1594, cap. 37, A.P.S. IV. 71.   [7] J. H. Stevenson, *Heraldry in Scotland*, 408.

the Continent, such a group is distinguished by all its members bearing the same basic surname. In the Highlands, only the chief and his immediate family used the surname at all. Most names were genealogical strings, such as " Alister MacIan MacSheumas MacIan Beg." Accordingly, where the members of the group were not bearers of the same name, the community was denominated a " clan."

Now, all *noblesse* or hereditary gentility flows—in legal theory at any rate—from the Sovereign,[1] or *Ard Righ*,[2] from whom, as the " Fountain of Honour," all rank and titular distinctions flow, and even under feudalism they flow—at least indirectly—from the Sovereign as ultimate superior, though some titles are held *in vavasoria* of subject-superiors.[3] Only by the sovereign directly or, since the fifteenth century, in titles and honours of *nobilitas minor* (*i.e.* gentility) by H.M. Commissioners—His Kings of Arms, to whom this branch of the Royal prerogative is delegated,[4] can any person be confirmed in, or his family received into the noblesse, as an order in the public life of the realm, as noble communities with hereditary insignia.[5]

Early grants or confirmations of arms expressly state that the patentee and his descendants (or other specified group) are received into, and henceforth to be " taken and numbered amongst the ancient nobles " of the realm,[6] and that the arms are " tokens of this nobility." [7]

In Scotland amongst the " communities " so taken cognisance of are not only the definitely affiliated families, but the broader, yet just as aristocratic groups, the *Clans* and *Names*. This is the import of the " Clan Chattan Declaration," 10 Sept. 1672,[8] wherein Lord Lyon Sir Charles Erskine of Cambo declares that the Clan Chattan comprehends Macphersons, MacGillivrays, Farquharsons, M'Quins, Macphails, MacBains, and others—

" And that I have given, and will give, none of these families any arms, but as cadets of the Laird of Mackintosh's family, whose predecessor married the heretrix of the Clan Chattan." [9]

---

[1] Nisbet, *Heraldry*, I., 9 ; J. H. Stevenson, *Heraldry in Scotland*, XII., note 1 ; A. C. Fox-Davies, *Heraldry Explained*, 1907, pp. 7 and 8 ; *Right to Bear Arms*, 1900, pp. 26–50 ; *Art of Heraldry*, 1905, p. 10.

[2] In early times it could flow from provincial *Righ* or *Mormaers* and from the Counts Palatine—*e.g.* Chester—in England.

[3] J. R. N. Macphail, *Highland Papers*, II., 241 ; W. C. Dickinson, *Court Book of the Barony of Carnwath*, 1937, xvi.

[4] *Macdonnell v. Macdonald*, 4 Shaw, 371, per Lord Robertson ; *Heraldry in Scotland*, 72.

[5] J. W. Woodward, *Heraldry British and Foreign*, 6–12 ; *Privy Council*, second series, III., 156.

[6] Webbe, 1550, *Miscellanea Genealogica et Heraldica*, third series, II., 156.

[7] Gerard Legh, *Accidens of Armory*, 1576, f. 16 ; A. C. Fox-Davies, *Right to Bear Arms*, 1900, p. 50, quoting patents.

[8] A. M. Mackintosh, *The Mackintoshes and Clan Chattan*, 32.

[9] Such certificates were not merely *pro bona memoria* or " for the satisfaction of the honourable recipient " (1938, S.L.T. 61), but are directed to " all nobles and persons competent by whatever eminence and authority, to take cognisance of titles " (*Cumming*, Register of Genealogies, I., p. 1, *see Juridical Review*, Sept. 1940, p. 201.

The 1672 Declaration was immediately sent north for the information of all concerned,[1] and was acted upon in future transactions
before Lord Lyon Brodie.[2] The fact impressed is that the Crown,
through Lyon, had received these families as all forming a " community," viz. the " Clan Chattan," which community was to be distinguished in the military, civil, and social life of the realm by the
award of certain basic insignia [3] differenced according to the circumstances of each case. Such groups, officially recognised by the Crown,
are denominated " Honourable " communities,[4] and the specified
families forming the branches of the Honourable Community are
each armorially treated upon their merits as regards their own branch-
members, *i.e.* the " absolute arms " of the branch-chiefs are cadet
arms *quoad* the chief of the ruling family of the confederacy. Thus
the family of MacBean is (conform to the Declaration) recorded in
1672 as " a branch of Clan Chattan," [5] whilst the Clan MacBrayne is
itself recorded as a branch of the great Irish tribe of O'Brien, and the
name of Maxwell as of the Clan MacSween. How far these descents
are historically or scientifically true is not the question.[6] Constitu-
tionally the position is that the Crown, in exercise of its prerogative,
was pleased, through Lyon, to *receive them as such*, and to devise differ-
ences, and award armorial bearings *on that basis*. So much is this
the case, that I recollect noticing a case where the Lyon Depute even
declined, as contrary to Scottish armorial practice, to give a member
of an " armigerous name " arms which would not infer dependency on
the chief whose name he bears.[7]

The " armorial significance " of the clan as a community is referred
to by Nisbet.[8] A clan, whether "Highland " or other, can thus be
defined in the law of Scotland, and in particular in the *Law of Arms*
in Scotland,[9] in these terms :—

[1] Macfarlane's *Genealogical Collections*, Scottish History Society Ed., Vol. I., p. 393.
[2] C. Fraser Mackintosh, *Dunauchtan*, p. 29.
[3] *Cf.* The "armigerous name" basis of arms design perceived by Lord Sands (1920,
Session Cases 802).
[4] " Honourable House of Mowbray " (R. R. Stoddart, *Scottish Arms*, II., 185); " Honourable Family of Clan Chattan," 1672 (*supra*); " Honourable Clan MacBrayne," 1770
(Lyon Reg. I., 130); " Honourable Clan M'Sween," 1773 (Ib. I., 489) ; " Honourable
House of Dick-Cunningham," 1850 (Ib. V., 16).
[5] Ib. I., 359.
[6] Just as one may question how far old women were really guilty of witchcraft ; but in
1672 the sorcery and the pedigrees were both subjects of conclusive legal decision!
[7] An *obiter dictum* in *Maclean of Ardgour v. Maclean*, 1938, S.L.T. 62, misapprehending
this heraldic point, suggests that Lyon's undertaking " as regards the future, went
beyond any legitimate legal act." Its nature, however, is really that of a *contract between
the Crown and the Clan*, that the heraldic authority would not countenance what we may
call the " armorial blackleg " who seeks to obtain arms inconsistent with his place or
membership in the clan-community under Scottish heraldic law.
[8] *System of Heraldry*, 1722, I., 268 and 425.
[9] The Law of Arms is regarded as really in the nature of an international law, and in
early times was identical in France, England, and Scotland (*Heraldry in Scotland*, p. 131),
but in detail is modified by the customs of each realm (Sir John Ferne, *Glorie of Generositie*,
1586, p. 297).

A clan is a social group consisting of an aggregate of distinct erected families [1] actually descended, or accepting themselves as descendants of a common ancestor, and which group has been received by the Sovereign through his supreme Officer of Honour, the Lord Lyon, [2] as an honourable community whereof all the members, on establishing right to, or receiving fresh grants of, personal hereditary nobility, will be awarded arms as determinate or indeterminate cadets, both as may be, of the chief family of the clan. [3] If such community comprehends only families of one surname, *i.e.* that of the chief family, then the community is or may be termed a " Name."

It will be observed I adopt the evolutionary theory of clanship, which in a primitive form must have been inherent in Pictish Alban as well as in Dalriada. [4] I hardly think that clanship was " ignored " in the twelfth to thirteenth centuries. Rather was it in process of assimilation with the Feudal system, by the machinery of which it was to be strengthened and preserved in Scotland, instead of withering as in other lands. It has been suggested that " clans " organised, as we understand the term, first appear in the fifteenth century. That is indeed a period at which most of our national organisations become more definite and apparent, and with these the clan, for the shape of patriarchal tribo-feudalism was by then leavening in its more organised mould. It is however significant, and has been entirely overlooked, that it is just prior to this period (*i.e.* in the later fourteenth century) that we find not one but a batch of Royal Charters assuming that the clan—like the noble family—is a community whose representership or chiefship was held *not* by election but directly of, and under, the Crown [5] and with an heritable destination. [6]

Such a group may, and in most cases would, have existed, anterior to the recognition or confirmation by the *Ard Righ*, but the constitutional theory is that, even assuming prior noble existence, confirmation by, or on behalf of, the *Ard Righ* as the Fountain of Honour is indispensable to affirm the position of the community as an " honourable clan " in place of a mere gang of *ignobiles* or " lawless limmaris." How many clan communities were officially recognised through their representatives, the loss of the ancient *Liber Insigniorum* [7] prevents

---

[1] Nisbet, *Heraldry*, II., iii., 15, 17. It also includes the *sencliathe* native men, and the tenants and servants forming the following (*Loyall Dissuasive*, p. 56 *n.* 1 ; *Privy Council*, 3rd series, III., 75).   [2] Ib. II., iv., 172.

[3] If the claim is, to be a branch of a " branch-family," there will be double or treble differencing as the case requires.

[4] *Cf.* I. F. Grant, *Social and Economic Development of Scotland*, 51–52.

[5] Great Seal, I., App. II., Nos. 912–914 and 982. The position of such a community could hardly be better expressed than in the Nomination by R. A. Macneil of Barra, 9 October 1913 : " His Britannic Majesty, the *Superior of the Chief and the Clan of Macneil.*" This is entirely consistent with the fourteenth-century charters of Chiefship, and the theory of " Honours."   [6] Great Seal, II., 509.

[7] Great Seal, V., 262. Scottish armorial patents as early as 1503 are known.

our knowing, but although no mediæval administration was exhaustive or perfect, the military importance of the clans and their leaders must have rendered the usual record of their titles and insignia [1] a necessary as well as a normal branch of the matters which were made of record under the Law of Arms.

THE CHIEF.

The Clan being a community cognisable in the Law of Arms, and recognised by the Imperial Parliament,[2] it is next necessary to define its chief. As already indicated, all tribal groups and all subdivisions of these are conceived, by the men who compose them, as descended from a single male ancestor,[3] or sometimes a matriarch.[4] Not only was the tribe or sept named after this *eponymus*, but the territory it occupied derived from him the name by which it was most commonly known.[5] Upon the death of the *eponymus*, one of his descendants became the " Representer " of him and of the group which was " his," *i.e.* within his patriarchal *potestas*. The successive chiefs were the judges,[6] public officers, and representers of the group,[7] and the very name king or *könig* means the head of the kindred.[8] This chief or primitive " King " formed the centre and *sacred embodiment of the race, i.e.* the supreme individual of the race giving to its race-ideal the coherence and endurance of personality.[9] Whilst the chief's influence was personal and tribal,[10] he owned an official estate or *earbsa* which descended only along with the chiefly office,[11] and for these territorial chiefs and chieftains to achieve the rank of *aire deisa* it was necessary to be " the son of an *Aire* and the grandson of an *Aire*," and to hold " the property of his house," or at all events the principal dwelling-place.[12] Sir George Mackenzie explains (expressly in relation to undifferenced arms) that :—

" By the term ' chief,' we call the representative of the family, from the French word *chef* or head, and in the Irish (Gaelic), with us *the Chief of the Family is called the Head of the Clan*." [13]

The *ceann cinnidh* or clan chief—or more properly the " *Head* " of the Clan "—is thus in nature precisely the same as the *chief of the family*. Both are the living individual who represents the founder of the tribe, and who is the sacred embodiment of the tribe itself.[14]

[1] Nisbet, *Heraldry*, II., iv., 172.   [2] *Clan Gregor Act*, 15 Geo. III. cap. 29.
[3] Sir H. S. Maine, *Early Hist. of Institutions* (1875), 78.
[4] R. A. M. Macalister, *Ireland in pre-Celtic Times*, 242.
[5] *Cf.* such titles as " *Laird of Mackintosh*," " *Laird of Macfarlane* " (A.P.S. and P.C. Reg.). " Laird " is indeed the *colloquial* Scots style for chiefs and chieftains."
[6] *Celtic Scotland*, III., 145.   [7] Maine and Pollock, *Ancient Law* (1930), 258.
[8] *Scotland under her Early Kings*, p. 27 ; Maine and Pollock, *Ancient Law*, 23.
[9] A. E. A. Joliffe, *Constitutional History of Mediæval England, s.v.* Tribal Kingship, 42, 47.
[10] *Sources and Literature of the Law in Scotland*, 427.
[11] *Celtic Scotland*, II., 145, 176 ; F. Brentano, *Old Regime in France*, 11, 44, 73.
[12] C. N. Starcke, *The Primitive Family*, pp. 47, 164 ; H. G. B. Westermarck, *History of Human Marriage* (1901), p. 110 ; *Old Regime in France*, 44, 267.
[13] Mackenzie, *Works*, II., 618, line 13 ; *cf.* Lyon Reg., XXXV., 15.
[14] See *Proc. of Soc. of Antiquaries Scot.*, Vol. 77, pp. 169–174, showing how the Representer, *i.e.* Chief, came as such to have a quasi-deified relation to the tribe and its family-ritual.

Heraldry, as already explained, is a science for distinguishing persons, families, and communities.

" Heraldry " (says Fox-Davies) " from its earliest infancy possessed two essential qualities. It was the definite sign of hereditary nobility and rank, and it was practically an integral part of warfare, but also from its earliest infancy it formed a means of decoration." [1]

Firstly, it was for distinguishing noble groups, and secondly, for distinguishing the chief of each noble group from the subordinate descendants thereof.[2] The basic, or absolute, shield and flag (for banners are older than shields and coats of arms [3]) exist for the practical purpose of distinguishing the leaders of family or tribe or feudal units, in the military, civil, public, and nobiliary life of the kingdom.

" Leaders wore their own devices . . . that they might be distinguished by their particular followers, hence the actual use in battle . . . of personal armorial bearings . . . and even yet the practice is not wholly extinguished, for the tartans . . . are a relic of the usage of former days." [4]

The cap-badges of our highland regiments, moreover, still display the crests of the chiefs who first raised the regiments, so that actual heraldry has come down *via* clanship into modern military uniform. Let us recollect there was *no such thing in the Middle Ages* as " representation in arms," apart from representation in national life [5]—*nor is there now.* It was part of the everyday machinery of that organised daily life—military and civil, Highland and Lowland.[6] Heraldry was a practical subject in an illiterate age, and had to be strictly controlled, since mistakes could lead to defeat in war,[7] or fraud in business.[8] Chiefs, being persons vested with high military authority, were, in consequence of that status, the very persons to whom ensigns armorial —especially armorial banners—were indispensable,[9] and whose " enseinzies " were controlled under the Law of Arms.

Amongst the other armorial insignia of Chiefship of " Clans " and of " potent families " [10] is the slogan which was shouted by the followers not only in battle but at tournaments and other honourable Gatherings. These are " allowed " by Lyon (*i.e.*, in the Middle Ages, slogan-shouting was evidently prohibited save with Lyon's sanction. Such slogans are recorded, often as a second motto, or as a " woord," [11] and are displayed running along the standard, whereas the motto should be, and usually is, depicted across it in transverse bands).

The chief, then, from his representing the founder of the race,

---

[1] *Complete Guide to Heraldry*, 1925, p. 24.   [2] Nisbet, *Heraldry*, I., i., 2 ; II., iii., 2.
[3] Innes of Learney, *Scots Heraldry*, p. 14.   [4] *Complete Guide to Heraldry*, p. 25.
[5] *Cf.* Fox-Davies, *Art of Heraldry*, 1905, p. 10 ; *Complete Guide to Heraldry*, 1925, p. 20 ; J. Woodward, *Heraldry, British and Foreign*, I., pp. 6–15.
[6] The tombstones at Iona and elsewhere show the early use of armorial shields by chiefs and chieftains (see fig. on p. 22).
[7] Battle of Barnet, see *Heraldry in Scotland*, p. 224.   [8] Ib. p. 31.
[9] Nisbet, *Heraldry*, 1722, Vol. I., p. 3, line 12 ; A. C. Fox-Davies, *Art of Heraldry*, 10 ; *Heraldry in Scotland*, 31.   [10] Mackenzie, *Works*, II., 633 ; Nisbet, *Heraldry*, II., iv., 24.
[11] *Macfarlane of that Ilk*, Lyon Reg., I., 377.

succeeded, upon his predecessor's death, to the insignia of the *eponymus* (or what was heraldically appropriate to the *eponymus*), his banner, his weapons, his helmet, his surcoat, and his emblazoned shield and his rallying-flag or standard. In the Middle Ages he succeeded to the *actual* accoutrements! The succeeding " Representer," and he alone, was entitled to bear the undifferenced shield of arms.[1] That is to say, when arms are assigned to a community,[2] only the Representer, *i.e.* chief, is entitled to these arms undifferenced. Any other course would

The Bellendaine standard of the Earl of Buccleuch with Scott slughorn.

have wrecked the whole value of heraldry, and in warfare would have rendered it a national danger. Its military value involved the im-

---

[1] In *Maclean of Ardgour v. Maclean* (1938, S.L.T., p. 37) their Lordships formed the strange idea that the chief of the " armorial family "—according to the Law of Arms—which notwithstanding its title they curiously supposed had no *military* association, *i.e.* the person entitled to the undifferenced shield, might be a different person from the chief of the clan, based on Lord Sumner's *dictum*, in the *Seaforth* case, that " Allangrange was chief of the Seaforth Mackenzies, which no one could gainsay, whatever arms he bore " (1922, S.C. (H.L.), 51). Actually, the assumption that Allangrange was Chief was quite unfounded. About five other claimants did gainsay it! (A. Mackenzie, *History of the Mackenzies*, p. 348). The deduction from Lord Sumner (whose observation was a mere *dictum*) is based on a misapprehension. A Scotsman may possess more than one coat of arms (Innes of Learney, *Scots Heraldry*, p. 77 ; A. C. Fox-Davies, *Complete Guide to Heraldry*, p. 348). What Lord Sumner correctly deduced is that, *e.g.* the Duke of Buccleuch is no less a Scott and a Duke of Buccleuch if he occasionally employs arms which he " and his heirs " possess " as proprietor of the Port and Harbour of Granton " (1866, Lyon Reg., VII., 41). It is not true of *pronominal* arms, which indicate (*a*) to which family/clan one belongs ; (*b*) whether one is chief of, or a cadet in, it. All the judges in *Seaforth* concurred that *the undifferenced shield of arms of the eponymus* (the simple *caberfeidh*) *could belong only to the chief of the clan*. Per Lord Dunedin : " If it was undifferenced as the head of the clan " (1922, S.C. (H.L.), 44, line 42). Lord Shaw : " The chief of the Mackenzie's coat, which is, Azure, a deer's head cabooosed Or " (Ib. 47, line 54). And said Lord Sumner himself : " As the chieftain he could have matriculated the ancient Seaforth arms . . . without any differencing " (Ib. 49–50). The Lords of Appeal were thus *unanimous* in holding the " chief of the arms " identical with the " chief of the clan." The idea underlying the *Ardgour* opinions of 1937 was indeed abandoned (see p. 51) in their 1941 judgment—most fortunately, since the 1937 ideas were unsound and contradictory of decision in the House of Lords. Lyon Court is, of course, bound by what was operatively decided in the House of Lords, and not by *obiter dicta* in *Maclean of Ardgour*, where chiefship of clans was not before the court, nor adjudicated on in the interlocutors (see p. 50), and, according to their Lordships' own expression, could no more be prejudiced than rights of junior heirs portioners (pp. 687, 692).
[2] And presumably to " all descendants " of its *eponymus* (Nisbet, *Heraldry*, I., 71, line 4), who can prove their descent, *i.e.* the *duine-uasail.*

mediate recognition of the leader of each group from his cadets, and this came from the leader displaying the undifferenced ensigns. Even if the chief was a kilted Highlander, the chief's banner (*i.e.* the undifferenced banner which had belonged to, or was scientifically appropriate to, the *eponymus*) devolved upon the successive representers of the community.

Chiefship of an honourable community is thus a title and dignity, even though of no higher rank than esquire,[1] held of the Crown and indicated by armorial bearings in terms of the Commissions of Visitation (" Visite " is a technical term in the Law of Arms),[2] and anyone who " challenges forth any name of tytle or honour or dignitie as Esquire or Gentleman *or other* [3] must ' justify the same *by the Law of Arms* ' " [4] ; and Lyon, in 1672, held that an assumption of Chiefship without his permission was unlawful.[5] The requisite proof is " by pedigrees, deeds, and such other evidence and matter of record and credit if need requires, as may justify the same." [6] Originally, under tribal custom, the chief was inaugurated like the *Ard Rìgh* in a solemn ceremony. The account of the form of inauguration of the High Chief of O'Neill by the Hereditary Inaugurator, The O'Cahan, is as follows :

" If any will take upon him to be O'Neill, being not named or chosen by O'Cahan, he is not to be obeyed nor taken for O'Neill, for if any undertake the name of O'Neill, not appointed by O'Cahan, the people will think themselves not bound in conscience to obey him " (Hogan, *Irish Law of Kingship*, 199).[7]

It will be observed there is no suggestion that O'Neill's *status as Chief* depended on election or recognition by the tribe, and in Eire to-day, succession of Irish chiefs is determined and recorded with their arms by the *Priomh-Aralt na h Eireann*.

Like the Royal Coronation, this ceremony included three features : (*a*) the selection or determination of the candidates' right to the Office [8]

---

[1] Highest category of the Precedency List, 1905, under which a chief could be grouped. *Cf.* Macpherson : Chiefship " setts you in the front of the first gentlemen of the Kingdome " (*Loyall Dissuasive*, 26), *i.e.* confers the rank of *Esquire*—which descends only to the *heir* of each person so hereditarily recognised by the King of Arms.

[2] 1592, cap 25, as interpreted by Lord Constable in *Macrae's Trustees v. Lord Lyon*, 1927, *Scots Law Times*, p. 292.

[3] A man may acquire gentility by office, but this dies with him. Only the chief of each family or branch is an " Esquire " by descent, *i.e.* the cadets are merely " Gentlemen " unless or until received by the King of Arms as *ecuyer*—feminine *ecuyere*. (*Encyclopœdia of Laws of Scotland*, *s.v.* Precedence, par. 33, 34.) Hereditary nobility can only be established by patent or confirmation from the Fountain of Honour, through a King of Arms (Nisbet's *Heraldry*, I., p. 2 ; Ferne, *Glorie of Generositie*, p. 67).

[4] *Ipsissima verba* of the Royal Warrant, *Right to Bear Arms*, 123. *Shrewsbury Peerage*, 1857, Min. of Evidence, 16, 18, 215 (Signet Library).

[5] Letter to Cluny-Macpherson (Macfarlane's *Genealogical Collections*, I., 393), consistent with the jurisdiction over " titles and designations " comprehended in the statutory term " visite " (1592, c. 29), *cf.* Gwillim, *Display of Heraldry*, 1724, p. 49.   [6] Ib. 127.

[7] The Hereditary Inaugurator of the Pictish kings was the Earl of Fife, who set the king upon the Stone of Scone, whilst the functions of the High Sennachie and Official Inaugurator of the Dalriad kings devolved, along with the red robe of the Sennachie and duty of declaiming the genealogy, upon the Lord Lyon King of Arms. (The Scottish Coronation, *Crown and Empire* (*Times* publication), 1937, p. 89 ; J. Sobieski Stuart, *Costumes of the Clans*, 1892, pp. 43–45 (notes) ; *Scots Heraldry*, p. 8.)

[8] In the case of the Crown the " destination " is now contained in the Act of Settlement.

C

by succession, nomination, or selection, as the case might be,[1] (b) the "Presentation," (c) the Inauguration.

The Recognition must not be confused with the antecedent determination of *title to succeed*, which is set forth in the Presentation, and depends on the ruling "destination" of the Office. The Recognition in Scotland was a mere acclamation,[2] and from essentially the people of the "country"—including tenants and "broken" men who had been taken on to the lands by "commendation," of whom much is heard in mediæval law—and who might withdraw, or support a rival claimant. The chief with a Crown-title or landcharter was in a far stronger position than the allodial chief in this respect, being, in case of dispute, entitled to the *Ard Righ's* assistance. Of course a substantial "failure" in recognition might lead to Civil War in the group, or to the resignation or assassination of the unpopular Chief. The Clanranald history illustrates both, but demonstrates the *ultimate* determinative influence of the Crown, whereby both land and arms were ultimately confirmed to Ian Muydertach and his line, which would not have been received as chiefs of Clanranald had the "substantial rights" not been satisfactorily settled in his line.

The "Recognition," in fact, relates to the "power" and membership, not to the Authority and Representation, of the community.

In days when the Royal power was none too strong and communications were difficult, the Crown no doubt found convenient formulæ for giving constitutional appearance to hard facts, but where a title *de Rege* existed, the Crown was bound to support the representative entitled thereunder to lands or chiefly insignia.

Reverting to the ceremony of the Inauguration : The new chief's genealogy was declaimed by the clan sennachie, and the insignia of rule—a white wand [3]—was formally delivered.[4] Such a ceremony is still appropriate, but (as in the case where the *Ard Righ* personally intervened to exercise his prerogative of inaugurating chiefs), if there be any doubt regarding the succession to the "representership" and relative armorial insignia, the *effective* "inauguration" is now a matriculation of arms in the Lyon Register, *i.e.* a constructive delivery *de Rege* of a picture on parchment, symbolising the *actual* shield, crest, and helmet of the former *ceann cinnidh*, which ensigns of honour for distinguishing the group, the chief (as its representer) holds of and under the *Ard Righ* as the Fountain of Honour at the hands of his Commissioner the Lord Lyon—*Qui facit per alium facit per se* [5]—who embodies, and has performed the *duties of*,[6] the high sennachie and

---

[1] See below, p. 39.   [2] Lord Clyde in A. & C. *in Civil Causes.*
[3] The official wand of a baron is also white (W. C. Dickinson, *Baron Court Book of Carnwath*, lxxxvi), which corroborates the connection of chiefship with the earliest baronial jurisdictions (Craig, *Jus Feudale*, 1–8–2).   [4] Marquis of Bute, *Scottish Coronations*, 16.
[5] Mackenzie, *Works*, II., 563 ; Sir John Ferne, *Glorie of Generositie*, 67.
[6] *Sources and Literature of the Law of Scotland*, p. 382.

official Inaugurator of the ancient Kings of Scots. Indeed, so that Lyon should be invested, to the extent of his Commission, with the full nobiliary prerogative of the King of Scots, he was summoned to dine at Holyroodhouse on the evening of his inauguration, when the Royal Crown of Scotland was set on his head.[1]

> " Whom royal James himself had crowned
> And on his temples placed the round
> Of Scotland's ancient diadem."   *Marmion*, IV., 159.

The Crown's recognition—direct or through the Supreme Officer of Honour—alone can qualify a chief to be *received as such in state or public ceremonial,* " whereof Lyon hath the management "[2]; and for any person to submit to, or assist at, an inauguration in opposition to a holder under the *Ard Righ's* protection and a destination of chiefly insignia held *de Rege* must necessarily be not only a nullity in effect, but an affront to the Fountain of Honour, and in the nature of treason. In such a matter, says Sheriff Sir Æneas Macpherson, " No subject could *vi et armis* maintain his right against the king *jure et impune.*"[3] In private life, bogus chiefs, like a bogus peer or baronet, or the *soi-disant* " Countess Cowley," may impose on humble neighbours, but they cannot be *officially* received by or accorded such titles, and are liable to be publicly denounced as *infamous* impostors,[4] or " interlopers and up-starts," [5] and public documents in which they are described as chiefs without the King of Arms' permission are liable to be rejected as irregular—*e.g.* the bonds of Cluny-Macpherson as " Chief of Clan Chattan," after Lyon had pronounced in favour of Macintosh. This would be an effective and sufficient enforcement of Lyon's decision [6] for all practical purposes ; if a " more efficient sanction " had been thought requisite in the Middle Ages, it would have been found in the execu-torial known as " Letters of Fire and Sword." [7]

CHIEFTAIN.

Whilst chief and chieftain, chiefship and chieftainry, are used pro-miscuously in Scottish records, the term *chief* probably does connote a greater chief, and consequently branch-chiefs have in later times

[1] Sir J. B. Paul, *Heraldry in Relation to Scots History and Art,* p. 85 ; Sir W. Scott, *Marmion.* canto iv., l. 159.   [2] *Scots Heraldry,* p. 9, n. 2.   [3] *Loyall Dissuasive,* 117.
[4] J. Dallaway, *Heraldic Enquiries,* p. 313 ; Boutell's *Heraldry,* 1891, p. 345 ; Macfarlane's *Genealogical Collections* (Scot. Hist. Soc.), I., 393.
[5] J. Gwillim, *Display of Heraldry,* 1724, *s.v.* Honour Civil, p. 49.
[6] A fact which the Court of Session likewise did not perceive, 1938, S.L.T., p. 58. This, it happens, is the practical sanction against bogus baronets (Royal Warrant, 1910, sec. II.), and this hereditary dignity is determined either directly by the Crown, on advice of the Secretary of State (the modern practice under secs. IV., VI., VIII.) or—alternatively—by the Kings of Arms, whose *jurisdiction* therein is politely saved by sec. XIII., whereunder Lyon's certificate was the authority on which the Lord Chamberlain received a man as Baronet (*Scottish Offices Inquiry Commission,* 1870, Evidence, par. 1984).
[7] *Social and Economic Development of Scotland,* pp. 512, 530. Difficulty of enforcement— a problem throughout the Middle Ages—had nothing to do with jurisdiction or validity of a decree.

come to be designated " chieftains " as being lesser chiefs. The word, originally French, may connote no more than the head of a territorial house,[1] and is not confined to " clan " groups, indeed is largely associated with feudal houses. Since the Ardgour hearing, when it was suggested the term " Chieftain of Ardgour " was without precedent in the Lyon Registers, such a term—viz. " Chieftain of Innermeath "—has actually transpired to be of record in the Public Register of Genealogies.[2] *Chieftain* is really a territorial title.

Indeed, the definition and the corresponding term, " *chevetainrie— propriété d'un chevetain, d'un seigneur,*" compared with the Scots term " chiftane of the cuntrie "[3] and the normal use of the title as annexed to a *locus, e.g.* " Chieftain of X——," obviously correlate the title with the *Grad Flaith*, territorial nobles of the Celtic polity.[4] The Chieftain thus appears, in this sense (*i.e.* of a country), as a personage combining the dual character of Representer of a family (or branch family) and leading person (as proprietor, tacksman, or occupier) in relation to the inhabitants of a specific district—" be place of thare duelling "[5]—as his *sencliathe*, vassals, and tenantry.[6] In short, he is a laird whose relations to the occupiers of his domain is quasi-tribal as well as economic (*i.e.* closer than " landlord and tenant "). In this sense a " recognition " by the " cuntrie " would obviously be a matter for proof in Lyon Court, and the " armorial " consequences of such a *nexus* (in addition to the allowing of badges, standard, slogan) could involve allusion in designing or differencing arms for members of such a synthetic " community " (recognised by Lyon), who might become themselves armigerous.[7] The " Recognition," as indicated further on, relates neither to the title nor right of succession, but to *membership* of the " community " forming such a following. It is comparable rather to the early British " commendation,"[8] which without the permanent bases of the clan/tribe and feudal connections proved evanescent. The strength of the clan system lies—as Stewart of Garth pointed out—in the *hereditary tribal bond*[9] around the " stem " or central family,[10] that is a feudal, *i.e.* " family " connection.

[1] Frederick Godefroy. *Lexique de L'Ancien Français*, 1901, p. 83.
[2] A. Cameron, *Juridical Review*, Vol. I., p. 72 (March 1938), " Diploma of Nobility of Thomas Cumming, 1727."
[3] *Acts Parl. Scot.*, III., 464.   [4] Skene, *Celtic Scotland*, III., 145.
[5] *Acts Parl. Scot.*, IV., 40.
[6] *Cf. Privy Council*, 3rd series, III. 75 ; *Loyall Dissuasive*, 56 *n. See* p. 15, n. 1 *supra.*
[7] *Cf.* Arms of " Clientage " and " Patronage," Nisbet's *Heraldry*, II., iii., 60, II., iv., 22, I., 268 ; *Heraldry in Scotland*, 273, 275.
[8] A. E. F. Jolliffe, *op. cit.* pp. 80, 99.
[9] The importance of the ultimate settlement by the *Ard Righ* of Chiefly and Chieftainly succession-disputes is obvious, since if this lay with " the clan " and not, as a determination of Representership, with the Fountain of Honour, the result would be dissension and weakness, *e.g. Macrae*, where rivals simply founded opposing " Clan Societies."
[10] The " Recognition," moreover, would seem to lie with the in-brought tenants, dependers and " broken men " who could resile from the new chieftain, as distinct from the *sencleithe* and " native men " who by three generations (conventionally eighty-one years or maybe three tacks of nineteen years) had become (by complement to the resultant Fixity

In any case, *grad flaith* or other, the branch-chief or chieftain—
and the term *branch* is in heraldry just as applicable to a family as
to a clan [1]—bears precisely the same relation to the members (*i.e.* actual
and assumed descendants of the branch) as " The Chief " does to the
whole clan or family group. The chieftain is simply " representer "
of the " first raiser " [2] of the branch. An interesting question is :
when is a branch so raised or erected that it becomes cognisable as a
" distinct house " ? In this there is a *consensus* of Celtic custom [3]
with heraldic law, that three generations, or apparently conventionally eighty-one years,[4] was necessary to perfect a coat-of-arms,[5] and
it would seem on comparison of these analogies that a branch is
not perfectly established until it has stood for three generations, in
fact until it has produced what in Celtic Law was termed a *gilfine*, or
five households.[6] Far from the title *chief* being a rare one in Celtic
civilisation, the popular unit was evidently the *gilfine* group under
a " *gilfine*-chief," [7] whom we to-day would conveniently term a
" chieftain," if " of " an estate or *grad flaith* house.

The question has been raised, whether chieftain of a clan has any
" armorial significance," but no judicial *proof* has yet been taken on
this important point. Seton [8] had evidently no doubt it had such a
significance. An hereditary chieftain,[9] in the sense of a " branch-
chief," would—in the heraldic view—be entitled to the arms of his
" branch-*eponymus*," without further *brisure*.[10] The term *chevtaine* is
definitely employed in early heraldic literature,[11] and " A cheivetayn's
hedd chappelled embattled Or " appears in an heraldic badge in 1562.[12]
This " chieftain's embattled cap," [13] inscribed with its owner's title
like a sailor's cap, is obviously the origin of the later stiff and un-
natural-looking Mural Crown, which (tinctured *Or*) has become more
or less confined to persons vested with high military authority,[14]

of Tenure) hereditary adherents whose membership would be implicit, whereas recently
" inbrocht " dependers—unless they had been specifically adopted (*see* p. 19), were on a
" commendation " basis until elapse of the requisite time when they automatically became
sencliathe.

[1] *Cunyham v. Cunyham*, 11 Dunlop, 1139, for use of the term.
[2] Nisbet's *Heraldry*, I., 176, line 51 ; II., iii., 17, line 41 ; *cf. Mackenzie of Coull*, Lyon
Register, I., 190.
[3] Skene, *Celtic Scotland*, III., 175.
[4] This seems the conventional three generations when applied to the *Senclaithe* (ib. III.,
173), who then became " native men "—hereditary followers.
[5] Nisbet, *Heraldry*, II., iv., 125, 147 ; *Heraldry in Scotland*, 79.
[6] *Celtic Scotland*, III., 179 ; J. Cameron, *Celtic Law*, 109, 111.
[7] *Celtic Scotland*, III., 180, 182.　　　[8] *Law and Practice of Heraldry*, p. 9.
[9] We are not here concerned with " Chieftains " of (*a*) Highland Gatherings; (*b*) Clan
Societies, but with " Chieftain " as a title and status of gentility—social or military rank.
[10] *Hamilton of Binning*, 1886, Lyon Reg., I., 329 ; *Scott of Sinton*, 1700, ib. II., 189
Grant of Auchernach, 1777, ib. I., 515 ; R. R. Stoddart, *Scottish Arms*, 306.
[11] *Book of St Albans*, 1486 ; J. Dallaway, *Heraldic Enquiries*, lxxv.
[12] Gerard Legh, *Accidens of Armory*, 1562 Ed., f. 101.
[13] *Herald and Genealogist*, I., 60.
[14] Fox-Davies, *Art of Heraldry*, 284. The true *Mural* Crown, as used on the continent and
shown in our older text-books, is embellished with three or five towers, thus distinguishing
it from the " chieftain's cap " pattern.

though the restriction is unfortunately not so close that it is not occasionally assigned to people who can claim to be neither chieftains nor military leaders.[1] It seems not unlikely that this mediæval chieftain's bonnet survives not merely in the Mural Crown of heraldry, but in the diced borders of military Highland bonnets. This border in its more primitive form was a broad surround of very large checks, a noticeable feature of the bonnet in which the Duchess of Gordon went recruiting.

The *provenance* and development of the military diced border accordingly deserves research, since its allocation to privates may easily have been a meaningless copying by regimental tailors of what had originally been an ornament restricted to chieftains' bonnets. It happens, however, that the chieftaincy of a " branch " *has* actually

been specifically taken cognisance of by Lyon Court in at any rate one case[2]— viz. *Campbell of Inverneill*,[3] who matriculated expressly to establish his position as chief of the *Clan Chearleich*[4] or "old branch or tribe of the family of Craignish," *i.e.* a branch of the great Clan Campbell. What Lyon awarded is illuminating :—The arms of Argyll, with a difference of immediacy from the stem of Lochaw, viz. a plain bordure Azure. The ground of the award was an acknowledgment 6 October 1795, by the " heads of families of the clan," including the " Clan Kater-Campbells in Breadalbane," the " Clan Tearlach Campbells," and the

Chieftain's cap (G. Legh, *Accidens of Armory*, 1562).

" Clan Iner of Ichtellegherne," who as the " representatives of the above five clans, bind themselves, their heirs, and successors to acknowledge Inverneil and his heirs and successors," on the ground of a traditional pedigree handed down, that Inverneill represented the eldest son, of whom he, according to their tradition,

---

[1] Leadbetter, 1900, Lyon Reg., XVI., 23 ; Beveridge, ib. XXIII., 31 ; Morris, 1917, ib. XXIII., 60. It would be within Lyon's prerogative to confer (or rather to *restrict* conference of) such a mural circlet of some colour on " chieftains," but many crests would not be improved by such circlets, so *chieftains' caps* may preferably, following 1562 precedent, be allowed in the *badge*—which with standard, is an " additament " of arms (*Stewart of Inchmahome*, ib. XXI., 74), allowed to those deemed to have "followings." It would be a more honourable practice than what occurred in 1917, viz. award of the mural circlet to an *architect*, presumably under a misapprehension of its nature, which the *Accidens of Armory* shows to have had nothing to do with mason work.

[2] Owing to Lyon Register, now existent since 1672, not being printed, it is difficult to say what may not, on a full analysis, be discovered in its voluminous pages.

[3] Lyon Reg., IX., 88, 18 Nov. 1875.

[4] Letter from Inverneil younger, 27 October 1875, that he and his father are " quite satisfied if it be proved that we are the chief of the race, tribe, or *Clan Chearleich of Ardeonaig*, without going to further expense " than £45. Inverneil omitted so to designate himself in the instances of his petition, though the chiefship is referred to *in gremio* of the matriculation, which was sought expressly to prove the chiefship.

was (they narrate) lineal heir male and representative, and the purpose of the declaration was to put on record their belief *in the pedigree.*[1] On this declaration, Lyon accepted the " pedigree " from a clan aspect, there being no documentary proof, and awarded the above chieftainly insignia, with destination to " descendants " (*not*, as in many patents, " heirs male "), conform to the legal implication of the term " heirs and successors." An interesting feature is, the existence of branch-clans subsidiary to *Clan Chearleich* (itself a branch of Clan Campbell), and, co-relating the number five with the *gilfine* number,[2] it may be assumed that *Clan Chearleich* was head of five sub-clans, whose sub-chiefs must each at least have been *gilfine, i.e.* chiefs of five houses.[3] The galley "cottise"[4] or compartment, is evidently a *reddendo* galley.

The development of branch-clans is illustrated amongst the Grants, *e.g.* Clan Donachie (Grant of Gartenbeg) ; Clan Allan (Grant of Auchernack) ; Clan Chiaran (Grant of Dellachapple) ; Clan Phadrick (Grant of Tullochgorum)[5]—again making, curiously enough, with the " stem family " of Freuchie, the *Gilfine* number of five.

The expanding nature of the Clan-groups of the later historical organisation is thus shown repeating what was evidently assumed to have occurred in the earlier

Achievement of Campbell of Inverneill, Chief of Clan Chearleich of Ardeonaig.

development of the *morthuath*, and the *Gilfine*-chief, rising to the status of " Chieftain " and then Chief/Chieftain of a branch-clan.[6]

SUCCESSION TO CHIEFSHIP.

A chiefless clan, like an orphan family, is an imperfect group. *Continuity under the bond of kin embodied in the perpetuation of the parental tie is the whole basis of the clan concept.* A clan without an hereditary

---

[1] *Cf.* Welsh Declaration of the *Hoby* Pedigree accepted by Garter and Clarencieux, 1598, *Misc. Gen. et Her.,* 1st series (1868), Vol. I., p. 142.   [2] J. Cameron, *Celtic Law,* 111.

[3] It must not be assumed that Lyon will forthwith launch an unlimited fleet of such galleys upon the sea of heraldry. Presumably he would insist on chieftainship of, say " 5 houses," or something of that sort, and/or the property involving the service or *reddendo*. On the other hand, Lord Lyon Swinton's last official act was to award such a galley to Campbell of Askomel (representer in the seventh generation of that house), an indication of the tendency (which has been the bane of heraldry) to extend insignia or *indiciæ* without a *defined* ruling of the extent and import of the award.

[4] Mackenzie, *Works,* II., 630.

[5] L. Shaw, *History of the Province of Moray,* J. F. S. Gordon, Ed. 1882, Vol. I., p. 93.

[6] Similarly the Macnabs claim to be a branch of Clan Mackinnon ; the Farquharsons are a branch of Clan Shaw, itself a branch of Clan Mackintosh, stem-family of Clan Chattan.

chief is a sorry organisation, alien to the whole idea of Celtic civilisation, wherein the chief is the sacred embodiment of the race. The question of succession to chiefship of, and chieftaincy in, clans, is therefore necessarily of the utmost importance and widest interest to Scotsmen.

We have seen that both Crown and Lyon treated the clan and its " representation " or chiefship as a heritable feudal fief.[1] Alike in the historic, heraldic, official, and popular view, the clan is a patriarchal community, based on the assumption of heredity and a " parent and child " *nexus*, and received, as has been shown, by and under the Crown, as an " Honourable Community."

Royal and judicial determination of its chiefship was accordingly not regarded as " grotesque " in the Middle Ages.[2] The Lord Justice-Clerk rightly says " The Chief was the Law "—but that " his authority was derived from his own people " is an idea utterly irreconcilable with the circumstances. His *power*, no doubt, depended on the number and loyalty of his people, but his *constitutional authority* over them was derived from his " representing " the *eponymus*. The *patria potestas* is not derived from the " children " ; no more is the chief's derived from his *clanna*.

The nature of this succession is, that what passed from patriarch to patriarch was " the community " as a " going concern," namely, " The public responsibility comprehended in the term *family*," [3] and that in many tribal communities it lay with the patriarch to determine which member of the family natural or adopted, should succeed to the public office of the patriarchate. The early Celtic system belonged to the type in which the succession was hereditary in the group, but sometimes selective in the individual. It was nevertheless strictly hereditary, and by whatever means ascertained, as Stewart of Garth explains, the " head of the central or stem family was the chief " *of the clan*.[4] The system, actually a most complicated one, was that it lay with the Chief to nominate his *Tanist*, or designated-successor,[5] as was the practice in many such early tribal communities [6] ; the whole ceremony of an early will-making being machinery for a Chief declaring who was to have the chiefship in succession to him. For the Chief to die intestate [7] without conferring his blessing on the heir was a great

---

[1] Great Seal charters and Clan Chattan Dec. Note legal import of "*heretrix* of the *clan*."
[2] *Loyall Dissuasive*, pp. 58, 116.   [3] Maine, *Ancient Law*, 205, 211.
[4] D. Stewart of Garth, *Sketches, &c., of the Highlanders of Scotland*, 1825, p. 24.
[5] By an analogous practice in old Scots burghs the old Council nominated the new.
[6] Sir H. Maine, *Ancient Law*, 215, 266, *cf*. Pollok's comparison with the Scots Trust Disposition and Settlement at p. 238.
[7] In the Ardgour proof, 4 July 1938, J. Cameron, Ph.D., likened Tanistry to Testate succession, and *derbhfine*-selection as Intestate succession to Chiefship (Evid. p. 13). The Law of Malcolm M'Kenneth ultimately introduced the Common Law of Succession, which in 1292 was held by Edward I's *Curia Centumvirale* to apply to all Scottish impartible successions (S.H.R., XVI., p. 7).

calamity, and it was in this contingency that the tribal Sennachie and Chiefs of Branches had to fill the blank by a ceremonial selection of a successor from a group called the *derbhfine*, consisting of his nine nearest kinsmen. The electors were apparently the chiefs of the other *derbhfines* within the clan, *e.g.* the " Seven Earls of Scotland " traditionally representing the " Seven Sons of Cruithne the Pict," were entitled to elect the *Ard Righ Albann* when the Crown fell *de facto* and *de jure* vacant. The nearest modern equivalent of a *derbhfine* is the official " Royal Family " as entitled to special coronets as grandchildren of the Sovereign, and to the prefix " Royal Highness." [1] If we imagined the sovereignty elective at an intestate demise from amongst all the living Royal Highnesses, and assume the electors were, let us say, the twenty-eight Dukes, and that these twenty-eight Dukes were each selected on an intestacy from amongst the persons who happened to have the courtesy title of " Lord " at the last Duke's death, we should *roughly* have an idea of what the system was like. The *derbhfine* was, generally speaking, a body of nine people descended from a great-grandfather, and in Ireland it was confined to persons connected by males, *i.e.* was of Salic form. In Scotland, upon Pictish precedent, the *derbhfines* were evidently *not* so restricted. The membership— that is, the electors and candidates—might be connected by females, and might even be females, because females succeeded to the Celtic mormaerships which in their original nature were the chiefships of *mortuaths*.[2] " The Law Clan Macduff," whereby certain privileges attached to individuals " within nine degrees of kin to Macduff, Earl of Fife," is regarded as really a privilege which belonged to Macduff's *derbhfine*.[3] *Now, this group included persons connected through females,*[4] so of course must have done the Royal *derbhfine*, from which the *Rex Pictorum* and later the *Ard Righ Albann* was selected.

This system of *derbhfine*-succession has been described as the " weakest feature of Irish polity." It led to perpetual intrigue and strife, and to lack of continuity in rule, and Professor Hogan concludes that :—

" Even from the native standpoint, probably the best thing that could have happened would have been the complete success of the attempts to establish primogeniture, or at least to fix a succession more strict and efficient than the traditional kingship by election." [5]

This seems precisely what the Scottish kings achieved, from a com-

[1] In the reigns of Queen Victoria and Edward VII. grandchildren of the sovereign, through daughters, were included in these privileges, which happen to correspond with what is found in early Scottish *derbhfines*.   [2] Skene, *Celtic Scotland*, III., 212.
[3] *Celtic Scotland*, III., 306. The survival of the Picto-tribal basis of the clan in Scotland is illustrated by the surviving assertion that a man may " wear a plaid of his mother's tartan," and the membership condition of certain Clan Associations : " Persons bearing a surname other than Mac . . ., but whose maternal parent or grandparent bore either the name Mac . . . or one of the said Septnames." This provision is analogous to a *gilfine* structure admitting, like the *Law Clan Macduff*, female connections.
[4] Skene, *De Verborum Significatione*, *s.v.* Law Clan Macduff ; E. W. Robertson, *Scotland under her Early Kings*, I., 255 ; *Scots Peerage*, I., 274.
[5] *Irish Law of Kingship*, 249 ; Cameron, *Celtic Law*, p. 120.

bination of the Pictish order of succession, the Hebraic code,[1] and the Roman *gens*. This evolution is attributed to King Malcolm Mac-Kenneth, 1005-34,[2] who is said to have laid down that the order of succession should be :—

" by whichever was at the time being the next descendant, that is, a son or a daughter, a nephew or a niece,[3] the nearest then living.[4] Failing these, however, the next heir begotten of the Royal or a collateral stock."

The last provision seems to have evolved into our Common-Law order of succession,[5] which soon came to ignore the " clan " or tribal element entirely,[6] but the petition of the Seven Earls in 1292 discloses that these magnates had a different interpretation. They submitted :—

" By the laws and customs of Scotland, from time whereof the memory of man was not, it pertained to the right, privilege, and members of the Seven Earls and *communitas* of the said kingdom, whenever the said Royal Seat should be vacant *de facto* and *de jure*, to constitute the King and to place him in the Royal Seat, and to yield up to him the Honours pertaining to the government of Scotland." [7]

By " Royal or a collateral stock," the Earls evidently contended that, if no heir existed *within the degrees of the Royal derbhfine*, and no *Tanist* had been designated, the succession was then for them to select from the collateral *derbhfines*.[8] The claim was rejected on the ground that the order of succession by next of blood (presumably Malcolm MacKenneth's Law) already applied to earldoms, baronies, and other "impartable tenures," and that the Scottish Crown devolved on similar principles. The earldoms (*mormaerships*) were really High-Chiefships,[9] and the early barons were likewise surmised to have been simply *capitani tribuum*.[10]

It may be doubted if the system was ever so " elective " in *Alba* or in Ireland. The Picto-Scots evidently saw, what modern historians point out, that the *derbhfine* system " would soon have reduced itself to an impossibility." [11] Rather, the characteristic tendency in Scotland

---

[1] Numbers xxvii. 8, xxxvi. 3.   [2] Skene, *Fordun*, II., 136.
[3] Perhaps *nepos aut neptis* meant grandson or granddaughter. If so, the first heads of Mackenneth's law of succession exclude sisters and their issue, which Stair adverts to in commenting on the case of Zelophahad's daughters (Stair, *Institutions*, III., 4-8). Sisters had usually married into other tribes already.
[4] Was *this* part of the basis of the Bruce's argument for the Crown?
[5] *Additional Case for Countess of Sutherland*, 1771, pp. 6 and 12.
[6] *Cf.* decision in *Bruce v. Baliol*, 1292, *Scotland under her Early Kings*, 21.
[7] *Mar Peerage Case*, 1875, Earl of Kellie's case, 99.
[8] Of course there were *derbhfines* beyond *derbhfines*, and apparently any *derbhfine* which had contributed a sovereign within three generations was eligible to provide a candidate—an appalling state of muddle (*Irish Law of Kingship*, 191, 193, 249 ; A. O. Anderson in *Scot. Hist. Review*, XXV., 383).   [9] *Scotland under her Early Kings*, 87.
[10] Craig, *Jus Feudale*, I.-8-2. Skene thought " Captains " were leaders subsidiary to "Chiefs," but A. McBain (*Highlanders of Scotland*, 1902, pp. 406, 413) holds *toisach*, captain, and chief, as synonymous, and that *capitanus* was the fourteenth to fifteenth century translation of *toisach* or *Ceancinnidh*. Comparison of the terms (Gaelic, French, and English) and the manner of their official usage, confirms this. The idea of " captain " as a subsidiary term is evidently a late one based on its use for an under-officer in the post-feudal and post-tribal Royal Army. The Hereditary Captaincy of Castles is consistent with either aspect, and probably passed from the one sense to the other. It was normally an hereditary and " chieftainly " tenure.
[11] A. O. Anderson, S.H.R., XXV., 283 ; J. Hogan, *Irish Law of Kingship*, 191, 249.

DIAGRAM OF *DERBHFINE* AND *GILFINE* SYSTEM OF FAMILY GROUPS

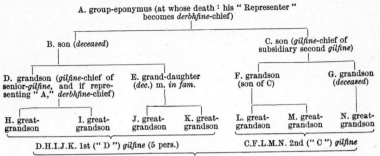

A. group-eponymus (at whose death [1] his " Representer " becomes *derbhfine*-chief)

B. son (*deceased*)

C. son (*gilfine*-chief of subsidiary second *gilfine*)

D. grandson (*gilfine*-chief of senior-*gilfine*, and if representing " A," *derbhfine*-chief)

E. grand-daughter (*dec.*) m. *in fam.*

F. grandson (son of C)

G. grandson (*deceased*)

H. great-grandson   I. great-grandson   J. great-grandson   K. great-grandson   L. great-grandson   M. great-grandson   N. great-grandson

D.H.I.J.K. 1st (" D ") *gilfine* (5 pers.)   C.F.L.M.N. 2nd (" C ") *gilfine*

D.H.I.J.K.C.F.L.M. *derbhfine* of " A " (9 persons), D being *derbhfine*-chief.

was *to make everything as hereditary as possible.* Indeed, *derbhfine* election in Scotland seems only to have been a form of intestate succession, as *Tanistry* was of testamentary settlement. Accordingly two practical measures modified the inefficiency of the *derbhfine* system and incidentally of primogeniture :

(1) By *Tanistry*, the ruling chief—like the Hebraic patriarchs— could nominate his successor, and thus interregnum and dispute were avoided. This was the practice in Roman and Hebraic law,[2] and in days of strife the tanist or *designatus*[3] was usually selected well in advance. Tanists are still traceable in the " Masters " as heirs to Scottish peerages.[4] Besides resignations and regrants of honours, Scots peerage law abounds with powers of " nomination " whereby peers had licence to appoint heirs to their dignities,[5] and in other cases a settlement by the peer himself has been given posthumous effect by Royal Warrant.[6] Similar practices in Chiefship, family representation and arms (" private rights " saved by Art. 18 of the Treaty of Union) subsist ; *e.g.*, numerous instances of Lyon giving effect as Crown Commissioner[7] to armorial settlements executed by will, tailzie, or *inter vivos* deed, and several involving chiefship specifically.[8] These are simply developments of the law of *Tanistry*.

[1] Few *derbhfiine-eponymi* could survive to reign, so representation is implicit.
[2] Maine, *Ancient Law*, 211, 215, 238, 266.
[3] John Riddell, *Peerage Law*, 210 ; S.H.R., XXV., 10.
[4] *Sources and Literature of the Law of Scotland*, 1936, p. 433.
[5] Stair Society, *Sources and Literature of the Law of Scotland*, p. 429.
[6] Lord Sinclair, *Scots Heraldry*, p. 87.
[7] *Scots Heraldry*, 87 ; J. Ferne, *Glorie of Generositie*, 67.
[8] *Grant of Auchernack, Chief of Clan Allan*, 1777, Lyon Register, I., 512 ; *Macneil of Barra*, 1915, ib. XXII., 60. In this case Lyon accepted a nomination by the late chief in favour of his second son, and awarded him the supporters, but (not having been referred to the Clan Allan, Scott of Synton, and other precedents, and from an apprehension the elder son might, as a U.S.A. citizen, be divested of arms) inserted a crescent in the chief's shield. Under 1672, cap. 47, however, Lyon is barred from awarding to any descendant of the family, its arms except those of the chief with an *added* brisure (*Cunningham v. Cunningham*, 11 Dunlop, 1139 ; *Clan Chattan Declaration*, 1672). So the true effect of the 1915 award would seem to be an alteration of the " chief arms " of Macneil, with the result that no branch-descendant could now matriculate except from the version including

The idea of an immutable descent of dignities is a mere reflection of late English peerage-law. As regards arms and chiefship it is contrary to the Act of Union,[1] and opposed to Scots common sense, which has naturally favoured passing over ne'er-do-weels, criminals, and fools, and also apportioning cumulated inheritances instead of merging them in one bloated line,[2] and selecting in each case for chief the most suitable son. Our institutional heraldic writers recognise the *right* to " adopt " and " settle " [3]—even upon a natural son [4] or a complete stranger,[5] which last is not approved by Scottish sentiment. Those who, when a settlement is made, within the tribe, talk of " disinherited rightful chiefs " are merely vapouring Anglo-Saxon nonsense.[6] *Tanistry* is still a recognised feature of our heraldic and clan law, and modern thought [7] would rather extend it to British peerages than restrict [8] the exercise, where occasion indicates, and subject to Official approval, of a useful and age-old patriarchal principle. Mackenzie and Nisbet distinguish settlement *within the blood*, which they regard as a matter of *right*,[9] from settlement on a stranger. Careful reading shows it is only in the latter contingency that they consider royal veto upon the transaction competent.[10] This explains the idea that Lyon is somehow bound to give effect to entail clauses to " enable the heir to take." Feudally, that cannot be, since (*a*) it would imply the subject could force the Crown's hand, (*b*) if Lyon refused, the condition would be " impossible " and void. Obviously the *true explanation* is survival in our Scottish family-law, and the Scottish Law of Arms which deals therewith, of the principle of *Tanistry*—the right of each patriarch to settle his successor (within the family), and only

the crescent which, in view of the statute, must be the ruling " chief arms " of Macneil. Many chief-arms have similarly been altered in detail in successive matriculations, *e.g.* Udny of that Ilk, Stirling of Keir, Hunter of Hunterston, Campbell of Aberuchill.

[1] Lord Sands delivered some *dicta* favouring this English (he didn't realise how alien !) doctrine in *Seaforth v. Allangrange*, 1920, S.C., 801—*giving no authorities*; whereas principles, precedents, and the constant practice of Lyon Court are opposed to this English absurdity.

[2] *Stirling-Maxwell of Pollok* and *Stirling of Keir* ; and the separation of the chiefships of *Grant* and *Colquhoun*, and of the *Earldom of Rothes* from *Haddington*.

[3] Sir George Mackenzie and Nisbet, and Macfarlane's *Gen. Colls.*, I., 125.

[4] *Lord of the Isles*, A.P.S., II., 189 ; *Maclean*, 1496, R.M.S. II., No. 2329.

[5] *Ross of Balnagowan*, 1732, Lyon Register, I., 208 ; *Heraldry in Scotland*, 353.

[6] Very likely thinking of the Jacobites and our " rightful king," but forgetting the proposition was that the Stuarts had been evicted by foreign force, and that the Hanoverian Kings were considered interlopers until Cardinal York settled his heirlooms on George III., making him heir by *tanistry*.   [7] *Hansard*, Dec. 1933, vol. 283, col. 374.

[8] Lord Sands' *groundless dicta* have not been followed in *e.g. Macleod of Macleod*, 1935, Lyon Register, XXXI., 74, and *Macgregor of Inneregny*, 1935, XXXII., 22, and, as in the old precedents of the seventeenth and eighteenth centuries, diversion of arms in the line of expediency or with the *duthus*, has continued. The correct difference of a superseded " heir " is a label, *cf. Duke of Windsor; Lindsay of Spynie*, Lyon Reg., XXXIII., 17.

[9] Nisbet's *Heraldry*, II., iii., pp. 56–60, also p. 33, l. 21, and 42, p. 34, l. 29, and p. 70, l. 24 ; referring to those who *have not* and those who " *have right* to dispose of the arms by way of testament or disposition."

[10] A person " assumed or adopted *by one of his own predecessors or family,* for these surely may bear the arms " (Mackenzie, Works, II., 616, l. 23) : " If lands were disponed to a *mere stranger* not upon condition that he should marry a daughter, but that he should bear the name and arms . . . the Receiver of the disposition cannot bear the arms (for that was not within the disponer's power to bestow) *except the prince consent*" (ib. l. 30).

if he makes a settlement outwith the group, or seeks to alter an existing specific destination, would a question of Royal veto or need for Letters Patent arise.[1] Otherwise the heir or nominee makes up his title by matriculation.[2] Unless the antecedent matriculation contains a specific destination, arms in Scotland thus pass by succession or nomination *in familia*, the former admitting of possession on apparency, the latter necessarily involving immediate rematriculation, which is technically requisite in every case,[3] to make up title to the arms and to establish the gentility and chiefship or chieftaincy denoted by the armorial achievement.

(2) The *Ard Righ*—even the Irish High-King—as part of his prerogative, could step in and settle troubles over chiefship, by determining the succession and causing one or other of the claimants to be inaugurated.[4] Similar power certainly came to be exercised by the *Ard Righ Albann* in the thirteenth century,[5] when, upon the chivalric principle of the " Fountain of Honour," the position was taken that chiefship—a " high social dignity " [6]—flowed from the Crown, and thus in the reign of David II. are found a series of charters confirming the office and diverting the order of succession of the *Kenkynol* of Carrick,[7] *i.e.* the chiefship of the Carrick and Kennedy " clans " and others; determining *who shall be* " Captain of " such communities as Clan Muntercasduff, Clan MacGowan, Clan Connan, and Clan Kennelman.[8] The very fact of the charters, not to add the terminology used, denotes the Crown's determination of a question, and that *clan* and *chiefships* were treated as heritable feudalised subjects.

By the thirteenth to fourteenth century the clans (*parentela*) were thus being held, like " noble families," to be " communities " whose status in public life flowed from the Crown (just as the " Seven Earls " were deemed to flow from the sons of Cruithne) and whereof the chiefships were dignities held of, and under, the Fountain of Honour.[9] The

[1] Although even an alteration of destination may (within the group, I assume) be made in a *matriculation* (*Heraldry in Scotland*, 127); no doubt a patent has often been craved in such circumstances, particularly if some ministerial declaration is desired in the deed ; and a patent is appropriate if a resignation has been formally made. If a petitioner asks confirmation by patent (and tenders the extra fees) he will naturally get it. In certain contests, a patent might also bar appeal, and force the opponent to sue a reduction if so advised, *cf. Dick-Cunyngham*, Lyon Register, V., 16.

[2] *Stewart-Mackenzie of Seaforth*, 1935, Lyon Register, XXXI., 56.

[3] *Fiscal of Lyon Court v. Murray of Touchadam*, 1778, Morrison's *Dict.*, 7656

[4] Chieftainship of the Burkes, 1595, *Irish Law of Kingship*, p. 199.

[5] If this period opened a new and " organised " basis of Clanship, obviously that organisation was based on the supremacy of the Crown.

[6] Per Lord Justice-Clerk in *Maclean of Ardgour v. Maclean*, 1937.

[7] Great Seal, I., 509 ; II., 379. [8] Ib. I., App. II., Nos. 912, 913, 914, 982.

[9] The Scottish nobiliary system has always differed from that of England in that whilst it appreciates the value of heredity, it also realises the inexpediency of immutable primogeniture. *Tanistry* was perpetuated in the regrants, nominations, tailzies, and other expedients whereby honours of every description *could*, as Chiefship and arms still *can*, be diverted into whatever channel from time to time seems most expedient (*Scots Heraldry*, 86), provided resort is made to the Fountain of Honour, and a satisfactory ground for the diversion shown by one having right to the honour to be diverted (Nisbet's *Heraldry*, II., iii., pp. 33, 34 ; *Scots Heraldry*, p. 86).

fifteenth century saw the development of armorial jurisdiction and the Court of Chivalry, *i.e.* Law of Arms ; also of the delegation of the Crown's prerogative of creating *nobilitas minor* (gentility as distinct from peerage) to the Kings of Arms—in Scotland to an officer already vested with the *genealogical* jurisdiction of the High Sennachie [1] —and consequently no more Royal " gifts of chieftaincy " pass the Great Seal. The " dignities " of Esquire and Gentleman were henceforth determined in, and matters of record in, the courts of the Law of Arms,[2] and it was there that claimants had to justify the same " *by* the Law of Arms." [3] The King of Arms, commissioned to " visite," inquired not merely into the armorial charges—which are a mere branch of heraldic duty [4]—but as judge inquired into all relevant matters of nobility including " pedigrees, titles or designations," taking cognisance of all and " degrading interlopers and upstarts." [5]

The clan has become the " honourable community," whose chief, as its " Representer," is " received and numbered amongst the ancient nobles of the realm," and distinguished by ensigns armorial, over which the Crown, for purposes of national safety, exercises a close control under the " Law of Arms." The chiefship has become a recognised social dignity, but of what rank ? A glance at the Precedency List, and at the degree of " helmets befitting their degree " assigned to chiefs in armorial patents, will show that the degree of this dignity is that of *Esquire*.[6] This exactly coincides with Macpherson's assertion that chiefship gave its holder precedence before " the first gentlemen of the Kingdom " [7] and the relative helmet.[8]

Now, it is entirely within the prerogative of the Crown whether a person or a community is to be received as a noble person or community amongst the nobles and noble groups of the realm or not.[9] If it be the Crown's pleasure to receive such community, the order of succession is absolutely dependent on the Crown's pleasure in making

---

[1] *Familie of Innes*, 1864, p. 46.

[2] *Scots Law Times*, 1937, p. 156 : J. Dallaway, *Heraldic Enquiries*, 309 ; Hailsbury's *Laws of England*, 1912 Ed., Vol. XXII., p. 289, par. 632.

[3] *Right to Bear Arms*, 1900, p. 123. Shrewsbury Peerage, 1857, Min. of Ev. 16, 18, 215.

[4] Sir J. Anstis, *Order of the Garter*, p. 326.

[5] J. Gwillim, *Display of Heraldry*, 1724, Honour Civil, p. 49.

[6] This and *Gentleman* may be relatively low in rank, but they are none the less hereditary honours, flowing only from the Fountain of Honour as the Royal commissions affirm, and a degree in the nobility as laid down in the Scottish statute, 1592, cap. 125, and the Baronetcy Warrants of Charles I. wherein the order of precedency is :—(1) Baronets ; (2) Equites, *lie* Knights ; (3) Barones, *lie* Lairds ; (4) Armigeri, *lie* Esquires ; (5) et Generosis quibuscunque, *lie* gentlemen. (Sir R. Douglas, *Baronage of Scotland*, p. 11 ; *Sources and Literature of the Law of Scotland* (Stair Soc.), p. 431 —where *Barones* marked for italics, was instead accidentally deleted !)

[7] *Loyall Dissuasive*, 26.   [8] *Scots Heraldry*, 22, n. 1 ; Denmiln MSS., 34–4–16.

[9] Whilst individual " nobility " depends on creation or proved descent, the Law of Arms has always recognised the existence of " noble " groups (" houses," " families," or " clans," *cf.* the patrician *gentes* of Rome) and persons are officially described as *e.g.* " of an auld honourable house " (A.P.S., II., 520 ; Lyon Reg., V., 16), and similarly of an " honourable clan "—which governs the *basis* of the arms—(*tesseræ nobilitatis*) which they will be awarded on receiving, by grant or confirmation, personal hereditary nobility, *i.e. duine-uasail*.

the grant or confirmation of *noblesse*, and any modification of the succession must be sought from the Crown by seeking a diversion of the
order of descent of the insignia conferred by the Crown for distin-
tinguishing this dignity.[1] As regards the descent of, and claims to,
chiefship, this was a subject which, in the seventeenth century, it was
not doubted was capable of legal determination, when the chiefship
of Clan Chattan was for five days debated in the Privy Council,[2] and
was then understood to have been previously argued before the Lord
of the Isles,[3] and not only was decree upon such a subject regarded
as enforceable,[4] but Macpherson seems of opinion that there was no
safe appeal from a Royal determination.[5] Only the party adjudged
chief " by the Law of Arms " (by which honours and dignities are
alone determinable)[6] could be received as chief[7] by the Crown and
public officials. Throughout the *Loyall Dissuasive* there is no suggestion that clan chiefship was elective, any more than there is in
the charters of David II. or the patents of chiefly achievements in
Lyon Register. If chiefship *had* been considered elective the " ornaments " (and arms) would, as in the case of corporations, have been
limited to "successors in office," not to various series of heirs. No
claimant such as John Moydertach of Clanranald could have any
security until his status had been acknowledged by the Crown.[8] In
constitutional principle, the only occasion where election has been
admitted is, where an " honourable community " exists, but the line
of chiefly succession has become extinct or cannot be established.[9]
In such a contingency, when the chiefship must otherwise have remained dormant, and the " honourable community " without a head,
the Lord Lyon—acting in accordance with the old tribal principle—
and exercising the delegated sovereign authority of the *Ard Righ*,
has awarded (heritably) the armorial achievement of the chief[10] to

---

[1] An *obiter dictum* in *Maclean of Ardgour v. Maclean* (1938, S.L.T. 57), that a " high
social dignity " can emanate from any source—such as an election—other than the Fountain
of Honour, was subsequently disregarded by the Court in 1941, being obviously untenable.
Chiefship being thus admitted a dignity, it is, however, immediately excluded from the
jurisdiction of the Court of Session (*Earl of Lauderdale v. Scrymgeour-Wedderburn*, 1910,
S.C., H.L., 44), and moreover becomes cognisable only in a court of the Law of Arms (1937,
Scots Law Times, 156 ; J. Gwillim, *Display of Heraldry*, 1724, Honour Civil, p. 49) and
must be established " *by* the Law of Arms " (*Right to Bear Arms*, 123).
[2] Sir Æneas Macpherson, *Loyall* Dissuasive, 58.   [3] Ib. 54, 115.   [4] Ib. 115.
[5] Ib. 117.   [6] W. Cruise, *Treatise on Dignities*, 251.
[7] *E.g.* if chiefs were ever again to be reviewed by the King as in 1822, or summoned
qua chiefs to Holyroodhouse, obviously only chiefs of whom there is official record would
be summoned, and the dignities of Esquire and Gentleman, within which chiefship falls,
are " of record " only in the Registers of a King of Arms (Halsbury's *Laws of England*,
1912, XXII., 289, par. 632 ; 1552, cap. 53, A.P.S. VII. 458). It is from Lyon alone that a
list of chiefs could be obtained. Accordingly, at the Lord High Commissioner's Holyrood
state dinner in May 1947, the Mackintosh, following his chiefship-decree 18th March 1947,
was placed much higher than *qua* naval officer in 1946.
[8] Moydertach's line was confirmed in the *earbsa* lands by the Crown before Lyon accepted
them as " chiefs."   [9] *Cf.* " *de facto* and *de jure* vacant," of the " Seven Earls' " Petition.
[10] That a clan election (actually Lyon's pro-regal discretionary patent to the electee) was
deemed to confer hereditary right on the line of the electee, see A. Murray Macgregor,
History of Clan Gregor, II., 271 ; *Campbell of Inverneil* (Chief of *Clan Chearleich*), 1875,
Lyon Register, IX., 88.

a nominee submitted by the clan or heads of its landed houses.[1] Mr J. H.
Stevenson, K.C., stated in the Macrae Case :—

"Nothing could be more erroneous than the opinion, or more inconsistent with the
character of the Highlanders, than to suppose that they ever in any degree admitted of
election." [2]

Obviously the Crown, through Lyon, could not be compelled to award
a chief's achievement and supporters ("feudal heritage") to an electee,
in despite of an heir under specific destination to these honours from
the Crown, unless the chief, under the existing destination, made a
demission of the insignia in Lyon's hands *in favorem*,[3] for although the
Crown of Scotland can accept resignations and implement entails or
settlements,[4] it cannot derogate from a right already conferred, without
the actual holder's initiative, nor can he on his part *complete* a diversion
without the King of Arms' consent *pro Rege*; though, as above-indi-
cated, it appears that where nomination *within the blood* is concerned,
the Scottish heraldic view is that the settler has the "right" to divert
the representation (*i.e.* chiefship) and relative insignia.

In the limited contingencies when an election *is* competent, such
will in the case of a chief be by nobles of the whole clan, and in case
of a branch-chieftain, of the branch.[5] Chiefship being a gentle dignity,
at least in the case of honourable (*i.e.* armigerous) communities, only
in such a contingency could an election arise without involving *pur-
presture* and treason. An *ignoble* community could elect whom it liked.
Not being *notilis* or known, such "limmers" would have no public
status, and their "chief" no dignity. As Sir Æneas puts it : If a
person was "of no family her father could not be a Cheefe"[6]; and
says Nisbet,[7] the "first raiser" of a family is he who first obtains a
coat of arms, *i.e.* the *indiciae* of *noblesse* which brings the community
(clan or other) within the cognisance of the Court and Social Life of
the Realm—and consequently of the Law of Arms.

[1] *Macnaughton*, 1818, Lyon Register, II., 172; *Macgregor*, 1795, ib. I., 565. The successful claimant got 880 votes (*Burke's Peerage*, 1937). In an earlier election, Macgregor of
Balhaddie had got 14 votes. A. M. Macgregor, *History of Clan Gregor*, 273.

[2] *Macrae v. Macrae*, 1909, Lyon Court, Report, p. 104. In some recent Clan disputes,
an "Association" elected one chief, then a rival "Society" elected another, and apparently
some overseas Clan societies were similarly electing Chiefs and High Chiefs. Such dignities
are of no more social or legal significance than "Lord Justice Clerks" elected by 19th century
drinking clubs (J. Henderson, *Annals of Lower Deeside*, p. 216), of no armorial significance,
and quite unrelated to the Clans and Chiefs of Scottish history recognised in armorial
jurisprudences.

[3] *Cf. Grant of Auchernach, Chief of the Clan Allan*, 1777, Lyon Register, I., 515; *Scott of
Sinton*, 1700, ib. II., 189., text printed in *Notes and Queries*, 27/4/1940, p. 293. A Roman
ould *sell* his clan to a *familiæ emptor*, but under chivalric feudal law, clan and chiefship
were matters of solemn settlement only "for grave and weighty considerations."

[4] 8 & 9 Vict. cap. 23, sec. 21; *Scots Heraldry*, p. 86; *Macneil of Barra*, 1915, Lyon
Reg., Vol. XXII., p. 60; *Campbell of Dunstaffnage*, ib. 34, p. 71; *Maclachlan*, ib. 35, p. 72.

[5] Lord Justice-Clerk in *Maclean of Ardgour v. Maclean*, 1938, S.L.T., 57, and per Lord
Mackay, by the principal *landed men*, of the clan or branch (a significant admission of the
territorial character of *chieftaincy*; *cf.* p. 32, *supra*), *i.e.* by the *duine-uasail*, *i.e.* the
nobiles armigeri.

[6] *Loyall Dissuasive*, p. 35. That is, to be chief of a clan one *must*, in Macpherson's view,
be the chief of the stem-family as recognised by the Crown's Officer of Honour.

[7] *System of Heraldry*, 1722, Vol. II., p. 3. The disinherited heir is termed in Spain *Pariente
Major* (*Juridical Review*, Sept. 1940, p. 220) and in Britsh Heraldry gets the arms differenced
by a label (Innes of Learney, *Law of Succession in Ensigns Armorial*, 46).

ORDER OF SUCCESSION.

As already indicated, the Scottish order of succession was derived from a Pictish basis, whose evolution is *attributed* to Malcolm Mac-Kenneth. Salic Law has never obtained in Scotland, and any attempt to introduce it has been repudiated as alien to our tradition and custom,[1] and in numerous clan traditions a fresh *eponymus* (really an " Incoming Husband ") is made to marry the heiress of an older Gaelic race.[2] It was apparently not because they were women that the clans objected to Mary Macleod and Anne Macpherson. There was a far graver reason—they married Campbells. The tribes had seen what happened with Muriel of Cawdor, and feared that two fresh branches of Clan Diarmid would arise on the ruins of Macpherson and Macleod. In the great Clan Chattan controversy, so strenuously argued in the seventeenth century, there is not a suggestion of Salic Law.[3] The Salic theory in the Scottish Highlands (argued, of course, from cases of tailzied nomination, etc.) appears to have been first propounded [4] by the notorious Simon, Lord Lovat, and the theory only occurred to him when he had failed to secure the chiefship by the abduction of either the heiress or the widow of his predecessor. The principle laid down by Macpherson—a lawyer and sheriff—and reiterated through his book,[5] is, in his own words :—

" Both from law and reason, we have the constant custome and practice of all the families of the Kingdome of our side to plead for us in this point, so much, That if you can instance us one familie in the whole Kingdome that owns one for their Cheefe for his being married to a daughter of the familie or ane heiress, *without his assuming the name and bearing (i.e.* the arms) of the family, we shall forthwith submitt " (p. 34). " It must needs follow that being himself M'Pherson, upon the same foot with us, that is, in memory of his predicissors office, *his daughter was so,*[6] and all that are come of her (if she was ane heiress), should be likewayes called M'Pherson, *without which* M'Intoshe do or say what he will, can never pretend to be our Cheefe ; for if he should to-morrow, or any time hereafter, assume the name of Cathone, that gives him no more title to be Cheefe of the *M'Phersons* than if he hade been married to the heiress of Struan, should think to be Cheefe of the Robertsons by calling himself M'Donell " (p. 48).[7]

Other high authorities took the same view as Macpherson. The destination of the *Cean Cinnidh* of Carrick was *heredibus,* and through

---

[1] W. Angus, Keeper of the Register and Records, *Sources and Literature of the Law of Scotland,* 268.
[2] *Social and Economic Development of Scotland,* 521, 580.; Nisbet *Heraldry,* II., Ap. 239.
[3] *Loyall Dissuasive,* Scottish History Soc. Ed., 29, 33, 34, 35, 39, 48, 55, 59, 71, 114, 116.
[4] Saving, perhaps, William Macpherson of Nuid, who was also *auctor in rem suam,* but who admitted the power of his chief to tailzie the succession *unless God prevented.*
[5] *Loyall Dissuasive,* 33. " M'Intoshe, his marrying (the heiress) *without taking the name and bearing of the family* could never make him Cheefe. That was *conditio sine qua non,*" failing *which,* the chiefship and following devolved upon the heir-male.
[6] Macpherson here recognises that the succession devolves on the heiress herself, and that the patronymic *M'Pherson* as a title would also devolve on her.
[7] Sir Æneas is silent concerning the Lord Lyon's Declaration, 10 Sept. 1672, and evades the point that neither Macpherson nor Mackintosh bore the name " Chattan," and that Lyon's decision was confined to (*a*) the aggregate community of " Clan Chattan," (*b*) the " Name of Mackintosh "—one of the components. Lyon never affirmed that Mackintosh was Chief of " the Macphersons " *as a unit within* the honourable community.

D

heirs-female it can be shown to have descended ; Walter Macfarlane of that Ilk, the great Antiquary, and Chief of his Clan, took the destination of his arms and chiefly insignia—*including the slogan*—to " heirs," *not* heirs-male,[1] and Maconnochie of Meadowbank, the Lord Advocate in 1819, likewise took the destination of the supporters granted him *as Chief of the clan*, to " the heirs whatsoever of the patentee's body." [2] None of these high authorities believed in Salic Law, or applied it to the succession awarded to their own houses.

Another significant point is that not only male heirs-apparent but an eldest daughter (being heiress apparent) was put out in fosterage.[3] This, and the label-differencing of an heiress-apparent's arms *vita patris*,[4] show how natural it was to treat the heiress exactly on the same footing as a male heir.   When she did succeed, Scottish heraldry —and Macpherson talks of " good " and " bad herauldrie " in relation to Clanship[5]—treated the heiress exactly as if the succession were uninterrupted, allowing her shield and crest[6] and even an " helmet befitting her degree," [7] so that the representation of the house continued heraldically—as genealogically—uninterrupted.

It will not escape the reader that Macpherson's principle, although it recognises the right being in the heiress herself—as the Royal and Lyon documents likewise expressly do[8]—treats the *son-in-law* as " Chief " *jure uxoris*.   This " Incoming Husband " is a feature of other tribal countries as well as Scotland.[9]   A recent authority writes :—

" It was recognised that whilst the actual muscle must be that of a man, the man held office by right of his descent or connection with a woman." [10]

" The Queen, through whom the Royal *Rank* and Blood came,[11] must have enjoyed an esteem which, when she knew how to use it, gave her considerable authority." [12]

There are, however, numerous instances of females taking command in their own right, even in the Middle Ages,[13] whereof Boadicea and Cartismandua of the *Brigantes* are instances, and mediæval heraldry even provided rules regarding the cut of armorial tabards to be worn

[1] Lyon Register, I., 377 (*heirs* includes females).   [2] Ib. II., 184.
[3] Mary Bisset, per Wardlaw MSS., p. 3 ; cited in *Macrae v. Macrae*, 1909, Lyon Court ; Proof, p. 79 ; and regarding education see Statutes of Iona.
[4] Janet Fenton of Bakie, *Scottish Armorial Seals*, No. 915.
[5] *Loyall Dissuasive*, 49, 63, 72.
[6] *Buccleuch*, Lyon Register, I., 34 ; *Robertson of Lawers*, II., 117 ; *Gibsone of Pentland*, II., 52 ; *Farquharson of Invercauld*, 1815, II., 130 ; 1936, XXXII., 34.
[7] *Buccleuch, supra*; *Cunningham*, I., 275 ; *Conti-White*, 1778, Reg. of Gen., I.
[8] *Loyall Dissuasive*, p. 48. Cf. Lord Royston (W. Fraser, *Earls of Cromartie*, II., 179).
[9] Sir E. B. Tayler, *The Nineteenth Century*, Vol. XL., p. 94.
[10] R. A. M. Macalister, *Ireland in Pre-Celtic Times*, p. 242. Our Scoto-Pictish customs may thus be " pre-Celtic " and indigenous to the realm of Scotland.
[11] As already pointed out, the " King " and " Mormaer " were just the highest variety of chiefs. The same *principles* were, *e.g.* in *Bruce v. Baliol*, held applicable to both.
[12] Henri Hubert, *The Rise of the Celts*, p. 210.
[13] J. Cameron, *Celtic Law*, p. 93, cites primitive instances of them going to battle in an inferior capacity, but in the Middle Ages Baronesses, etc., were summoned to the Royal Army "with horse and arms " (Rymer, *Foedera*, I., p. 753).

by women commanding in the field.[1] That heraldry may relevantly be referred to in *Clan* matters is evidenced by Sir Æneas Macpherson, who refers to " good " or " bad herauldrie." He appreciated that chiefship was a subject to be " justified by the Law of Arms." [2] In her father or husband's absence, a *Ban-Tigherna* had no doubt not infrequently to take the rôle of a " Black Agnes " or a " Helen Macgregor."

In the Middle Ages an heiress was either married or put in a convent at the age of fourteen (in Celtic Scotland), so the independent *Chieftainess* [3] seldom emerged in practice. If the heir was under fourteen, an acting-chief was chosen, who held office, or anyway *title*, for life, but on the direct heir attaining full age they ruled jointly.[4] This explains the " joint reigns " found in our early history, and similarly Mackintosh of Benchar acted as Chief, pending the majority of his nephew ; but by 1609, this Tutor-like office apparently terminated at the heir's majority,[5] as the Clan Chattan band explains.

The express right of a woman to hold " chiefship " personally, which is recognised in the armorial patents such as Lord Advocate MacConnochie's and the destination of the *Kenkynol*, however, was necessarily and formally recognised in the case of the Crown, or highest " chiefship " of all, when the " Maid of Norway " [6] was received as Queen. For the Scottish coronation involved receiving the *Ard Righ* as " Chief," [7] and though the " Maid " died before her coronation, Mary Queen of Scots *was* crowned, and *must*, according to the usual ceremony, have (*omnia rite acta esse presumunter*) been installed " chief."

The principle enunciated by Sir Æneas was re-stated in Council in November 1672 by the Earl Marischal,[8] and so confident of its correctness was Macpherson, that he applies it in favour of Glengarry's claim, through the heiress of Lochalsh, to the chiefship of Clan Donald,[9] on which the Privy Council had already taken the same view.[10]

---

[1] G. Legh, *Accidens of Armory* (1562), fol. 96 ; E. J. Millington, *Heraldry in History, Poetry, and Romance* (1858), 296.   [2] *Loyall Dissuasive*, pp. 49, 63, 72, ref. to " bearings."

[3] This term, which appears in the fifteenth century and is sanctioned by Sir Walter Scott (*New Oxford Dictionary*), is considered unnecessary by the Court of Session, on the ground that a female Chairman is not called a " Chairwoman." But in the more punctilious and chivalric atmosphere of the Law of Arms, the title of a dignitated female is normally feminised. One does not call a Queen-regnant a " King," nor a Countess in her own right an " Earl." The Gaelic dictionary provides feminines of almost every rank in Scotland. The Lord Justice-Clerk's view that *Chief* is a term applicable to either sex is, however, borne out by Trevoux's French Dictionary (1743) : " *Il se dit aussi au feminin* " ; see also *La Dictionaire de L'Academie Française.*

[4] W. F. Skene, *Highlanders of Scotland*, 1902 Ed., p. 105.

[5] It has been suggested that for convenience such an *ad hoc* " chief " or " chieftain " should be styled " Chieftain-Wardatour," as the term " Sheriff-Wardatour " was used in hereditary sheriffdoms. It has been objected that this sounds " French " ; but the very words " chief " and " chieftain " are French, so the only question is really what to call him in Gaelic. Had an appropriate term existed there would not have been the existing historical confusion over " joint reigns."

[6] Titles of this description are incidentally matter of record in Lyon Register, *cf.* " Fair Maid of Moray," Lyon Register, I., 528, being of course factual " pedigree matter."

[7] Nisbet's *Heraldry*, II., iv., p. 155.   [8] *Loyall Dissuasive*, 59.

[9] Ib. 118. Many complicated considerations are, however, involved in Clan Donald's chiefship.   [10] *Privy Council*, 3rd Ser. III. 552.

The principle thus laid down by a distinguished seventeenth-century lawyer (whose party-interest was assuredly to propound the Salic Law —if anything of the sort had existed in the Scottish Highlands) explains not only many clan successions, but much armorial practice of the Lyon Court, and the terms of the Royal charters, *e.g.* of *Kenkynol.* It happens to be the principle also found in the quasi-agnatic families of some other countries, where the *incoming husband* [1] is a recognised feature. Sir George Mackenzie considers such a husband ought to drop his own name and arms entirely,[2] and when any possibility of confusion exists, that is the only safe course,[3] as it is in any event the only proper course, unless two " houses " are merged in one line.[4] In the Clan Chattan case (whereof Macpherson makes so much, but of Lyon says little—since he had decided against Macpherson), Sir Charles Erskine's decision was obviously based on the principle that since neither Mackintoshes nor Macphersons bore the name " Chattan," that chiefship passed to the eldest flow of the blood within the clan, nor did the Privy Council overturn Lyon's decision.[5] Cluny-Macpherson's matriculation was of date the day following.[6] Whatever procedure was then preliminary to the issue of a Declaration from the Lord Lyon King of Arms,[7] its official value was such that it was received and acted on by the Crown, to the extent of even awarding differenced versions of the Royal Arms.[8] Since the succession to " Clan Chiefship " appears—save where competently diverted by tailzie or settlement, with consent of the Crown through its King of Arms (*i.e.* in a matriculation of arms or supporters), or where the Crown has similarly received as chief some particular or nominated member of the group—to be in " the eldest line of the eldest blood " bearing the Name, it only remains to observe that where such chiefship devolves upon a female, it appears that on her marriage, or within due time,[9] her husband *must also take the clan name,* and that the heir-male—who is then the principal cadet of the family—has a prominent status at the immediate

[1] *Erbtochtermann* and *Iri Muko.* Sir E. B. Tayler, *The Nineteenth Century,* Vol. XL., p. 94; H. B. G. Westermark, *History of Human Marriage,* 1901, p. 110.
[2] *Works,* II., 490, 616; *cf. Scots Heraldry,* 107 (non-armigerous husband).
[3] *Cf.* Nisbet's *Heraldry,* II., iii., 48. Nisbet failed to perceive what the chiefs evidently realised. Had the later chiefs of Clan Mackenzie, founding on their ancestress's matriculation, 1815, refrained from quartering Stewart, the great Seaforth litigation, 1920–22, need never have arisen.   [4] Innes of Learney, *Scots Heraldry,* p. 88.
[5] Naturally not—having applied same principle to Clan Donald on 18 July !
[6] Cluny's matriculation of 12 March 1672 was necessarily reduced prior to 10 Sept. 1672, at least *quoad* the *description.* Whether the reduction itself was *in foro* we have no evidence— perhaps not—Cluny, for example, was not a " baron " as he had averred, and presumably did not defend. The Declaration, far from being for private edification, was promptly sent north for publication (Macfarlane's *Genealogical Collections,* I., p. 393).
[7] And these are directed to " all persons of eminence having power and authority to take cognisance of titles." (*Familie of Innes,* p. 45 ; *Cumming,* 1727, Reg. of Gen., I., p. 1.)
[8] *Lundin of Lundin,* 1679, Nisbet, I., 66; Warrant, *John* (formerly Drummond) *Lundin of that Ilk,* "incoming husband " of the heiress Sophia Lundin of Lundin.
[9] *Loyall Dissuasive,* 39 ; presumably within *anno deliberandi* (year and day) unless she (Matheson of **Achany,** *Scots Heraldry,* 152) and her child keep her name independently.

right-hand of the heir-female chief[1] who is the " premier head " of the race.[2] Until a break occurs in lineal male succession this post of honour belongs to the eldest cadet. Indeed, in many clan cases the so-called " eldest cadet " would probably now appear to be actually the collateral heir-male where the name, arms, and chiefship have passed to an heir-female.

The foregoing has been the view of all our great jurists and states the *real law,* and in Crown, Peerage, and Chiefships, this Scots order of succession has in practice proved itself expedient. It is always disruptive if continuity of the sacred race-embodiment be interrupted, or confusion and discord supervene, or the racial representation be separated from the *earbsa*-land. In the present age of smaller families and high death-duties, we must recognise that perpetuation of male succession is deplorably likely to become progressively rarer. It is therefore of practical importance that, as in the case of our highest chiefship, the Crown, the dignity of a clan chief or chieftain duly passes in the old Pictish order of *the directest succession*—the basis of our Common Law succession—*provided the heiress, at least, and her husband retain, or take, the name and title of the clan*—a *sine qua non,* legally a " resolutive condition." Owing to the modern English predilection for double-barrelled surnames, Sir George Mackenzie's emphasis upon the necessity of taking the heiress's name *alone,* must be reiterated. For the succession of the heir of line, we have the considered opinions of Scots Privy Council, the Earl Marischal, the Lord Advocate, three Lords of Session, four Lords Lyon, and Sir Æneas Macpherson. Riddell, the celebrated peerage lawyer, has pointed out " the constant devolution of *all* our older peerages to heirs general besides the later female descents," and the 19th-century Salic ideas, when applied to Scotland, have been described as " a perversion of the facts and misconstruction of the ancient law of the country." [3]

DETERMINATION OF CHIEFSHIP.

The Chiefship of a " noble and armigerous family " has always been a subject capable of judicial determination, either in Pedigree, or in relation to its Arms (*tesserae gentilitatis*), but, being a " dignity," is also capable of ministerial determination by the Crown, or its Supreme Officer of Honour, the King of Arms, in a Birthbrief, of the form entitled *Diploma Stemmatis,* with which, as an exercise of the Pre-

---

[1] *Loyall Dissuasive,* 52. [2] *Clan Cochrane,* Reg. of Genealogies, I., 2 (Earl of Dundonald).
[3] H. Doubleday, *Complete Peerage,* VIII. 854. A *second* earldom *was* also created 1565. *Maclean of Ardgour,* 1941 S.C. 616 : proposed findings 16, 19, 20, and Warrant 2nd, sustained for Lyon's decision *in foro* (p. 658) and approved by L.J.C. p. 630–35; Mackay, p. 651 ; Wark, p. 654, 656.

rogative, and a " ministerial " function of the King of Arms—a Minister of the Crown—the Courts " cannot " interfere.[1]

A clan, or *parentela*, as it is called in the Great Seal Charters,[2] is similarly an incorporeal nobiliary " fief," and a heritable subject —of which there can be an " heir " or " heretrix "—and a heritable destination,[3] like a " family " as above-mentioned ; and in the Ardgour proof in July 1938 the whole basis of the Division's preliminary (1937) opinions (referred to on pp. 51-2 of this book, 1938 ed.) was over- turned by the expert witnesses, including Dr L. Maclean Watt's evidence :

" Clan and Family mean exactly the same thing. . . . Yes, Clan and Family are the same. . . . Stem or stock [4] is a good word perfectly understandable in dealing with High- land matters." [5]

Indeed, the more so when related to Sir George Mackenzie's pronounce- ment (subsequently declared authoritative by Lord Aitchison) about undifferenced arms and heraldic differencing, viz. :

" such difference or brisure as might . . . distinguish their families from that of their *Chief*, *for so we call the Representative of the Family*, from the French word *chef* or Head, and in the Irish (Gaelic) with us *the Chief of the Family is called the Head of the Clan*.[6]

This completely equates the Highland Clan, and its *Ceann-Cinnidh*,[7] with the "noble armigerous family" and its Chief; and with the Law of Arms, and heraldic differencing, pursuant to the statutes 1592 c. 125 and 1672 c. 47,[8] and with Lords Dunedin and Shaw's opinions (the operative decisions in the Seaforth case) in the House of Lords in 1922 (see p. 28, n. 2).

[1] Admitted by 2nd Div. in *Maclean of Ardgour v. Maclean*, 1937, *see* 1941, S.C. p. 638 ; the qualification, " which can be brought before *us* as a question of law," left the subject of nobiliary descriptions—such as hereditary chiefships of all " Honourable communities "—in Lyon's exclusive jurisdiction, agreeably to Sir Charles Erskine's Clan Chattan letter (see p. 53 *infra*, and also *Juridical Review*, Sept. 1940, pp. 182, 194, 204, 208). A Birthbrief, being Ministerial (as admitted by Lord Mackay, 1941, S.C. 642), is immediately placed completely outwith the appellate jurisdiction of the Courts ; just like the Scottish Secretary's " Letter " in *Royal College of Surgeons, &c.*, which, as an expression of *his* official opinion, and the manner in which *he* would act, could not be muzzled, or varied (save by the Sovereign.) The same applies to Lyon's *Diplomae* in matters pertaining to his sphere of duty. Accord- ingly it was *ultra vires* of Lord Mackay (or the Court, as Lord Aitchison perceived, S.C. p. 638) to say what Lyon might or might not put in it !—as was laid down of Ministerial Writs in the words " cannot interfere " ; per Lord Robertson in *MacDonell v. Macdonald*, 1826, 4 Shaw 371 (see *Heraldry in Scotland*, p. 73).   [2] See p. 41.

[3] Kenkynol of Carrick, R.M.S., I., 539 ; Clan Chattan Declar., 10 Sept. 1672, see p. 51. [4] The purpose of Arms for distinguishing those of " noble stok " is set forth in 1592 c. 125. [5] Ardgour Evidence, p. 517.   [6] Mackenzie, *Works*, II. 618, line 18. [7] The Chief, or *Ceann-Cinnidh*, has to be distinguished from the War-Leader, *Ceann-Cath* (See *Notes and Queries*, 15 Aug. 1942, pp. 96–98) who in the eighteenth century was styled the " Commander of the Clan " (*Historical Papers*, New Spalding Club, pp. 357, 358, 362, 368). Chiefship is hereditary, " War-leadership " selective (E. W. Robertson, *Scotland under her Early Kings*, p. 27, analysed in *N. & Q. supra*, p. 96). [8] Lyon accordingly, on 19 Dec. 1938, thought himself precluded from calling anyone chief, chieftain, or representer (1941, S.C. 644–5) in consequence of the Division's Interlocutor of 17/7/37 erroneously pre-assuming that *clan* and *family* were different (and excluding evid- ence on clan-branch chieftaincy)—since by determining Representer/Chiefship *of Family* (as expressly held competent) he would (in light of the evidence in proof) incidentally and automatically determine Chiefship/Chieftaincy of or in the clan. Lyon, of course, *should* have just determined the Family Representer/Chiefship as remitted, even though it had transpired on proof that this would incidentally determine " clan " chiefship or chieftaincy. Accordingly Lyon—on the Lord Justice Clerk's holding there was nothing to prevent him (p. 687) and, by the Division's interlocutor 18/7/41—directed to " proceed as accords " with the Petition of the party found in right of " the old family seal of arms " (1941, S.C. 713–14)—then duly described the heir in the arms (*Pub. Reg. of Genealogies*, IV, No. 26, 26 Feb. 1943) in the terms laid down by Sir George Mackenzie ; and judicially 11th July 1944.

The Court of Session had accordingly quietly to extricate itself from the situation mistakenly adopted in 1937 ; and, looking indeed to Lord Aitchison's definition of *right to the undifferenced arms as coincident with chiefship*, laid down, per Lord Justice-Clerk Aitchison, that there was nothing to preclude Lyon Court [1] affirming that the heir in the estate and the " family arms " is the Representer of the Family, which Mackenzie had authoritatively declared synonymous with " Head of the Clan." This affirmation Lyon thereafter duly performed, in a *Diploma Stemmatis*, 26 Feb. 1943, and subsequently by decree, 11 July 1944, in a re-matriculation. The Jurisdiction of Lyon Court thus, in such matters, remains what it was always believed to be ; and the undifferenced Arms represent the chiefly character attributed to them by all heralds and jurists, and by the House of Lords. In accordance with this principle several important Clan Chiefships have since been decided.[2] The 2nd Division acknowledged that in 1672 the Lord Lyon made a *Declaration of Chiefship* of Clan Chattan, and of the " Innes tribe " in 1698, and naturally did not lay down that Lyon as a Great Officer of the Crown [3] can be prevented from investigating and forthwith making such a " Declaration " ; and as regards the effect of such a declaration, it is the case that until the institution of the Roll of Baronets, Lyon's certificate was the normal evidence accepted by the Lord Chamberlain regarding a right to the dignity of Baronet.[4] Such declarations and certificates of genealogy, etc., are frequently in the form of Patents, and therefore are ministerial acts of the King's representative, and as such, outwith any judicial review.[5] In this connection, Lord Lyon Erskine's letter to Cluny-Macpherson, after the pronouncement of the Clan Chattan Declaration, indicates the situation and Lyon's *official authority* in such matters :—

"You, *without having got leave from us*, have represented yourself as chief of the Macphersons, and moreover *without my permission* . . . have designed yourself chief of the Old Clan Chattans."

Two points are noticeable : (1) Sir Charles Erskine drops into the regal or viceregal " us " of a King of Arms' most formal documents.[6]

[1] The Court of Session has no jurisdiction to make pronouncements about such nobiliary titles, of no patrimonial value, see p. 54 *infra*.
[2] *Maclachlan*, 1946 ; Lyon Register, XXXV., 72 ; *Rose*, 1946 ; ib. XXXVI., 8 ; *Mackintosh of Clan Chattan*, 9 April 1947 ; ib. XXXVI., 36 ; *Macdonald*, 1947 ; ib. XXXVI., 44.
[3] *Cf.* Scottish Secretary's intimation regarding *Roy. Coll. of Physicians*, 1911, S.C. 1054.
[4] *Scottish Offices Inquiry Commission*, 1870, Min. of Evid., par. 1984; Baronetage Warrant, 11 February 1910, see XIII. In this Warrant, 11 February 1910, the Crown acknowledges —as Lord Dunedin says it may (1911, S.C. 1060)—the existence of the Kings of Arms' (including Lyon's) jurisdiction in the higher hereditary dignity of Baronet. In the preamble of the Warrant the phrase " without any *just* right " is significantly similar to Lyon's phraseology in the letter to Cluny-Macpherson concerning the Chiefships.
[5] *Macdonnell v. Macdonald*, 4 Shaw, 374. Unless the Crown has infringed any existing right which (per Lord Justice-Clerk in *Maclean of Ardgour v. Maclean*) could be raised before a Civil court as a question of law. As regards this, allusion may be made to the Lord Chancellor's ruling in *Lauderdale v. Scrymgeour-Wedderburn*, 1910, S.C. (H.L.), 44 :—
" In respect of the Office or dignity now in question, the decree is wholly outside the jurisdiction of the Court of Session of that day, or of any day, and to that extent a nullity."
[6] *Heraldry in Scotland*, 121. " We Schir Lord Lyon Forman of Luthrie," 1567.

(2) Insistence that the dignity of chiefship must not be assumed without leave or permission from the Crown through its armorial representative in nobiliary status, the King of Arms.[1] It was not until 1873 that by decree of Lord Lyon Burnett, Cluny-Macpherson was allowed the chiefship of the Macpherson Clan, and awarded the incident armorial ornaments.[2]

The text of the Clan Chattan Declaration is, for students of Clanship, also an instructive document. An inquiry (judicial, "Departmental," or other) must have preceded it,[3] but the Certificate is not this deliverance itself; it is the "Letters Patent"[4] following thereon, and making known "to all concerned" the Lord Lyon's decision :—

I, Sir Charles Areskine of Cambo, Knight Baronet, Lord Lyon King of Arms, having perused and seen sufficient evidents and testimonies from our histories, my own registers, and bonds of manrent, do hereby declare that I find the Laird of Mackintosh to be

(a) The only undoubted chief of the name of Mackintosh, and

(b) To be the Chief of the Clan Chattan, comprehending the Macphersons, Macgillivrays, Farquharsons, MacQueens, Macphails, Macbeans, and others, and

(c) That I have given and will give none of these families any arms but as cadents of the Laird of Mackintosh's family, whose predecessor married the heretrix of the Clan Chattan, anno 1291,

and that in particular I declare,

(d) That I have given Duncan Macpherson of Cluny a coat of arms as a cadent of the foresaid family,

(e) and that this may remain to posterity,

(f) and may be known to all concerned, whether of the foresaid names or others.

I have subscribed these presents with my hand at Edinburgh the tenth day of September 1672, and have caused append my seal of office hereto.[5]

The document falls into three sections : (a) and (b) are two declarations of Chiefship ; (c) and (d) declarations of the armorial consequences ; (e) and (f) the purpose and consequences of the decision.

The judges concurred in regarding it a *Certificate*, not a judicial act. It is in fact a *Diploma Stemmatis*.[6] The Lord Justice-Clerk, after saying it was "in no sense a finding pronounced in a *lis* or contested

---

[1] Cf. Guillim's *Display of Heraldry*, 1724, Honor Civil, II., p. 49, regarding King of Arms prerogative in "visitation."

[2] Lyon Register, Vol. IX., 45. Supporters are *incidents* of Chiefship and other high positions. They are not *indiciæ* of anything. They are "exterior ornaments." A Chief was distinguished by his shield, surcoat, and banner, not by "supporters." No chief went into battle with a stuffed dog and a gollywog nailed to the corners of his shield to show he was chief—the idea is ludicrous. No, the chief in the field was known to his followers, and amongst his cadets, by the *plain arms* of the *eponymus* he represented, and the armigerous cadets springing from that eponymus bore the same arms with *brisures*. Nevertheless an award *qua* chief of supporters by Lyon, whether by patent or in a matriculation, involves the *acknowledgment* by Lyon as H.M. "Supreme Officer of Honour" of such person as "Chief" of the community in question. An award of these *incidents* of Chiefship *can thus be a conclusive determination of Chiefship*, and resolve any question which might exist as to whether the shield bore "chief arms"—a fact which Lyon can set forth in the matriculation, cf. *Scott of Harden*, Lyon Reg., II., 189.

[3] The *Innes of that Ilk* Birthbrief of 2 Dec. 1698 is more precise; it describes the taking of a proof, wherein documents were examined; and officially transcribes the Memorial wherein it is averred that Lyon was "judge competent in the lyke cases" and declares the correctness of such statement (*Familie of Innes*, 1864, pp. 1, 46).

[4] Cf. *Campbell*, 1762, Reg. of Genealogies, I., p. 82.

[5] H. Paton, *The Mackintosh Muniments*, 1903, p. 549 ; A. M. Mackintosh, *The Mackintoshes and Clan Chattan*, 32.   [6] *Juridical Review*, Sept. 1940, pp. 194, 204.

process," [1] proceeds : " It vouches nothing beyond that in this particular case *Lyon made a declaration of chiefship*." [2]

That, however, is " everything " ; for this *official* writ contains not one but *two* Declarations of Chiefship—one of these being the Chiefship of a " Clan." The important and necessary deduction from Lord Aitcheson's opinion is that *since it was not judicial, it was a ministerial Declaration.* The parties mentioned in the Clan Chattan declaration were assuredly " contestants " for this Chiefship of Clan Chattan, which was here declared to be in Mackintosh—a pronouncement officially fatal to his opponent. A matriculation of 12 March preceding in favour of Cluny had just been rescinded, and a fresh matriculation agreeable to this " Declaration " was issued 26 November.[3] Moreover, amongst the evidence cited is the Lyon's Registers, which accordingly must (*a*) have contained evidence of Chiefship, (*b*) have been evidence of the rightful tenure of this dignity, just as they were Registers in which other dignities were of record.[4]

We are thus, with the high judicial sanction of the Lord Justice-Clerk, brought to recognise that " Chiefship " is both judicially and *ministerially determinable by Lyon*, whose " permission " as H.M. Supreme Officer of Honour for such an assumption was, by the seventeenth century, regarded as necessary and whose testimony was " conclusive," since the Court of Session regards such a matter as beyond review in a Court of ordinary Law."

Scotsmen would, no doubt, prefer that chiefships should be matter for judicial proceedings—as indeed they now are—as " titles or designations " under Lyon's judicial function of " Visitation " [5] ; and as held

---

[1] Quite so, but what of the antecedent reduction of the Macpherson's matriculation ; judgements were written on the Petitions, and not preserved (*Heraldry in Scotland*, 458, i. 16). Since both the parties mentioned in the Declaration (Mackintosh and Cluny) were claimants to the Chiefship, and Cluny's matriculation (or that part of it certifying the Chiefship) was reduced, it seems reasonable to presume Lyon heard both—if Cluny appeared—and that the Extracts from " my own Registers " and the " histories " were put before him as evidence. Certainly Lyon was not likely to find the Bonds of Manrent for himself—they could only be produced from the parties' charter chests. In the Innes case (Certificate as *Phylarchus*-Chief of tribe), 1698, the Petition bears to adduce evidence " upon such authentick grounds as may induce those, *to whom judgement in the lyke cases is competent, such as the Lyon and Lyon Clerk* " (the Lyon Clerk was also Lyon-Depute in 1698)). In the certificate following, Lyon not only confirms—but officially transcribes—the Petition *including this averment of jurisdiction*—which is therefore officially approved (*Familie of Innes*, 1864, pp. 1 and 45). In this case likewise the Interlocutor is not extant —though both Petition, or presumably a copy of it (for the original went into Lyon Court), and the certificate, embodying the certified version, are extant (Roxburghe Charter Chest). Forbes of Culloden (the Lord President's father), who prepared the Petition, evidently regarded the proceeding as judicial—and so did Lord Lyon Erskine—but the document following is of course a Ministerial Certificate. Such a *Diploma Stemmatis* proceeds of course on a ministerial warrant; but it may include an official pronouncement regarding an antecedent judicial decision of the *Curia Militaris*. [2] Ib. p. 58.

[3] A. Macpherson, *Glimpses of Church Life*, pp. 432–433.

[4] Peerage, Baronetcy, Knighthood, and feudal baronies were (and *are*) all matter of nobiliary record in the Lyon Registers. (J. Riddell, *PeerageLaw*, 629.)

[5] 1592, cap. 29, A.P.S., III., 554 ; interpreted by Lord Constable, 1927, S.L.T., 292: " Visitations are in the nature of the circuits of our judges " (J. Gwillim, *Display of Heraldry*, 1724, Honour Civil, p. 49).

by the House of Lords, in relation to matriculation of " undifferenced arms." But for this, the tendency might have been to increase in Scotland a policy long since adopted by the Earl Marshal and English Kings of Arms, of determining and administering the Law of Arms departmentally as Ministers [1] of the Crown rather than judicially in the Court of Honour. In such cases the *Diploma Stemmatis* is issued by Lyon as Lieutenant [2] of the *Ard-Righ*, the Fountain of Honour and " Chief of Chiefs " [3] in exercise of the supreme parental Prerogative.[4]

The determination of Chiefship, whether effected ministerially or judicially, is, however, a matter of more than academic importance and one which is really the basis of Scottish Heraldry. Most Lyon Court litigations have been directly or indirectly connected with this subject. From its social importance as a binding-force in the community, it is manifestly expedient that such disputes *should* be capable of conclusive settlement.[5]

" For the disciding of sutes concerning honours and for the preserving unto everyman the right of his fame or dignity, the natural tribunal, seat or court for the nobility is everywhere called by this name *militaris* . . . and commonly the Court of Chivalry." [6]

Visitation conferred on Lyon by 1592, cap. 29,[7] has been found by the Court of Session a technical term explained by reference in the Royal Commissions of Visitation,[8] and these visitations [9] :—

" are in the nature of the circuits of our judges " wherein the Kings of Arms " enquire into all matters concerning nobility and gentility such as arms, crests, pedigrees,[10] *titles or designations*, and taking still as they go cognisance of all, and degrading interlopers and upstarts."

---

[1] Halsbury's *Laws of England*, Vol. XXV., p. 69. par. 163. This work is cited only for its bearing on the *Law of Arms*, see *Grey v. Hastings*, 1411, where the Respondent pleaded " the law and custom of England are not admissable in this most high Court of Chivalry for that the laws and customs of England ought not to be confounded with the Laws and customs of the said Court nor be put forward or alleged in a cause of arms except in so far as they were accordant with the laws and customs of Arms." Grey, the plaintiff (an heir-female), having in reply claimed not only the arms but the *name of Hastings*, the Court, " after good deliberation and the advice of divers sages of the law and usage of arms " found the plaintiff had proved his right to the " entire (undifferenced) arms " and decerned accordingly. (*Herald and Genealogist*, II., 13.)

[2] Denmiln MSS, 34–11–7 ; *Scots Heraldry*, 157 ; and *cf. Juridical Review*, 1940, p. 218— Diplomas issued *virtute officii* by the Spanish Kings of Arms as " in the Royal Name."

[3] Toast " The Chief of Chiefs, The King " *Historical Account of H.M. Visit, 1822*, p. 242, and *cf.* p. 12 *supra.*

[4] Mackenzie, *Works*, II, 446 ; F. Brentano, *Old Regime*, 7, 21, 145 (King " father of all the fathers " and " Head of the Family ; and *cf.* pp. 30, 41 *supra.*)

[5] Had the Erracht dispute not been disposed of by Lyon in 1795 (Lyon Register, I., 567) Clan Cameron would have been rent in factions to-day.

[6] Milles, *Political Nobility*, 1612. W. Cruise, *On Dignities*, 251.   [7] A.P.S., III., 554.

[8] Lord Constable in *Macrae's Trustees v. Lord Lyon*, 1927, S.L.T., 292.

[9] J. Gwillim, *Display of Heraldry*, 1724, Honour Civil, ii., p. 49 ; *cf.* Hubback, *Evidence, of Succession*, p. 546.

[10] The Court of Session has no jurisdiction in " pedigrees "—and remitted such to the Macers—who it happens were the nearest available officers of Arms! (A.P.S., III., 449)— procedure consistent with the original jurisdiction of these in pedigrees (1937, S.L.T. 156, *n.* 1). Far from being precluded from determination of nobiliary descent, or bound by Retours (as surmised by Lord Mackay, 1938, S.L.T., 61), Retours and Judgements of Civil Courts (*cf.* case of *Earl of Banbury*) however effective for civil purposes are not conclusive in honours and require, as in Spain, to be presented as evidence for a confirming nobiliary decree by the Chronicler King of Arms in the case of *nobilitas minor* (dignities of Baronetcy and Gentility) and ultimately of the House of Lords in a peerage case.

Chiefship has been accordingly adjudged within " the Law of Arms " and conclusively determinable by the King of Arms as " His Majesty's Supreme Officer of Honour." [1]

CLAN SOCIETIES.

The past century has seen the development of numerous Clan Societies and associations, whose services in maintaining the existence of clanship and identity of the clans has been invaluable, though it is unfortunate that few of them have yet gone beyond the sphere of dinners, whist-drives, and bursaries, in place of the wider and more permanent scope of acquiring heritage in the clan country, and starting, even in a small way with a few crofts, to re-settle the clan races upon the soil of their native districts. It seems now important to define the relationship of the Clan Society to the " clan," the more so as a number of clan societies [2] have recorded armorial bearings. It will be noticed that in each case the arms are a differenced version of the chief's, and that the Association is treated as a corporate *persona*. In other words, the clan society is—according to the Law of Arms, wherein the "clan" is nowadays alone cognisable [3]—simply a "corporate clansman," though no doubt a very important one—in fact, when it becomes armigerous, a corporate *duine-uasail*—an "indeterminate cadet." But the position of "chief" or president [4] *of the clan societies* and *chief of the clan*, although they may concur (as in the Stewart Society) in the same individual, are not necessarily synonymous, for the chief, chairman, or moderator of the clan society is simply the "representer," for the time being, of the corporate *duine-uasail*, and is—like a branch-chief (chieftain)—subordinate to the *hereditary chief of the clan*, as denoted by the chiefly insignia, holder of the hereditary " high social dignity " of representership of the *eponymus* and " his " clan as a noble community under the *Ard Righ* as Fountain of Honour. [5]

Since corporations never die, the clan society as a corporate *duine-uasail* certainly can, or will, become the most important member of the clan, and is the " clansman " on whom will fall many duties which formerly were, roughly, inherent in the Clan Council. Indeed, the Council of the Society may become the permanent Clan Committee.

---

[1] Nisbet's *System of Heraldry*, 1742, II., iv., 172. This, as in old peerage practice, probably explains why there is "no inflexible rule" (per Lord Jeffrey) and how "each case has been judged on its own merits " (per Lyon, 1920, S.C. 776) : for practical reasons the Crown and its High-Sennachie, Lord Lyon, had a " wide discretion " (see pp. 40–41).
[2] *Stewart Soc.*, 1919, Lyon Register, XXIV., 1; *Clan Buchanan Soc.*, ib. XXIII., 27 ; *Clan Dhai (Davidson) Assoc.*, 1935, ib. XXX., 80.
[3] *I.e.* in regard to arms—Nisbet, *System of Heraldry*, I., 268, 425; supporters—Lord Justice-Clerk, *Maclean of Ardgour v. Maclean* ; " Name "—the Macgregor Act, 1775, cap. 29, and Lyon Court Act, 1867, Sch. B.   [4] *Moderator* or *Convener* is the correct title.
[5] In the constitutions of noble clan societies, chiefs and chieftains appear by titles only, *e.g.* *Macleod of Macleod*, so that whoever succeeds to the estate and arms, is *ipso facto* chief or chieftain in the society—which is thus kept strictly related to the Laws of Honour and to Clanship as a legal subject.

The " sacred embodiment of the race " must (from the nature of the *clan* and of the Law of Arms, wherein it is cognisable) remain in the line of hereditary chiefs, even if it is occasionally necessary (from a chief's business abroad, etc.) for the society to recommend the chief to appoint (or he to do so by his own prerogative) a " Commander of the Clan " at home (p. 50, n. 7), a post which should not be coincident with that of chairman or convener/moderator/" president " of the Clan Association, as their functions are different.

Amongst important duties which must presently devolve upon these associations, must be the compilation and maintenance of a Roll of the Clan.[1]

MEMBERSHIP OF THE CLAN.

Since the clan has now been shown to be a subsisting group recognised by the Imperial Parliament, 15 George III. cap. 29, and whose representative is entitled to legal rights under the Law of Arms, it becomes of definite importance to determine the extent and membership of the organisation, and to indicate at least what privilege such membership confers, points which were raised from the Bench in *M'Gillivray v. Souter*, but apparently were not answered. By the custom of the Law of Arms, members of the clan, like other dependers of the chief of a noble group, enjoyed the privilege of displaying their chief's livery, but in a peculiarly Scoto-Highland form, namely, the wearing upon their person of the chief's crest and motto, within the well-known strap and buckle, the origin whereof is, that chiefs distributed to their dependers a silver plate engraved with their crest, which was attached to the arm of the doublet, or bonnet, by a short strap, as still seen in porters' number plates. This, in a conventional form, has become the armorial badge of clanship, and is a valuable privilege, because to use the crest without (*a*) the strap and buckle, or (*b*) without being a member of the clan, involves a statutory offence in Scotland, penalty £8, 6s. 8d. sterling.[2]

Now, *who* are members of the clan, and as such, entitled to enjoy these armorial privileges ? The Statutes indicate [3] persons depending upon the " *capitanis, chieffis, chiftanis*," by " pretence of blude or place of their dwelling." The former of these are the actual and indeterminate cadets cognisable in the Law of Arms, and the second category, as appears from the Privy Council's bonds,[4] are the vassals, tenants, and occupiers of land under a territorial, or *grad flaith*, chief and include the *sencliathe* or ancient adherents, *i.e.* those who have followed the chief for over three generations.[5] Not all tenants and

---

[1] But that does not mean that it has power to usurp or assume the parental functions of the Chief (representer of the *eponymus*) or Chieftains (the hereditary noble heads of branches of the stem demonstrated by arms with " immediate " marks of cadency).

[2] The statutory penalty is in force, and has been recently exacted (*Fiscal of Lyon Court v. Macrae*, 1925 ; *Warrantholders and Fiscal of Lyon Court v. Alexander & Co.*, 1933).

[3] 1587, cap. 59, A.P.S., III., 464 ; 1593, A.P.S., IV., 40.

[4] *Privy Council*, 3rd Series, iii. 75   [5] *Celtic Scotland*, III. 145

vassals were followers of their laird as his clansmen. Often, they depended on a patriarchal chief of their own, and similarly all blood-descendants are not necessarily members of their " biological " clan. Since surnames came in, bearing the chief's race-name, or one of the approved sept-names, has been the normal criterion of clan member-ship, and the statutory phrase, " depending upon the directions " of the chiefs, may equally, and can now only, apply to " peaceful pageantry"—though whenever a war breaks out, the War Office is thoughtful to exploit the clan spirit ! The power of even French families to exclude pretended members [1] and the bonds of adoption,[2] and specific instances of adoption of clansmen by a chief, *e.g.* " to *be* Gordons depending upon the noble house of Huntly," [3] indi-cate that, apart from descent within the name or sept-names, the *consent of the chief*, although it has been only occasionally applied for solemnly,[4] was the requisite step to acquire membership of the clan. Indeed, most chiefs endeavoured to persuade their tenantry to join their clan.[5] Similarly in armorial administration there are many cases where—*e.g.* in difficult pedigrees—the chief is invoked to give a certificate that he accepts the party as a member, even if indeter-minate, of his community.[6]

With the development of the permanent Clan Association and modern availability of records and filing, business methods must gradually develop, and the Clan Cameron is compiling an official Roll of Member-ship, with numbered certificates signed by Lochiel, the Chief. It will only be a further, and natural step, to make such a roll definite, and a certificate of membership the evidence of right to wear the strap and buckle crest, and for a permanent Clan Association acting under the chief to institute prosecution of individuals infringing the armorial privilege without having become sanctioned members of the clan as an organised and honourable community.[7] To these sentimental and armorial privileges, which thus form the cog-nisable and legal basis of clan membership under the chief of the clan as a statutorily recognised community, it is to be hoped that ere long the material advantages of country club membership, etc., may in most cases be developed, rendering membership of the clan a valuable social privilege. The Courts have drawn a clear distinction [8] between the " clan " (*i.e.* " family ") [9] and a " clan Society," which is a piece of clan-machinery—indeed, the " clan civil service."

[1] Seton, *Law and Practice of Heraldry*, p. 421.   [2] Cameron, *Celtic Law*, 220.
[3] Spalding Club, Misc., III., 234.
[4] Most chiefs were delighted to accept any adherent who would till land and could wield a claymore ; *cf.* references cited in process in *Macgregor of Inneregny*, Lyon Register, XXXII., 22.   [5] *Social and Economic Development*, pp. 500–505.
[6] *E.g. Carstairs*, Lyon Register, II., 147 ; *Colquhoun* (Cahun), 1781, ib., I., 528 ; *Macleod*, 1947, ib. xxxvii. p. 36.
[7] Tartans (incidentally) recorded in Lyon Register are clearly " cognisances."
[8] Lord Jamieson in *Ardgour*, 1941, S.C. 707.   [9] See p. 50, *supra*.

ARMORIAL BEARINGS.

The science of Armory, or Heraldry, as a system of identification, was evolved in the twelfth century. Leaders adopted simple and outstanding devices which they painted on their shields and banners, so that their followers might recognise them in war, and the same device was repeated on the shirt worn over the armour, hence the term " coat of arms." In Scotland the *leine croich*, or saffron shirt of war, was in some cases evidently the basis upon which heraldic objects were depicted, but in other cases a small shield was embroidered on the back and breast of the yellow *leine croich*. Armorial bearings, when invented, were a personal mark of identification, but necessarily became hereditary in the second generation (end of twelfth century), when the son who succeeded to estate or Chiefship naturally continued the banner, shield, and surcoat which his father's followers had learnt to recognise, and since a coat of arms could only distinguish one individual, his younger brothers were obliged to bear marks of cadency to distinguish them from the head of the house. In peace the banner above a house, or arms carved upon it, indicated the owner, and a wax seal displaying a representation of the owner's shield was attached to charters, and served as a signature, which could be recognised by those who could not read.

Great Seal of King David II., showing armorial shield, tabard (surcoat), and horse-trappings (ordinary lairds carried their own banners, but the King's banner—also showing the tressured lion rampant—is carried by the Chief of the Scrymgeours). This illustration shows just how arms were used. (No crest is depicted—they were often omitted in battle.)

Arms, from their nature and the position of those who first used them, became marks of *nobility*, and as grants of nobility included a grant of arms, a grant of arms became legally a patent of nobility and proof of inheritance of arms a proof of nobility.

A coat of arms consists of (1) The shield, displaying the arms. This is the most important item, and sometimes the only part existing. (2) The helmet, which varies in shape with the wearer's rank. (3) The mantling, a cap which kept the sun off the helmet. (4) The wreath or torse, covering the joint between helmet and crest, and often depicted as a " wreath bar." (5) The crest, which, until the seventeenth century, was granted only to important personages, but since the seventeenth century to all above the rank of esquire, including ladies who have succeeded to the representation of their house. A crest cannot exist except as subsidiary to a coat of arms. (6) Supporters (sometimes a comportment), an honour only granted to Peers, Chiefs of Clans and ancient families, feudal Barons older than 1592, and Knights Grand Cross. (7) The motto. (8) In the case of Chiefs a slogan—to be shouted by their followers. (9) A badge and standard—or rallying flag as distinct from the *personal* flag—*i.e.* the armorial banner. In order to secure easy recognition, the devices on the shield are simple and conventional, and there are 5 colours and 2 metals, which, if they have to be depicted in black and white drawing, are distinguished as follows :—

Silver	Gold	Red	Blue	Green	Purple	Black	Ermine
Argent	Or	Gules	Azure	Vert	Purpure	Sable	Ermine

A shield may contain one coat of arms, or, if impaled (*i.e.* divided down the centre), the arms of a husband and wife : the husband's being on the dexter, *i.e.* his right hand, when the shield is held in front of him ; the wife's on the sinister. Quartered shields arise from marrying heiresses, or inheriting offices or fiefs.

To prevent mistakes in battle, and fraud in sealing deeds, etc., the King had to arrange for control of heraldry, and settlement of disputes. Since this involved genealogy the matter was delegated to the Royal Sennachie of Celtic Scotland, as chief genealogist, who became the Lord Lyon King of Arms, and who—since he represents the King—was given a tabard of the Royal Arms. It was soon held that only arms granted or confirmed by Lyon were admissible. In 1592 and 1672, the Scottish Parliament forbade the use of arms not so confirmed, and established the *Public Register of All Arms and Bearings in Scotland*, which is kept in the Court of the Lord Lyon, H.M. Register House, Edinburgh. Under the Act of Parliament it is unlawful to use any arms which have not been matriculated in that Register, or to use the registered arms of any person of whom you are not the lawful heir (*i.e.* senior living descendant in terms of the patent or last confirmation).[1] A coat of arms when registered, descends, like a peerage, to each successive senior heir.[2] Daughters (non-heiresses) use the arms for life on a

---

[1] Penalty £8, 6s. 8d. and costs for each offence, confiscation of moveables bearing the "unwarrantable" arms and deletion from heritage (*Scots Heraldry*, 65).

[2] Unless varied by special provisions ; see pp. 39-40.

" lozenge," or for impalement in the shield of an armigerous husband. Younger sons must apply to Lyon for a matriculation, costing £20, when the Lord Lyon registers a differenced version of the arms, usually with a bordure indicating the applicant's relationship to the Chief or Chieftain. " Virtuous and well-deserving persons," who cannot by proof connect their pedigree to a coat of arms already registered, may get a grant of arms (cost £48), and since the fees are payable to H.M. Treasury, the Lyon Court is a source of national revenue.   Since armorial bearings are for distinguishing individuals, Scottish clans as such have neither arms nor crests, though the Chief's arms form the *basis* of the arms to be accorded to all members of the Clan, and a Chieftain's arms the *basis* of arms accorded to all members of his branch.   The arms depicted in this book are in every case those of the Chief, or some prominent Chieftain of the clan.   Some clan societies have registered arms which are used on stationery, etc.

It was the custom for Lords and Chiefs to give their retainers a silver plate of their crest, to wear as badge, and which was affixed by a strap. When not in use, this was coiled round the crest, and this in its conventional form constitutes the crested cap badge worn in Highland bonnets.[1]   A Chief, Chieftain, or armigerous *duine-uasail* wears his crest and motto alone, or in a plain circlet.   The strap and buckle implies a follower or clansman, wearing his Chieftain's crest to indicate that he, or she (ladies wear them to hold sashes and *arisaids*), is the clansman or clanswoman of the Chief, Chieftain, or Chieftainess, whose crest is displayed.   The lion sejant crest seen on Scottish Government stationery is Crown property, like the tressured lion rampant coat of arms, and may not be used by unauthorised persons, but any Scotsman may display the silver cross of St. Andrew—as badge or National flag.[2]

SLOGANS OR WARCRIES.

The Slughorn, Slogan, or Warcry is reckoned one of the " exterior additaments " of armory.[3]   It served as a watchword in cases of sudden alarm, in the thick of battle, or in darkness of the night.   In peace it was " shouted out cheerfully " at Gatherings and tournaments by the adherents of Chiefs on their arrival, or during rival contests. It sometimes consisted of a prominent mountain in the clan district such as " Cruachan," the slogan of the Campbells ; or an island such as " Clar-Innis " in Loch Lomond, associated with the Buchanans. It might also be the remembrance of some gallant deed performed by a prominent clansman, or some act which shed lustre on the clan.   Of this latter nature is the warcry of the MacLeans, *Fear eil' air son*

---

[1] This form of strap-and-buckle badge is worn by any acknowledged clansman-cadet, however high his own rank—even a Duke's brother.
[2] See fig. on p. 67.   [3] Nisbet, *System of Heraldry*, II., iv., 21.

Eachainn! (another for Hector), which records the loyalty of the clansmen to their chief, Sir Hector Roy, at Inverkeithing. Often the name of the chief, twice or thrice repeated—" A Home, a Home, a Home "—was employed. Many of these slughorns will be found at the top of each clan sketch. The right to cry a slogan was naturally subject to official control, or grave confusion would have arisen, and they " were not allowed to any but to the Chiefs of Clans and great men who had many followers, vassals, and dependers." [1] Falling within the jurisdiction of the Law of Arms, they are " allowed " by the King of Arms, and whilst many have latterly been registered as secondary mottoes, the older practice was to record them on a scroll issuing from a be-helmeted head painted beside the achievement.[2] Sometimes they are expressly recorded on the " compartment." [3] Slughorns could still be " cried " at clan and Highland Gatherings. To use them on a public occasion without Lyon's official " allowance " would be a Breach of the Peace as well as of the Law of Arms.

DESIGNATIONS OF CHIEFS AND LAIRDS.

Scottish Law and nobiliary practice, like those of many other European realms, recognise a number of special titles, some of which relate to Chiefship and Chieftaincy of families and groups as such, others being in respect of territorial lairdship. These form part of the Law of *Name* which falls under the jurisdiction of the Lord Lyon King of Arms, and when officially recorded by him as Supreme Officer of Honour, are recognised by the Crown, Lord Chamberlain, etc.[4] At the instance of the Lord Advocate they have even been subject of important legal decision involving estates, and also entail disputes.[5] As regards these chiefly, clan, and territorial titles, by Scots Law each proprietor of an estate (including " undifferenced arms ") is entitled to add the name of his property to his surname, and if he does this consistently, to treat the whole as a title or name, and to get officially recognised as such in a matriculation, thenceforth to be so received " amongst all nobles and in all places of honour," and under Statute 1672 cap. 47, to subscribe himself so.[6]

The chief of a family, whose surname and title both came from his land, was known as, *e.g. Udny of that Ilk*, and the title *of that Ilk* has thus come to imply chiefship, even if there be no land.

Chiefs of patriarchal clans, in order to denote their chiefship, adopted the same style, one of the earliest examples being *Maclachlan of that Ilk*. A number of them have latterly preferred to

---

[1] Sir G. Mackenzie, *Works*, II., 633.
[2] Forman, Lyon Office MSS. ; Nisbet, *Heraldry*, II., Pl. 31.
[3] *Macfarlane*, Lyon Register, I., 377 (destined to heirs female).
[4] Sir R. Douglas, *Baronage of Scotland*, 11; Prestonfield Act, 8 & 9 Vict. cap. 23, s. 20.
[5] See Innes of Learney, *Scots Heraldry*, Chap. XV.
[6] Stevenson, *Heraldry in Scotland*, 441, *e.g.* " Jas. Campbell of Glenfalloch." Only peers and bishops are allowed to sign without prefixing Christian name or initial. Wife and daughters of course similarly use the territorial title in signatures.

E

reduplicate the patronymic, *e.g. Macleod of Macleod*, but the ancient practice was for all chiefs to use the form *of that Ilk*, which is the more characteristically Scottish form of title, and *Lamont of that Ilk* was officially recognised under that title in 1909.[1] Even where no land estate existed, chiefs were styled, *e.g. Laird of Macleod* and *Laird of Mackinnon*, meaning high chief of the Macleods and Mackinnons, and of the clan country. The designation was, however, normally, *e.g. MacSporran of that Ilk*. All Scottish rank, Celtic as well as feudal, was characteristically associated with land—the *carbsa* or *duthus*.

The wives and unmarried daughters of chiefs, chieftains, and lairds are all entitled to use these titles, and the heir-apparent prefixes the word *younger* (or *ygr.*) to the title. In formal deeds or columns, where " full *name* " has to be inserted, he usually puts the complete name and title, affixing the word *younger* afterwards, *e.g. Ian Mac-Sporran of Glenbrachan, younger*. The reason is that Southern officials might otherwise suppose " younger " was a Christian name.[2] In speech, etc., he is " MacSporran younger of Glenbrachan " or " Young Glenbrachan," and his visiting-cards :—

Mr and Mrs MacSporran

younger of Glenbrachan

Only the actual head of the house, his wife, and heir, normally use the style *of that Ilk*, *e.g.* Mactavish of that Ilk ; Madam Mactavish of that Ilk ; Ian Mactavish, younger of that Ilk ; but his sister would be, Miss Jean Mactavish of Mactavish.

All unmarried daughters bear these titles, but younger sons, younger brothers, and collaterals do *not* bear the designation of the house. According to Scottish principle, they have to make their way, and found houses of their own.[3]

Observe that the ambit of these titles in Scottish practice corresponds exactly with the persons who are by the Law of Arms entitled to bear substantively or derivatively the undifferenced arms of the house—and the heir of course with his temporary label *brisure*.

Celtic, chiefly, and territorial titles should be supplied and carefully used on all official occasions and in official documents. They, of course, regularly appear in the Scottish Registers of the Great Seal, as an examination of the printed volumes will show, and without them these registers would be valueless to the historian and genealogist. Unless, however, (*a*) the succession is by immediate descent, or (*b*) the person is actual owner of the estate, officials usually require pro-

[1] Lyon Register, XX., 24.

[2] Nevertheless *Malcolm Alfred Laing, younger of Crook*, appears—and quite properly—in a Royal Commission, 1892, Great Seal, Lib. 46, No. 211.

[3] On the Continent, it is the practice for younger male branches to continue the designation of the house, and to add the designation of their own property, thus forming long-stringed surnames, *e.g. Boucher-de Crèvecœur-de Perthes*. The practice in Scotland is to add the cadet's own estate-title direct to the basic name.

duction of a Lyon Court matriculation of arms, or statutory certificate
of recognition by the Lord Lyon as a voucher. This is consistent with
the King of Arms' jurisdiction in matters of name [1] and designations
and titles,[2] and the fact that Lyon's permission or declaration is
necessary for the assumption of chiefly titles.[3] In France, where
similar conditions obtain and the laws of nomenclature are stricter
than in Scotland, a celebrated French lawyer, editor of the *Annuaire
de la Noblesse de la France*, observes :—

" In your interests and those of your children, if you possess or can vindicate a nobiliary
title or territorial name, *surnom terrien*, you should be careful that these are regularly
employed in all registrations of Births, Marriages, or Deaths."

As in France, however, you are likely to be asked to produce official
evidence that you have been recognised by the proper department
(in Scotland, the Lord Lyon)—unless you actually own the property.
Care upon such points, in regard to vital registration, commissions,
etc., is just as requisite in Scotland as in France, if Celtic and chiefly
titles are to be preserved unquestioned. It need hardly be pointed
out that official recognition is only accorded where such titles are
ordinarily used, and that officials cannot be expected to accept an
alias which has been assumed for the night of the Caledonian Ball, or
the day of some Highland Gathering, and is thereafter dropped for the
remainder of the year ! Signature on *cheques* is a good test !

The words *Chief, Chieftain*, and *Laird* are each a statutory *nomen
juris* found in use both by the Kings of Scots and in the records of
Parliament ; and—as indicated—a Chief is often referred to as " the
Laird of Mackintosh." It is simply an affront to a laird to describe him
as a " proprietor " or a " landlord " (which is technically a publican !),
and " The Laird " or " The Laird of Glenbracken " are *the proper
Scottish terms* in which to refer to our *Grad Flaith* (territorial houses).

In personal address, the title alone is used, *e.g.* " Lochiel," " Glengarry," " Monaltrie "—(no " Mr ")—or in Gaelic the patronymic, if
any, *e.g.* " Mac Cailean Mhor," [4] " Mac Mhic Alein." [5] It is characteristic of our tribally democratic custom that such address is used by all
ranks. It is *rude*, not " respectful," to address " *Clanranald* " as " Mr
Macdonald " or the *Laird of Keir* as " Mr Stirling."

In address writing, or in lists, *Esquire* is not normally added, the
designation being taken to infer it. Where esquire is used, and that is
usual in deeds and useful on the Continent, the word follows the territorial or chiefly designation, *e.g.* Alexander Irvine of Drum, Esquire.[6]

[1] Forlong, 1870, II. Rettie, 910.
[2] J. Gwillim, *Display of Heraldry*, 1724, Honour Civil, 49 ; *Right to Bear Arms*, 123.
[3] Macfarlane, *Genealogical Collections*, I., 393 ; Lyon's letter to Cluny. [4] Duke of Argyll.
[5] Clanranald (*Ian Muydertach*); titles like *Mac Mhic X*—— do *not* denote the chief of
X——'s line (*Loyall Dissuasive*, 102) ; but—as examination shows—a prominent cadet.
[6] " Alexander Irvine, Esquire, of Drum Castle," would be doubly wrong, since one does
not use the word " castle " as part of one's title, for one presumably owns the whole lairdship (or superiority) of which a castle is the *caput*.

Similarly, where the title Baronet, C.M.G., D.S.O., are used, these honours follow *after* the territorial or chiefly title, *e.g.* " Colonel Hugh Rose of Kilravock, C.B." ; " Sir James Burnett of Leys, Bt." [1]

In personal letters, a Scottish laird or chief, *e.g.* " Campbell of Glenfalloch," is addressed " Dear Glenfalloch," not " Dear Campbell," which would be as rude to Glenfalloch as to Lord Breadalbane, for the laird or chieftain of Glenfalloch has just as much a " title " as the earl.   The old prefix of a laird or chief was " The Much Honoured," and letters are still sometimes addressed, *e.g.* " The Much Honoured the Laird of Glenfalloch " [2]—they arrive quite safely.

Where husband and wife are referred to, the correct styles are, *e.g.*, " Glenfalloch and Lady Jean Campbell of Glenfalloch," or " Mr and Madam Gordon of Cluny."   Such a description as " Mr Mactavish of Dunardrie and Mrs Mactavish " is *wrong*, and suggests that the unfortunate lady is not his wife ; any respectable hotel would be justified in turning them out !   Under Scots Law, a wife or widow has certain rights in her husband's estate, and in our law of families and titles *she has corresponding rights in the name and title of her husband*.

Territorial and chiefly titles are of course used upon visiting-cards, where they should strictly be on the same line as the name, without " Mr," and a chief or chieftain places his crest above.   In the 19th century the designation was sometimes (less correctly) placed slightly below :—

GENERAL LEITH   MISS FYFFE-DUFF
   OF FREEFIELD   OF CORSINDAE

In nobiliary practice, titles are normally feminised, *i.e.* when an earldom devolves upon a female in her own right, she is designated a *countess*, and a female baronet is a *baronetess*.

Similarly, there is no such thing as a " woman laird." [3]   When a lairdship devolves upon a female, she has been, in Scottish official documents and judicial proceedings, normally, formally, and officially described as, *e.g.*, " Lady Invercauld " if proprietrix, and similarly in the case of wives, *e.g.*, Lady Invergelly (wife of Robert Lumisden of Invergelly),[4] Lady Craigcaffie (wife of Gilbert Neilson of Craigcaffie).[5] This feudal title of *lady* is not a " courtesy " but a proper legal description of the female.   The wife of a knight or baronet was invariably described as *Dame*.   In modern practice, the latter have, by courtesy, been accorded the title of " lady " *properly belonging to the wives of lairds*, and a laird's wife is now ordinarily known as " Mrs Neilson of

[1] *Encyclopædia of the Laws of Scotland*, *s.v.* Name and Change of Name ; *Scots Heraldry*, Oliver & Boyd, 1934, Chap. XV.   [2] *Cf.* J. Stirton, *Crathie and Braemar*, p. 96.
[3] This horrible description appeared in one or two instances in the press—autumn, 1937.
[4] Mor. Dict. 5944.   [5] Ib. 5922.

Craigcaffie." [1] Nevertheless, " *My Leddy* " [2] (Gaelic, " *Mo Bantigherna* ")
and the terms " laird and leddy " [3] (*e.g.* " Leddy Glensnooks ") are *still*
the normal and *correct* (also legal) way of addressing a laird's or chief's
wife in rural Scotland. Away from home it may, under modern conditions, be simpler to use the form—well recognised since the 18th
century—" Mrs Snooks of Glensnooks "—but the *designation* should be
carefully insisted on by those entitled thereto—and regularly *used* by
its holder.

The terms *chief, head*, and *representative* (*Cean Cinnidh* and *Cean-
tighe*) are of course grammatical terms as applicable to a female as
to a male,[4] and there has been no occasion to feminise such ; but *Chieftain*, which more commonly indicates the representer of a territorial or
grad flaith house, has—like other such titles—been where necessary
feminised since the fifteenth century in the recognised form of *Chieftainess*, and this is the normal equivalent of the Gaelic *Ban Flaith* and
Ban Tigherna—which last is the proper form of Gaelic address for a
Chieftainess or for the wife of a laird or Chieftain.

The principles and practice regarding these titles has been dealt with
at some length, since their preservation and correct use is important
in preserving the structure and spirit of our native Scottish social system.

CLANSHIP AND THE SCOTLAND OF THE FUTURE.

A generation ago, it was supposed that clanship as an institution
was a matter of the past, and one having no immediate bearing upon
everyday affairs. The principles upon which an historic sovereign-
state has been evolved and which enabled the children of that inheritance to consolidate a world-encircling empire,[5] are not to be thus
rashly dismissed, and in recent years not only have the principles of
Celtic civilisation re-established themselves as subjects of enthusiastic
art and culture, but even in our law-courts have again become the
subject of debate.

Concern grows over the steady depopulation of the Highlands,
and many remedies are suggested. None of these has yet proved
effective, and none such is likely to do so. It is urged we have
" the land, the people—and (it is hoped) the spirit." What spirit ?
The only spirit which will serve us here is *the clan spirit*—the tribal
pride instinctive in the clan, whose members feel for their racial home
an affection transcending mere material affluence. Many improve-

---

[1] If a chief, chieftain, or feudal baron's wife, then more correctly *Madam Neilson of
Craigcaffie*, as used in Ireland (chiefs' wives) and France.
[2] For this see *Burt's Letters*, and Scott, *Waverley*, cap. 9.
[3] Analogous to the distinction between *lord* and *laird*. Mackenzie, *Works*, II., 549–550.
[4] *Maclean of Ardgour v. Maclean* (1937) ; Trevoux, *French Dictionary* (1743), *s.v. Chef*;
Edmond Huguet, *Dict. de la Langue Française du 16me siècle* (1925) " *chef* "—(*inter alia*
" *Princesse,*" *Capitainesse—chef*).
[5] **The British Empire is really the *creation of the Scots*, for prior to the Union, England
could not even retain the territories** which it from time to time inherited.

ments in Scottish rural life are requisite, but ironically enough those thrust on the Highlands most vigorously [1] are, many of them, inimical to the very prosperity they seek to promote. The clan spirit alone will maintain our Highland population, and it is to *this* rather than whist-drives and dances that our Clan Societies should devote their energies. Every clan should have a permanent home, even if it begins only with a croft and a few acres. The only forces which make practicable permanent settlement in the remoter districts under modern conditions are the tribal organisation and pride of inheritance, inherent in the clan. Only by a unity of purpose—a linking of *the tribe and its own native soil,* and under the inspiration of its hereditary race-chiefship, can this ideal be realised. Sir John Orr has aptly remarked of the re-organisation of rural Scotland : [2]—

It could all be done in a decade if our industrial magnates, instead of concentrating their attention entirely on moneymaking, would take a pride in the number of men their territory can support and boast of the high standard of living enjoyed by the men in their industry . . . if they would boast, not (*only*) about the number of salmon and grouse they have killed, but (*also*) of the health and physique and intellectual standard of the children in their domain.

That is just a return to the old Chieftainly point of view. As the chronicler records of the sixth Lord Lovat, " There was no earthly thing he put in balance " with his clan, whom he kept ever so far as possible within the Fraser country, and regarded as his " glory and honour " ; whilst a celebrated bard of a later age has aptly said, " Woe unto him who chooses a four-footed clan."

The trouble lies in a social policy which has long deprecated both Chiefship and Lairdship, scattering the ancestral inheritances and belittling so far as possible the titles, precedence and influence of those whom the old Scots Kings and constitution saw fit to honour in relation to the extent of their " following." To quote Sir John again :—

" What we want is not more money, but leaders. Will our Dukes and Lords and our Highland Chieftains come forward to build the new Scotland ? "

Very likely they will—if they get the chance ; but what rural Scotland *does* require is to be saved from the extraction by Death Duties of its inherited capital, a process which (far more thoroughly than any clearances)—being the antithesis of Fixity of Tenure—has divested it of its people, and transferred the broad acres of the clans to Southern sporting profiteers. Under modern conditions we must envisage corporate racial ownership. We must in fact revert to the spirit and the social organisation of the clan, and our hereditary leaders should, as of old, act with the corporate weight and power of the " clan and good men of the cuntrie," *e.g.* the " Mutual Bond " of 1555 between

---

[1] By-laws of urban character unsuitable in rural conditions of life and weather.
[2] A. Maclehose, *The Scotland of Our Sons*, pp. 87, 106. Italics are mine, Love of " The hunt " is Celtic and wholesome.

Argyll (*MacCailean*), "with the consent and counsel of the clann M'Quibhne (*O'Duine*) and the good men of Argyll on the one part," and O'Donnell (of Antrim) " with the consent and counsel of the good men of Tyrconnell on the other."[1] Not only leaders are needed, but behind them the united *spirit of the tribe*, permanently organised in *clanship*. Such is the system which could lead to real progress in Scotland.

In the political sphere, politicians shout glibly for a social order in which " class barriers shall be broken down," regardless of the exist-ence within their midst of a Celtic civilisation in which these " class barriers " have no official existence, and in which the great principle of kinship and clanship has made the enjoyment of honours, titles, and dignities, the pageantry of heraldry and the glorious pride of race, sources of pride and inspiration to all ranks and orders of the Kingdom.[2] The momentous divisions amongst Scotsmen have been not *class* divisions but *clan* divisions. Those, with the consequent sense of brotherhood and ties of lineage, and the extension of the principles of aristo-cracy throughout, not merely a select class, but the whole body of a clannish nation, have combined the interests which produce individuality with those which in other circumstances tend to produce socialism, keeping both wholesomely balanced. Men who believe, however humble their position, that they are sprung of an ancient and  historic lineage, that they have traditions to maintain and kinship with a Chief or Chieftain, who has fellow-clansmen to support, and who have an " inordinate pride in noble birth,"[3] have a very different outlook on life from that of the Sassenach " man of the people," facing the world with a class grievance and a sense of inferiority. For forty generations, Scotsmen have been reared to these principles of clanship, kinship, and pride of ancestry, and our whole legislative and constitutional system was based, as much unconsciously as consciously, on building up a nation in which every one was imbued with a sense of pride and co-operation. These instincts of *Tribality* and *Inheritance*, enshrined in Clanship and its theory of an aristocratic brotherhood, glorying in lineage, ancestry, and love of their romantic native clan-countries, represent a civilisation of which the glamour has grown with the ages, and which carries a message of loyalty and inspiration to Scots throughout the world.

---

[1] J. R. N. Macphail, *Highland Papers*, IV., 214 ; *cf.* I. F. Grant, *Social and Economic Development*, p. 522 ; *Familie of Innes*, pp. 97–98.
[2] *Scots Magazine*, April 1931, p. 50.
[3] Per John Major, *Scotland Before 1700*, p. 56.

THE HIGHLAND DRESS AND HOW TO WEAR IT.

THE Highland dress as presently worn is the result of a process of evolution. Prior to 1600 the dress of the Gaels of Ireland and Scotland was the *léine-chroich* or saffron shirt. M. Nicolay d'Arfeville, Cosmographer to the King of France, who visited Scotland in the sixteenth century, writes: "They wear, like the Irish, a large and full shirt, coloured with saffron, and over this a garment hanging to the knee, of thick wool, after the manner of a cassock." About the beginning of the 17th century this saffron shirt ceased to be necessarily part of the Highland dress, and the *breacan-féile* or belted plaid (see p. 138), and the *féile-beag* or little kilt remained. The former was a combination of kilt and plaid, and consisted of twelve ells of tartan (six ells of double tartan) neatly plaited and fastened round the body with a belt. The lower part formed the kilt, while the other half, being fixed to the shoulder by a brooch, hung down behind and thus formed the plaid. It was possible to display considerable skill and neatness in arranging the plaits, so as to show the sett of the pattern. The *féile-beag* was made of six ells of single tartan, which, being plaited and sewn, was fixed round the waist with a strap, half a yard being left plain at the ends, which crossed each other in front. This is really the modern form of that part of the Highland dress.

For everyday wear the Highland dress should consist of a kilt, jacket, and vest of tweed, with horn buttons, strong *brogs* or shoes, plain knitted hose, garters, and a bonnet of the style of the "Balmoral" or "Glengarry." The sporran should be of leather, or the head of a fox, badger, or other such animal. A plaid about 4 yards long by 1½ wide, and fringed at the ends, is often worn, and Highland cloak or "Inverness cape" is more appropriate than any "greatcoat." The kilt should reach the centre of the knee-cap. The *sgian-dubh* is worn in the stocking, on the outer part of the right leg. The bonnet should contain a brooch showing the crest of the wearer (if he is the owner of one) or a badge consisting of that of his chief within a "belt and buckle" bearing the motto. This denotes he is a clansman of the chief whose crest is displayed—even if the clansman is a Duke's brother.[1]

The *full dress* Highland costume consists of a kilt or *féile-beag* and plaid of some regular tartan, with hose either made from the web of tartan or knitted in check of its prominent colours in the proper proportions, a doublet of cloth, velvet, or tartan with lozenge or diamond-shaped silver buttons (if an open doublet is worn, which is that usually affected by civilians, the waist-coat may be of scarlet, white or tartan), low-cut shoes, silver-mounted sporran, and broad bonnet with

---

[1] To wear without the "strap and buckle," a crest to which one is not entitled as grantee or heir is "conduct unbecoming an officer and a gentleman," and on inquiry leads to humiliation!

badge or crest, a brooch to fasten the plaid, a waist belt, and a baldric or sword-belt ; the arms—a claymore or broadsword, dirk, *sgian-dubh*, a pair of pistols, and a horn.

KILT.—If a member of a clan possessing one or more tartans, such as " clan," " hunting," or " dress," the person should wear one of his own tartans. On " dress occasions " the " dress " tartan is generally worn. If belonging to a sept of any clan, he should wear the tartan of the clan of which he is a sept ; if the sept has a special tartan, he should wear it. When the wearer is entitled to both a " clan " and a " district " tartan it is admissible to wear kilt and hose of the latter and doublet or plaid of the former. It is not considered proper to combine either " clan " or " hunting " tartan with " dress " tartan. If one is to wear " dress " tartan, the kilt, plaid, and hose must be uniform.

PLAID.—The long shoulder plaid should be worn, or alternatively the square " belted " plaid which is more suitable indoors. The hose correspond with either the kilt or plaid. The long plaid (see p. 238) is usually worn over the sword-belt, and removed in the ballroom. On the Border (Eastern March) when the kilt is not worn, the tartan plaid may appropriately be worn with tweeds and bonnet, or even trews.

BONNET.—The bonnet should be broad and blue, somewhat akin to what is called the " Balmoral." The " Glengarry " is preferred by the Gordons and some branches of the Macdonald clan. The bonnet should bear the crest and motto of the wearer if he has one, or the chief's crest within a " belt and buckle " surround, also the evergreen badge of his clan or sept. A *duine-uasail* wears one eagle feather, the chieftain of a branch two, and the chief or chieftain of a whole clan, or family, three.[1]

GARTERS.—The garters should be of scarlet worsted, about an inch in width, pattern and knot correct. There is a special knot, called in Gaelic *snaoim gartain*, or garter knot. Garters ornamented with rosettes date from the seventeenth to eighteenth century.

DOUBLET.—The jacket or doublet may be of velvet or cloth, or tartan cut on the cross. The jacket must be of proper Highland pattern. The oldest form is the *còta-geàrr*, something like what is commonly called a " swallow-tail," but cut short in the tails, or even like an ordinary shooting coat, but short, and with Highland pocket flaps and cuffs. The buttons may be round or diamond-shaped, bearing the wearer's crest if he has one, or may show cairngorms.

TIE.—The evening tie may be either black or white, or a lace jabot— which is the oldest style. The black tie generally favoured commenced as a narrow ribbon tied round the jabot towards the end of the seventeenth century. Some chiefs, *e.g.* Mackintosh, wear a black tie, others, such as the late Marquis of Huntly, wore a white one.[2]

[1] The use of feathers by " those entitled to them " is referred to in Levee Dress.
[2] In origin, the black tie may have a military association—in so far as it is noticed in portraits of persons who had military commands. I do not say it had any military significance.

SPORRAN.—Goat skin—black, grey, or white—with or without tassels; otter or badger is now more usual. The mounting of the sporran should show the crest or shield of the wearer, if armigerous, and the ornamentations thereon should be Celtic in design, and correspond with those on the brooch, belt, and buckles.

SHOES.—The shoes should be low cut. Buckles should be uniform in ornament with the belts, buckles, etc.

BELTS.—Sword-belt, etc., of ornamented leather, bearing crested buckles, etc. (patent leather is undesirable).

CLAYMORE, &c.—A double-channelled blade with basket hilt, lined with scarlet cloth or tartan to correspond with the dress. Dirk of proper pattern, and bearing uniform Celtic ornamentations. *Sgian-dubh* of proper pattern, uniform with dirk in design.

The shoulder belt for claymore was specially restored by the Act of 1782, and the sword is still appropriate at court and on formal occasions.

PISTOL, &c.—The proper pistol is a single-barrelled muzzle-loading belt pistol of antique pattern, having the ramrod attached to the barrel.

POWDER-HORN.—This, suspended by a chain rather than a strap, is worn on the right side, with the mouthpiece to the front. It was originally the chieftain's blowing-horn, in the 17th century "a tup-horn filled with *usquebai*"—as now—often adapted as a refreshment flask.

LADIES.—For day wear, a kilted skirt, which to be graceful must for anatomical reasons be cut on somewhat different lines from a man's, is worn with a tweed or other jacket, and diced or other long stockings *covering the knees* are worn with brogues. The sporran is *not* worn by ladies, and the travesties of male attire worn by dancers at Highland Gatherings are an affront to the Gael. For evening wear, a skirt of tartan silk or other light material is worn with any suitable corsage, usually decorated with Celtic embroidery and the graceful *arisaid* of silk hangs down the back, and is gathered on the breast by a Celtic or heraldic brooch. Sometimes the smaller *tonnag*, or shoulder-shawl, of tartan silk or light woven material is similarly worn. With ordinary evening dress a sash is worn across the shoulder, fastened with the badge-brooch. Such sashes look best when fairly voluminous. A chieftainess wears her crest[1] in her hat along with the two feathers of a chieftain or three of a chief, as the case may be. Other ladies wear the ordinary "strap and buckle" badge displaying the crest of their chief or chieftain.

[1] The idea that ladies are not entitled to crests is a modern one, based on a confusion between ordinary daughters (who are not entitled to crests) and heiresses who, by the pure Law of Arms, both take and transmit crests. Examination has shown that seventy per cent. of the ladies for whom arms were matriculated in the early volumes of Lyon Register got crests.

GENERAL.—It has been suggested that anyone not bearing a clan surname may adopt the tartan of their mother's clan or sept should she possess a clan surname.[1] If a person belongs to no clan the correct course is to wear a " District " tartan if any suitable one exists, or else " Jacobite " or " Caledonia " tartan, which are admissible even when the wearer belongs to no clan.

The day-dress of vegetable-hued hard tartan, and ordinary tweed jacket is simple and workmanlike. For formal wear the Highland dress naturally lends itself to the glittering ornaments, cairngorms, braiding, and velvet or tartan doublets, which combine with the tartans to enhance that rich variety of costume which accords with the history and instincts of the Highlander. Attempts by self-conscious lowlanders to convert the picturesque dress of the Gael into a " quiet style " and to deprive the garb of its ornaments or reduce it to the drab monotony of Anglo-Saxon evening clothes are un-Scottish and contemptible.

FLAGS AND BANNERS.

The ensign has always been an important instrument of command, and figures much in Celtic, as in other mediæval literature. Flags are " ensigns armorial," and fall within the Laws of Arms.

BANNER.—This is a square or rectangular flag. Its whole surface is covered by the shield-device of its owner, whose personal flag it is. The best-known " banners " are the quartered " Royal Ensign " of H.M. the King and his tressured lion rampant banner of the King of Scots. Most chiefs and chieftains use banners, both as their house-flag and on a pole at Gatherings, where the banner is set near the chief's pavilion or *lonquard*.

STANDARD.—This is a long narrow flag [2] with St. Andrew's cross next the pole. The remainder of the flag is parted of the livery colours of the chief or chieftain, and upon it is depicted his crest, badge or sometimes shield, and his motto or slogan. Sometimes the chief's arms are placed next the pole instead of the national cross. The standard is the rallying flag of the " following." The ancient forms of banner and standard should be carefully adhered to, as they alone combine utility with the simple beauty of ancient heraldry.

PIPE-BANNERS.—These, like other banners, should display the shield-device over their *whole* surface. They should *not* include the crest and supporters. The older examples are of the form above mentioned. Crests, coronets, and supporters are only found in the later debased examples. The pipe-banners of the Royal Company of Archers, and those recently presented by H.R.H. the Princess Royal to the Scottish Signals are of the ancient form here recommended.

[1] This is really a survival of the *non-Salic* Celtic organisation under which the children can belong to their mother's clan or tribe—which in origin depended largely on whether the " house " was established in the " country " of husband or wife. Since *Name* has become the index of clan-membership, it follows that nowadays *one is not entitled to wear the mother's tartan unless one assumes the mother's name*, or happens to bear it or other sept-name.

[2] In the 18th century, by an accidental slip of the Privy Council, the word " standard " was applied to the quartered royal ensign. This arose from the depiction on *guidons* (a short swallow-tailed flag, sometimes made rectangular) of the whole coat of arms—crest, shield and supporters ; and a number of these debased flags were used as, or for, banners during the 18th century. *Both on principle and from practical considerations such flags are incorrect*, being of poor effect and unrecognisable at any distance.

ANDERSON

(MACANDREW)

THIS surname means literally the son of Andrew, but as held by families of Lowland origin, denotes, it has been suggested, a "servant of St. Andrew," the patron saint of Scotland. The name is common all over the Lowlands, as well as in Aberdeenshire.

The Gaelic equivalent of Anderson is "Mac Aindrea," son of Andrew, or "Gilleaindrais"— Gillanders, or St. Andrew's *gille*, so that these Andersons are probably an off-shoot of Clan Aindreas (Ross). These MacAndrews are regarded as a sept of Clan Chattan. Kinrara (1676) after recording the association of the MacQueens, or Clan Revan, says :—"And sick-like Donald MacGillandrish, of whom the Clan Andrish are named, came out of Muidart, with Mora Macdonald, Lady Mackintosh" (Clan Ranald's daughter).

The descendants of MacGillandrish settled in Connage of Petty. In course of time the name was anglicised as MacAndrew. Gillanders is another variation of the original Gaelic.

One of the noted members of the MacAndrews was an archer "Iain beag MacAindrea"—Little John MacAndrew of Dalnahatnich—in Duthil, who in the year 1670 took part in what may be regarded as the last *creach* or cattle-lifting expedition to Inverness-shire. It was committed by Macdonell of Achluachrach in Lochaber, and a party of twelve men, who fell on the lands of Kilravock and drove away the cattle of the Baron and his tenants, in the course of one night. The tenants in a body pursued, headed by William Mackintosh of Kellachie, who was accompanied by his faithful attendant on such occasions, John beag MacAndrew.

The cattle-lifters had settled for the night in a small hut or bothy in the heights of Strathdearn. An arrow was shot into the hut. Achluachrach came out, and falling on a hide, which was slippery, instantly received an arrow from MacAndrew which killed him. Kellachie killed the next who came out, and then by a shower of arrows poured into the hut at the door, window, and small holes, all the band were killed. It is said that, with the exception of the faithless sentry, not a single individual survived to carry the tale to Lochaber.

The most prominent branches of Clan Anderson have been the Andersons of Dowhill, traced from 1540, the Andersons of Wester Ardbreck, in Banffshire, and the Andersons, lairds of Candacraig in Strathdon for ten generations prior to 1865. Arms were awarded in the 16th century to "Anderson of that Ilk" but this family has not been identified. No *place* "Anderson" ever existed and what the registration implies is that one of the Lindsay Lord Lyons, in the exercise of the Crown's armorial prerogative vested in the Lyon's Office, "received and numbered" one of the Anderson chieftains as representer of the "clan"—as henceforth an "honourable community" whereof the successive heirs of *that* house would be received in public ceremonial as Representers of the race or *clan* of Anderson.

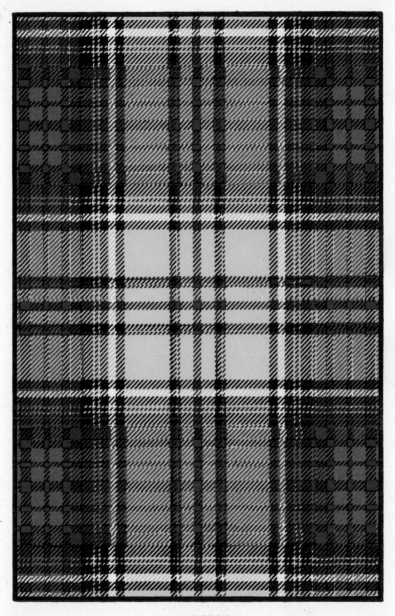

I. ANDERSON

ARMSTRONG

INVICTUS · MANEO

BEFORE 1376 the Armstrongs are found in Cumberland, but in that year the first of the family in Scotland is found at Mangerton, in Liddesdale. This place was then and afterwards the seat of the chief of the clan, and Whithaugh was the home of the next most important chieftain of the family who was apparently the " eldest cadet." Simon of Whitehaugh 1510–25 is the first of this branch on record, and he was executed in 1536. At one time the clan owned the greater part of Liddesdale, which forms the southern portion of Roxburghshire, and at a later time they became so numerous that they spread into Eskdale and Annandale. In 1528 they were able to put —it is said—3000 horsemen in the field.

About 1525 John Armstrong, brother of the Laird of Mangerton and who is known in history as " Gilnockie," settled on the lands of Canonbie, and built the Hollows Tower, which still exists in fair preservation. In 1526 the Armstrongs had seized the greater portion of the Debatable Land, and built on it a number of towers. Lord Dacre, the English Warden, determined to drive them out, and in 1528 he attacked and burned the Hollows Tower, and the Armstrongs retaliated by burning Netherby, in Cumberland. In 1527 the Laird of Johnston killed " Meikle Sym Armstrong," and in the following year the Armstrongs, incited by Lord Maxwell, attacked the Johnstons in force.

King James V. determined to put down the lawlessness of Liddesdale in person, and in 1530 John Armstrong of Gilnockie was induced to meet the king. Not suspecting harm, he rode up, unarmed and " brawly " accoutred, with fifty followers. Whenever the king saw him he exclaimed, " What wants yon knave that a king should have ? " and gave orders for the party to be surrounded and captured. When this was done, all were ordered to be hanged. Gilnockie made several offers to the king if he would spare his life, but without avail ; so turning to James V., he said, " I am but a fool to seek grace at a graceless face, but had I known you would have taken me this day, I would have lived in the Borders despite King Harry and you both."

Poor John Armstrong and his followers were buried in Caerlanrig Churchyard. The story is told in the spirited Border ballad, " Johnie Armstrong " :—

" Farewell ! my bonny Gilnock Hall,
   Where on Esk side thou standest
      stout !
Gif I had lived but seven yeirs mair
   I wad a gilt thee round about.

John murdered was at Carlinrigg,
   And all his gallant companie ;
But Scotland's heart was ne'er sae
      wae
   To see sae mony brave men die."

A descendant of the Gilnockie branch, William Armstrong of Morton, or Kinmont Tower, known as " Kinmont Willie," was captured by the English during a truce and imprisoned in Carlisle. In 1596 the Scottish Warden, Sir Walter Scott of Buccleuch, being refused his release, assembled his followers, rode to Carlisle, and rescued " Kinmont Willie."

Of the chiefly house, " Alexander Armgstrand " was Laird of Mangerton in 1378 and they kept the lands until 1610 when Archibald Armstrong of Mangertoun was " put to the horn " as a rebel, and soon after the rest of the Armstrong lands passed to the Scotts.

2. ARMSTRONG

BARCLAY

THE Barclays in Scotland claim to be a branch of the great English house of Berkeley of Berkeley Castle, Gloucestershire, and to derive from John, son of Roger de Berchelai, who is said to have come to Scotland 1069, and to have had three sons, Walter, 1st of Gartly, Alexander, who founded the line of Towie-Barclay, and Richard, of Ardrossan, living 1140.

Sir Walter Barclay of Gartly, Lord of Redcastle and Inverkeillor, was Chamberlain of Scotland under William the Lion, and Sir John de Barclay of Gartly signed the Ragman Roll 1296. The male line of Gartly ended with Walter Barclay of Gartly, Canon of Moray in 1456. His sister married the Laird of Towie-Barclay, and thus carried the chiefship to the House of Towie as recorded in Wyntoun's *Cronykill*. Gartly was thereupon apparently settled upon a younger son, William, founder of the subsequent house of Barclay of Gartly, whilst the chiefship continued in the eldest blood, represented by the house of Towie-Barclay, whose representative, Sir Patrick Barclay of Towie, rebuilt the castle of Towie-Barclay about 1598 with its splendid vaulted hall. The succession again passed to an heiress in 1668 when Elizabeth Barclay of Towie married John Gordon of Rothiemay, and was eventually succeeded by her daughter Elizabeth, wife of Sir George Innes of Coxton, who took the name and title of Barclay of Towie, was out with the Chevalier, and died shortly after Sheriffmuir. His granddaughter, Isobel Barclay, married the Earl of Lauderdale's brother, who took the name of Barclay-Maitland, but sold the estate of Towie in 1755, and upon their descendants ceasing to bear the name and arms of Barclay of Towie, the chiefship accordingly passed to the heir male, The Rev. John Barclay, Minister of Delting, lineally descended from George Barclay of Auchreddie, son of Walter Barclay of Towie, the chief who was murdered at Edinburgh in 1587. The minister's line failed in 1844, and the chiefship ultimately passed to the line of his brother, James Barclay of Mill of Towie, whose descendant, Charles Alexander Barclay, was awarded the chief arms by decree of Lyon Court, 1901. His son, Charles James de Tollie Barclay, the present chief, resides in California.

The most important cadets are the Russian Barclays de Tollie, deriving from Andrew Barclay, a kinsman of the Laird of Towie in the sixteenth century. Of this line, Field-Marshal Michael Andreas Barclay, Commander of the Russian army which defeated Napoleon in 1812, was created Prince Barclay de Tolly, a dignity now held by his grand-nephew Nicholas, Prince Barclay de Tolly-Weymarn.

Another distinguished branch were the Barclays of Mathers and Urie, of whom Captain Robert Barclay-Allardyce of Urie and Allardyce, was a celebrated sportsman and pugilist. From this line come also the Barclays of Buryhill, descending from Robert Barclay, the apologist for the Quakers.

The Barclays of Collairnie in Fife were long a distinguished house, whose picturesque tower is still embellished with splendid heraldic ceilings.

3. BARCLAY

F

BRODIE OF BRODIE

Badge :—Periwinkle.

THIS name is from the local place-name Brodie (Gaelic, *brothach*). The old writings of the family were mostly carried away or destroyed when Lord Lewis Gordon, afterwards (3rd) Marquis of Huntly, burnt Brodie House in 1645. From Malcolm, Thane of Brodie, living *temp.* King Alexander III., descended Alexander Brodie of Brodie, Honble. Lord Brodie as a senator of the College of Justice, 1649, who was one of the commissioners sent from Scotland to Charles II. during his exile at the Hague. His son and successor, James Brodie of Brodie, born 1637, married in 1659 Lady Mary Ker, daughter of William, 3rd Earl of Lothian. Leaving nine daughters but no son, he was succeeded by his cousin, George Brodie, son of Joseph Brodie of Aslisk, and grandson of David Brodie of Brodie, brother of Lord Brodie. In 1692 he married Emily, fifth daughter of his predecessor. He died in 1716, leaving three sons and two daughters. James Brodie of Brodie, the elder son, died in 1720, and was succeeded by his brother, Alexander, born 1697, Lord Lyon King of Arms of Scotland 1727. He died 1754. By his wife, Mary Sleigh, he had a son, Alexander, his heir, and one daughter, Emilia. Alexander Brodie of Brodie, born 1741, was succeeded by his second cousin, James Brodie, son of James Brodie of Spynie. This chief was Lord-Lieutenant of the county of Nairn. Born 1744, he married Lady Margaret Duff, youngest daughter of William, 1st Earl of Fife. He died in 1824, leaving two sons and three daughters. Their son, James, was drowned in his father's lifetime, leaving two sons and five daughters. The elder son, William Brodie of Brodie, Lord-Lieutenant of Nairn, born in 1799, succeeded his grandfather in 1824, married in 1838 Elizabeth, daughter of Hugh Bailie of Redcastle, M.P., and had Hugh Fife Ashley Brodie of Brodie, born 1840, died 1889. His son, Ian Brodie of Brodie, D.S.O., born 1868, died 1943, was succeeded by his son Montague Ninian Brodie of Brodie, the present chief, whose seat is the ancient Castle of Brodie, in Moray, " chief chymmes " of the ancient Thaneage of Brodie.

The other branches of this clan are Brodie of Lethen, Brodie of Idvies, and Brodie of Eastbourne, Sussex. Sir Benjamin Brodie, a distinguished surgeon of the Royal Family, was made a Baronet in 1834.

4. BRODIE OF BRODIE

BRUCE

OUR patriot monarch, King Robert the Bruce, belonged to the Norman family De Bruis, which, in the person of Robert De Bruis, came to England with the Conqueror in 1066. This knight received the lands of Skelton in Yorkshire, and his son, Robert, who was an associate of the prince who afterwards became David I. of Scotland, obtained the Lordship of Annandale. At the Battle of the Standard (1138) Robert Bruce fought on the English side; while his son, Robert, 2nd of Annandale, fought under David and was taken prisoner, it is said, by his own father. He had two sons, Robert and William. Robert, the elder, died before 1191. William, his brother and heir, died in 1215, and was succeeded by his son, Robert, 5th Lord, who died in 1245, having married Isabella of Huntingdon, great-granddaughter of King David I. Their son, Robert de Bruce, was in 1255 nominated one of the Regents of the Kingdom of Scotland, and guardian of Alexander III. In 1290 he claimed the Crown of Scotland, as nearest heir of King Alexander III. King Edward I. overruled all the pleas of Bruce, and adjudged the Kingdom of Scotland to Baliol, whose claim was strictly the preferable under the law of succession attributed to King Malcolm Mackenneth. Bruce died in 1295, aged eighty-five. His eldest son, Robert de Bruce, was born in 1245 and died in 1304. By Margaret, Countess of Carrick, his wife, he left a large family. His eldest son, Robert the Bruce, born 11th July 1274, asserted his claim to the Scottish Crown (which had fallen vacant by reason of Baliol's disgraceful renunciation of his throne). He ascended the throne of his ancestors, and was crowned at Scone, 27th March 1306. After many vicissitudes, the power of King Robert I. was finally cemented by his splendid and decisive victory at Bannockburn, 1314. He died at Cardross, in Dumbartonshire, 7th June 1329, aged fifty-five; he was interred in the Abbey Church of Dunfermline.

The Earl of Elgin, descended from Bruce of Clackmannan, who sprang from a cousin of King Robert's, is now acknowledged chief of the family. His seat is at Broomhall, in Fife, and the old fortalice of his house, Clackmannan Castle, is a picturesque tower whose battlements still overlook the valley of the Forth. The Earldom was conferred in 1633 on Thomas, 3rd Lord Bruce of Kinloss, who descended from Sir David Bruce, 7th Baron of Clackmannan.

5. BRUCE

BUCHANAN

Slogan :—" Clar Innis " (An island in Loch Lomond).
Badge :—Dearc bhraoileag (Bilberry) or Darag (Oak).

ABOUT the middle of the 13th century, Gilbert, seneschal to the Earl of Lennox, obtained from the Earl a part of the lands of Buchanan in Stirlingshire and took his name from them. An ecclesiastical origin is claimed for the surname, as in Gaelic a Buchanan is known as *Mac-a'-Chanonaich*—the Son of the Canon—and the place-name Buchanan (*Both-chanain*) really means the canon's seat, but the name is obviously a territorial one. Part of the lands may thus have been held on a pre-charter tenure on some of the Celtic hereditary clerical tenures. The arms are noticeably different from those of scions of the House of Lennox.

Donald, 6th Earl of Lennox, renewed to Maurice of Buchanan the grant conferred by a former earl on his ancestor, and the King granted a charter of confirmation to his successor of the same name.

Sir Maurice, 9th Laird of Buchanan, was the first who assumed the surname from the lands. His eldest son, Sir Maurice, succeeded him, whilst the second, Allan, married the heiress of Leny of that Ilk and founded the first line of Buchanan of Leny. John, 12th Laird of Buchanan, married the sole heiress of these Buchanans of Leny. Their eldest son, Sir Alexander, distinguished himself as a soldier, and was slain in the battle of Verneuil in 1424. His second brother, Walter, succeeded to Buchanan, and his third to Leny.

Walter Buchanan of that ilk married Isabel, daughter of Murdoch, Duke of Albany, the Regent. Their eldest son, Patrick, married the heiress of Killearn and Auchreoch.

Patrick's son, Walter, married a daughter of Lord Graham. Patrick, who fell at Flodden, by his wife, a daughter of Argyll, left two sons—George, 12th of Buchanan, Sheriff of Dumbarton in 1561, and Walter, the founder of the House of Spittal.

By Margaret Edmondston of Duntreath, George had John, his heir, and by his second wife, Janet Cunninghame of Craigends, William, founder of the now extinct line of Auchmar.

The principal line became extinct in 1762 on the death of John, 22nd and last laird of Buchanan (with which he had to part in 1682), and the chiefship passed to Buchanan of Spittal ; and though in 1878 Mr. Francis Hamilton Buchanan of Spittal established his claim as Chief, his grandson, Mr. J. H. Buchanan of Spittal, died 1919 without issue, since when the chiefship has been dormant.

The Buchanan lands are now possessed by the Duke of Montrose. The principal estates which subsist are the Buchanans of Powis, Drumpellier, Auchintorlie, Scotstoun, and Leny.

There is a Buchanan Society in Glasgow, possessed, it is understood, of considerable funds, and which might advantageously devote itself to the territorial re-establishment of the Buchanan clan. It received by gift of a *duine-uasail* the historic island of Clare Inch.

6. BUCHANAN

CAMERON

Slogan :—" Chlanna nan con thigibh a so 's gheibh sibh feòil " (" Sons of the hounds, come here and get flesh ").

Badge :—Darag (Oak) or Dearca fithich (Crowberry).

THE original possessions of the Camerons were confined to the portion of Lochaber lying on the east side of the loch and river of Lochy, held of the Lord of the Isles as superior. The more modern possessions of the clan—Lochiel and Locharkaig—lie on the west side of these waters. The MacGillonie Camerons are generally regarded as the oldest family of the clan, but under the Law of Tanistry a House, Cameron of Lochiel, sometimes designated as once the senior cadet, came to be the chief line and " stem " of the clan.

Tradition says he was a distinguished knight who became chief of the clan by marriage with the heiress of the old line. The first chief of the clan definitely found in historical records is Donald Dhu (*cir.* 1411) (reckoned 11th Chief). He married an heiress of MacMartin of Letterfinlay and left two sons—Allan, Constable of Strone Castle, who succeeded him; and Ewen, who is generally regarded as the progenitor of the Camerons of Strone. Allan, styled Captain of the Clan Cameron in 1492, left two sons, Ewen and John.

Ewen, 13th Chief, first who took the title " of Lochiel," married first a daughter of Celestine of Lochalsh. For him the estates of the chiefly line were erected into a barony of Lochiel in 1528. Since then the Chief's title has been " Lochiel "; and it was settled by litigation at the instance of the Crown that these titles are part of the Chief's ordinary name. His eldest son and heir, Donald, died before his father, between the years 1536 and 1539. He married secondly, Marjory, daughter of Lachlan, second son of Malcolm Mackintosh of Mackintosh, by whom he had Ewen, the progenitor of the family of Erracht, and John, progenitor of the Camerons of Kin-Lochiel. Ewen was succeeded by his grandson, *Eoghan Beag*—Little Ewen—who was the father of a natural son, the famous Black Tailor of the Axe.

He was succeeded by his brother, Donald, father of Allan, 16th Chief, who fought under Huntly at Glenlivet, and was grandfather of the famous Sir Ewen Cameron of Lochiel, 17th Chief, born in 1629. He built the old Achnacarry Castle, burned in 1746, when the country was overrun and wasted after Culloden. Achnacarry was rebuilt early in the nineteenth century, but not completed till 1837. Sir Ewen married first, Mary, daughter of Sir James MacDonald, first Baronet of Sleat, and secondly, Isabel, daughter of Sir Lachlan Maclean of Duart, and thirdly, Jane, daughter of Colonel David Barclay (XVII.) of Urie. He died in 1719, aged ninety.

He was succeeded by his son, John, who married Isabel, daughter of Campbell of Lochnell, with issue—Donald, who succeeded, and John of Fassiefern, who died 1747 or 1748.

He was succeeded by Donald, his eldest son, known as " The Gentle Lochiel," who followed Prince Charlie. After Culloden he escaped to France, where he died in 1748. He was succeeded in the chiefship by his son, John, who was succeeded by his brother, Charles. He died in 1776, and was succeeded by his son, Donald, who in 1795 was established by decree of Lyon Court as Chief of the Family of Lochiel and Chief of the Clan Cameron. He died in 1832. He was succeeded by his son, Donald, who died in 1859, and his son, Donald, 24th Chief, died 1905. His son, Sir Donald Walter Cameron of Lochiel, K.T., is the 25th Chief. Achnacarry Castle is the seat of the chiefs.

There is an organisation called " The Clan Cameron," with its headquarters in Glasgow, which has recently been taking steps to form a " Clan Company " to take over part of the Lochiel estates.

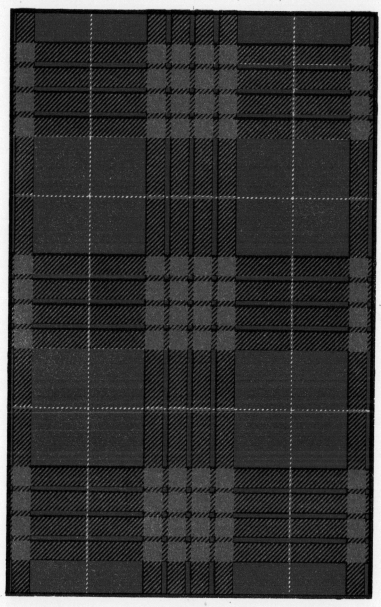

7. CAMERON CLAN

CAMERON OF ERRACHT

Badge :—Darag (Oak) or Dearca fithich (Crowberry).

THIS family were known locally as *Sliochd Eóghain 'ic Eóghain*, or "the children of Ewen, son of Ewen." The first representative of the family was Ewen Cameron, son of Ewen, by his second wife, Marjory Mackintosh.

Donald Cameron, 7th of Erracht, was born shortly before the Rising of 1715. Some thirty years later he joined Prince Charles, and, under Lochiel, was second in command of the Camerons at the historic Glenfinnan.

After fatal Culloden, Cameron of Erracht was for three years a homeless wanderer among the mountains. He had four children, the eldest of whom was afterwards the famous Sir Allan Cameron of Erracht, K.C.B., who in 1793 raised the 79th or Cameron Highlanders. He was appointed Lieutenant-Colonel Commandant, and led the 79th through the severe campaigns of 1794–1795 in Flanders, till it embarked for the West Indies. In 1797 the battalion was broken up, and 210 joined the Black Watch.

Colonel Cameron and his officers repaired to the Highlands, and in 1798 soon raised a second 79th regiment, 780 strong. In 1804 he formed a second battalion, 800 strong. After taking part in many engagements in foreign parts, he retired from active service, and died at Fulham in 1828.

What is known as the "Erracht Cameron Tartan" was specially designed for the 79th Cameron Highlanders by Mrs Cameron of Erracht (Allan's mother), a daughter of Ranald MacDonell of Keppoch, who, by blending the tartan of the MacDonalds with that of the Camerons, solved the difficulty which presented itself, and in this way the sentiment of both clans was respected.

In 1792 Erracht impetrated from Lyon Court a patent recognising him as chief of the clan, but on a petition by Lochiel in 1795 this was reduced and annulled by a judgment of Lyon Court—Lochiel being declared the true chief.

Clansman's badge of
Clan Cameron.

8. CAMERON OF ERRACHT

CAMPBELL

Slogan :—" Cruachan " (A mountain near Loch Awe).
Badge :—Roid (Wild Myrtle) or Garbhag an t-sléibhe (Fir Club Moss).

DIARMID O'DUINE is generally regarded as the founder of the clan *Duibhne* or Campbells, and in 1368 a Crown Charter acknowledges Duncan MacDuibhne as progenitor of the Campbell lords of Lochow. Duncan appears to have lived in the reign of Alexander II. and, according to tradition, Eva o'Duibhne, heiress of the line, married the first Campbell and carried with her the chiefship of her tribe. This seems probable ; and the word *Cam*-bell (involving *crook*), traditionally a place-name, seems related to Castle-Campbell, in the Lordship of Gloume, and noticeably near " Crook of Devon " at Dollar, presumably the *duthus* of Eva's husband.

The real founder of the family of Argyll was *Cailean Mór*, from whom the Chief gets his patronymic of *MacCailean Mór*. This Colin was slain at *Ath-Dearg* (Red Ford), in Lorn, 1294. The early titles were *de Ergadia* and Lords of Lochow. His descendant, Sir Colin Campbell (*Cailean Iongantach*) succeeded his father, Sir Archibald, who died in 1372. He died in 1413, and was succeeded by his son, Sir Duncan, who was Lord Campbell prior to 1427. He died in 1453.

Archibald Roy succeeded his father, and was succeeded by his son, Colin, who was created Earl of Argyll in 1457. He died in 1493, and was succeeded by his son Archibald, 2nd Earl of Argyll, who fell at Flodden. He was succeeded by his son, Colin, 3rd Earl of Argyll. Archibald, his son, succeeded him. He died in 1558, and was succeeded by his son, Archibald, who died without issue in 1575, and was succeeded by his brother, Colin, 6th Earl of Argyll. Archibald, 7th Earl, reduced the MacGregors in 1603. He was succeeded by Archibald, his son, in 1638 as 8th Earl. He was created Marquis of Argyll in 1641. He was beheaded in 1661. His estates, after being forfeited, were restored to his son, Archibald, with the title of Earl of Argyll. For the part he took in the Monmouth rebellion he was beheaded in 1685. His son, Archibald, 10th Earl, was created Duke in 1701. He died in 1703, succeeded by his son, John, 2nd Duke of Argyll and Earl of Greenwich. He died 1743. His brother, Archibald, 3rd Duke, who died 1761, was succeeded by his cousin, General John Campbell of Mamore. He died in 1770, succeeded by his son, John, 5th Duke, who died 1790. He left two sons—George, 6th Duke, who died 1839 ; and John, 7th Duke, who died in 1847, leaving George, 8th Duke, who died 1900. He had five sons of whom the eldest, John, 9th Duke, born 1845, married Princess Louise in 1871. His nephew, Niall Diarmid, became 10th Duke in 1914 and died 1949. His cousin, Ian, 11th Duke, is the present Chief, and is Hereditary Master of H.M. Household. His seat is Inveraray Castle, and he is Keeper of the Royal Castles of Dunoon, Carrick, Dunstaffnage, and Tarbert. Dunstaffnage and Saddell are held under him by races of hereditary Captains.

The Dukes were also Hereditary Lord Justice General and are still Admirals of the Western Coasts and Isles of Scotland.

9. CAMPBELL OF ARGYLL

CAMPBELL OF
BREADALBANE

Badge :—Roid (Wild Myrtle) or Garbhag an t-sléibhe (Fir Club Moss).

AFTER the House of Argyll, the leading family are the Campbells of Breadalbane, whose ancestor was Black Colin of Glenorchy, second son of Sir Duncan Campbell, Knight of Lochow, 1st Lord Campbell, by his wife, Lady Marjory Stewart. Hence the patronymic of the House of Breadalbane—*Mac-Chailein-Mhic-Dhonnachaidh* (son of Colin son of Duncan). In 1432 Sir Colin received from his father, Glenorchy, from which the McGregors had been driven.

Sir Colin, who built the romantic castle of Caolchurn, got by his second wife, Margaret Stewart, co-heiress of John, Lord of Lorn, one third of Lorn, and died in 1498. His descendant, " Black Duncan," 7th of Glenorchy, was created a baronet 1625.

Sir John, 4th Bart. and 11th Campbell of Glenorchy, known as *Iain Glas*, was the 1st Earl. Born in 1635, he was created Earl of Caithness in 1677, having married the widow of the 6th Earl and bought up most of his estates ; but Sinclair of Keiss establishing his right to the Caithness Earldom, Glenorchy was in 1681 created Earl of Breadalbane. He was a celebrated statesman, but his line failed in John, 3rd Earl, died 1782. John, 4th Earl, created Marquess of Breadalbane, 1831, succeeded as lineal descendant of Colin of Mochastar, second son of Sir Robert, 3rd Baronet. John, 2nd Marquess and 5th Earl, succeeded his father in 1834. He died without issue in 1862, when the Marquisate became extinct, and the Earldom passed to the Glenfalloch branch, in Sir John Alexander Gavin Campbell, 6th Earl of Breadalbane. His son, Gavin, 7th Earl, was created Marquis of Breadalbane, 1885, but died without issue, 1922, when the Marquisate expired, the Scottish honours devolving on his nephew, Iain, 8th Earl, who died 1923, succeeded by a kinsman, Charles William, 9th Earl of Breadalbane and Holland. Taymouth Castle, the principal seat of the House of Breadalbane, became an hotel, but the Earl still holds large estates, including Glenorchy. There are many cadets of the house ; Campbell of Glenlyon, who executed the massacre of Glencoe, was the most celebrated—or notorious. The baronets of Barcaldine, Hereditary Keepers of the picturesque Castle of Barcaldine, are also cadets.

There is a Clan Campbell Society, with its headquarters in Glasgow.

10. CAMPBELL OF BREADALBANE

CAMPBELL OF CAWDOR

Badge :—Roid (Wild Myrtle) or Garbhag an t-sléibhe (Fir Club Moss).

JOHN, 7th Thane of Calder or Cawdor, married, in 1492, Isabel Rose, daughter of Kilravock, and, dying in 1494, left one posthumous child, a daughter, Muriel. Kilravock intended this heiress for his own grandson, her first cousin ; but Kilravock being pursued in a criminal process for robbery in joining Mackintosh for spoiling the lands of Urquhart of Cromarty, Argyll, the Justice-General, made the process easy to him, got the ward of Muriel's marriage of the King in 1495, and she was carried to Inveraray in the year 1499. In autumn of 1499 Campbell of Inverliver, with sixty men, came to receive the child on pretence of sending her south to school. As Inverliver came with little Muriel to Daltulich, in Strathnairn, he was pursued by Alexander and Hugh Calder, her uncles. A sharp conflict took place and seven of Inverliver's sons were killed. When asked whether this was not too heavy a loss, since the heiress might die, Inverliver replied, "The lassie can never die sae lang as there is a red-headed lass on the shores of Loch Awe."

Muriel was married in 1510 to Sir John Campbell, third son of Argyll. He resided permanently at Cawdor from 1524 till 1546, the year of his death. Lady Muriel died in 1573, resigning her Thanedom in favour of her grandson, John (III.). Sir John, early in the 17th century, sold Croy, and disposed of Ferintosh to Lord Lovat, and mortgaged other lands in order to purchase, or rather to conquer, the island of Islay. The Cawdor family kept possession of Islay from 1612 to 1726, when it was purchased by Daniel Campbell of Shawfield.

Sir John Campbell, son of Sir Alexander (VII.), succeeded his father. He married Mary, eldest daughter and co-heiress of Lewis Pryce, and died in 1777. He was succeeded by his son, Pryce Campbell of Cawdor, M.P., who was succeeded by his son, John, who was elevated to the Peerage in 1796 by the title of Lord Cawdor of Castlemartin, Pembrokeshire. He died in 1821, and was succeeded by his son, John Frederick Campbell, Earl of Cawdor (*cr.* 1827). He died 27th June 1860, and was succeeded by his eldest son, John Frederick Vaughan Campbell, 2nd Earl of Cawdor. He died in 1898, and was succeeded by his son, Frederick Archibald Vaughan Campbell, 3rd Earl of Cawdor, who was born in 1847. The 5th (and present) Earl, John Duncan Campbell, succeeded to the title in 1914.

Cawdor Castle, built in 1454, is one of the finest feudal fortresses in Scotland. Tradition says the Thane dreamt that he should place a coffer of gold on an ass's back and build the castle where the ass stopped. This it did beside a hawthorn tree, which still flourishes in the vault of the great tower of Cawdor.

Cawdor Castle.

11. CAMPBELL OF CAWDOR

CARNEGIE

JOCELYN DE BALLINHARD, living 1203, is reckoned founder of this race, which derived its name from the lands of Carrynnegy, which in 1358 were confirmed to John, the son of Christian, the son of John de Ballinhard. The direct line of the Carnegies of that Ilk expired before 1563, and from Duthac de Carnegie, second son of John de Ballinhard, derives the chiefly House of Southesk. His son, also Duthac, acquired Kinnaird by mariage with Mariota de Kinnaird, about 1409, and fell at Harlaw. John, 4th of Kinnaird, fell at Flodden, and Sir Robert, 5th of Kinnaird, was a Lord of Session, 1547, and Ambassador to England 1556. Sir David Carnegie, 8th of Kinnaird, was created Lord Carnegie of Kinnaird, 1616, and Earl of Southesk, 1633. James, 2nd Earl, a Royalist who was imprisoned by Cromwell, was known as "The Black Earl," having learned magic at Padua. His grandson, James, 5th Earl, was out in the 1715, and proclaimed King James at Montrose, and entertained him during winter 1715–16. In consequence of this, he was attainted, and dying without issue, the representation devolved upon his cousin, Sir James, 3rd Baronet of Pitarro, descended from a younger son of the 1st Earl, M.P. for Kincardineshire, who repurchased the forfeited estates of Southesk. Sir James, 6th Baronet, got the attainder reversed 1853, and consequently became 9th Earl of Southesk. He was a Knight of the Thistle and a distinguished antiquary. Charles Alexander, 11th Earl of Southesk, is the present chief. His seat is Kinnaird Castle, Angus. The Carnegie tartan is based on that of Glengarry, and seems to have been adopted during the Rising of 1715, when Lord Southesk and Glengarry acted in close co-operation in the Jacobite Army.

The Earls of Northesk, whose seat was Ethie Castle, derive from John, younger brother of the 1st Earl of Southesk, who was created Lord Lour in 1639, and Earl of Ethie 1647, but had the latter altered to "Northesk" in 1666. Of this line, George, 6th Earl, was a celebrated Admiral, as also his son, William, 7th Earl, Third-in-Command under Nelson at Trafalgar, and Commander-in-Chief of the British Navy, 1821–30. Andrew Carnegie of Skibo, the multimillionaire and philanthropist, born in Dunfermline, founded the Pittsburg steelworks, and with his wealth established the Carnegie Free Libraries and Scottish Universities Students' Trust. The Carnegies of Balnamoon are cadets of Southesk, and those of Lour (both in Angus) of the Northesk line.

[Continued from page 96.

Heretrix of the Clan. On the death without issue of his son Lachlan, 1734, the Chiefship, following the *duthus* lands of Lochaber, then passed to the heir of tailzie, William, 22nd Chief of Clan Chattan and 21st of Mackintosh, and thereafter under an entail of Sir Aeneas, 24th Chief, passed to successive cousins in male-tail until the death in 1938 of Alfred Donald Mackintosh of Mackintosh, 29th Chief of Clan Chattan and 28th of Mackintosh, when, the last of the Clan Chattan lands being sold, and a special settlement made of the Mackintosh *duthus* and Chiefship, not including the arms and Chiefship of Clan Chattan, Alfred was succeeded in the latter by his granddaughter, Arbell Mackintosh of Mackintosh, until she became "conventionally dead" on taking the non-Clan Chattan name of "Mrs. Warre of Dalcross" on her marriage in 1942, when the Chiefship of Clan Chattan (no longer attracted by the entailed *duthus*) passed to her cousin, the next heir-general within the clan (a descendant of Aeneas Mackintosh of Daviot, 2nd son of the 26th Chief), Duncan Alexander Eliott Mackintosh of Mackintosh-Torcastle and Clan Chattan, to whom the arms and Chiefship were confirmed by Lyon Court, 1947, as 31st Chief of Clan Chattan. He is the present *Gillichattan Mor*, and resides on his estate at Fairburn, Felixburg, S. Rhodesia.

12. CARNEGIE

THE CLAN CHATTAN

Slogan :—" Clan Chattan."
Badge :—Red Whortleberry.

THE Clan Chattan, deriving its name from the title of its Chief, *Gillichattan Mor* (the great servant of St. Catan) is derived by modern historians from the *co-arb*, or the bailie, of the Abbey of St. Catan, probably Kilchattan in Bute, where the surname *Cattanach* was long common. In the reign of Malcolm II., or III., the Gillichattan became possessed of Glenlui, Loch Arkaig and Glen Spean in Lochaber, and appears as *Gillichattan Mor O'Gualav*, with his seat at Torcastle, and is reckoned 1st Chief of the Clan Chattan. His son, Dugal or Diarmid, had two sons, (1) Gillichattan (*Muriach-Mor*), reckoned 3rd Chief, and (2) David Dow of Invernahaven, ancestor of Clan Dhai. The 3rd Chief had two sons, (1) Kenneth, *Tanastair* or Chief, who may or may not have succeeded, but died without issue, and (2) Muriach, Celtic Prior of Kingussie, who upon the opening of the succession was called to leave the Church, was styled *Gillichattan-Clerach*, and as 4th Chief married in 1173 a daughter of the Thane of Cawdor and had, (1) *Gillichattan-Patrick*, his heir, (2) *Ewan Ban*, described as " son of the Prior," *Mac Parson*, and eponymus of the Clan Macpherson, (3) *Neil Crom*, claimed as progenitor of all the name of Smith in Scotland (!) and (4) *Ferquhard Gilliriach*, ancestor of Clan MacGillivray.

The eldest son, *Patrick Gillichattan*, 5th Chief, was father of *Dugal Doul*, 6th Chief of Clan Chattan, who left an only daughter, Eva, Heretrix of the Clan, who in 1291 married Angus Mackintosh, 6th of Mackintosh, who in her right became 7th Chief of Clan Chattan. Their second son, John, was progenitor of the Mackintoshes and Shaws of Rothimurchus and Tordaroch, whilst the eldest, William, born 1292, became 7th Chief of Mackintosh and 8th Chief of Clan Chattan. In the time of his son, Lachlan, 9th Chief, originated the dispute between Clan Mackintosh and Clan Macpherson, from a dispute at the battle of Invernahaven, 1384, as to whether the Davidsons, as eldest cadet of Gillichattan, or Kenneth Mac Ewan Ban Macpherson, as heir-male, was entitled as principal cadet of Clan Chattan to command the right wing of the Clan under Mackintosh as Chief, through the heiress, commanding the centre and whole clan. Mackintosh had quite reasonably upheld Davidson, but the dispute being carried into the Scottish Court of Chivalry in the " Clan Battle " of 30th August 1396 at the North Inch of Perth, this " Trial by Combat " settled that in such circumstances the heir-male has precedence of the eldest cadet and has first place at the right of the heir-of-line Chief. His son, Ferquhard Mackintosh, 10th Chief of Clan Chattan, abdicated about 1409 (his descendants being styled the *Slioch Ferquhar vich Lachlan*) in favour of his uncle Malcolm, 11th Chief, from whom the Chiefships of Mackintosh and Clan Chattan descended to Sir Lachlan Mor Mackintosh of that Ilk and Torcastle who, in a celebrated bond of 1609, received the fealty of the " haill kin of Clan Chattan as it was of auld according to the Kings of Scots their Gift of the Chiftainry " (alluding to Crown confirmation of Ferquhard's abdication). Sir Lachland died 1620, and his successor William was father of Lachlan Mackintosh of that Ilk and Torcastle, 20th Chief of Clan Chattan and 19th of Mackintosh, who in 1672 (Cluny Macpherson having impetrated through Stacy, Ross Herald, an armorial confirmation as " only and true Representer of the antient and honourable famile of the Clanchattone ") succeeded, 10th September 1672, in a litigation before Lyon Court in having Cluny declared a cadet and himself to be *Chief of the Name of Mackintosh* and *Chief of the Clan Chattan*, from descent through Eva as

[*Continued on page 94.*

96

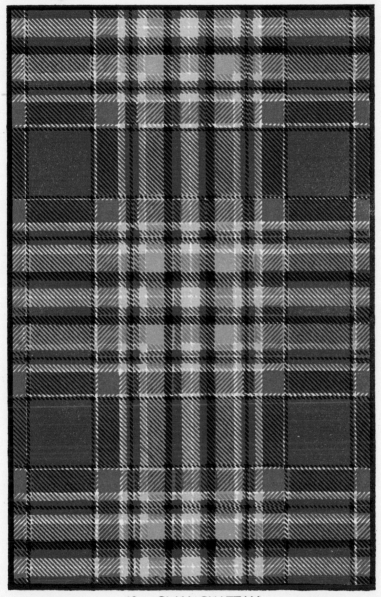

13. CLAN CHATTAN

CHISHOLM

Badge :—Raineach (Fern)

THE Chisholms in Scotland are first found on the Borders, in Roxburghshire. This clan is of Norman origin, and the name was originally spelt De Cheseholm. Their original Border seat was the Barony of Chiesholme in Roxburghshire, which long continued in the house of Chisholme, afterwards Scott-Chisholme of Chisholme. The last chief of these Border Chisholmes, Colonel John Chisholme of that ilk and Stirches, was killed in the charge at Elandslaagte, 1899. In the 14th century, Sir Robert de Chisholme was Constable of Urquhart Castle, and his son, Alexander de Chisholme, having married Margaret, Lady of Erchless, daughter and heiress of Weyland of the Aird, had a son, Thomas de Chisholm, 1403, from whom the Chisholms of Comer and Strathglass descend. In accordance with the Clan Chattan decision of 1672, the Chisholms would have become chiefs of Margaret's "clan," if no "del Aird" surname was in use—and at that period and locality it was no doubt only a designation. The Chisholms are therefore quite properly chiefs of a Highland clan. For John Chisholm, great grandson of Thomas Chisholm, the lands of Erchless and Comer were erected into baronies 1538-39. The direct line terminated with Alexander Chisholm, 1793, whose daughter Mary, married James Gooden. She is celebrated in the highlands for her opposition to the "clearances." The chiefship and estates passed under entail to his brother William, whose two sons, Alexander and Duncan, died without issue, leaving a sister Jemima, Mrs Chisholm-Batten, while the estates passed to a cadet, James Sutherland Chisholm, great-grandson of Alexander Chisholm of Muckerach, whose son, Roderick Chisholm, The Chisholm, died without issue 1887, and was succeeded in Erchless by his sisters, at whose death Erchless passed to Edmund Chisholm-Batten, grandson of Jemima. This picturesque fortalice in Strathglass, for centuries the seat of the race, was recently sold. In 1887, Roderick, the last chief in the male line by possession of the estates, having died, and Jemima's descendants having taken the principal name and arms of Batten, James Gooden-Chisholm, eldest son of Mary, Mrs Gooden-Chisholm, heiress of the direct line, claimed and was awarded the undifferenced arms of the race, with supporters, and was thereafter designated *An Siosalach*, and received as chief of the Clan Chisholm. The name of "Gooden" has since been dropped and the title "Chisholm of Chisholm" officially recognised in Lyon Court. Captain Roderick Chisholm of Chisholm was succeeded by his grandson, Alistair Chisholm of Chisholm, The Chisholm, present Chief of Clan Chisholm, who resides at Coldbrooke House, Herts, and Cnoc - an - Fhurain, Barcaldine, Argyll.

Erchless.

98

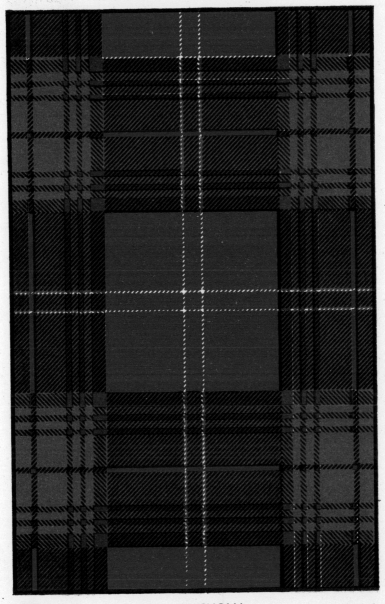

14. CHISHOLM

COLQUHOUN

Slogan :—" Cnoc Ealachain."

Badge: —Braoileag nan con (Dogberry) or Caltuinn (Hazel).

COLQUHOUN is a territorial name, and is derived from the Barony of Colquhoun, in the parish of West Kilpatrick, Dumbarton-shire. The Chief of the clan is Colquhoun of Luss, and the clan's territories are on Loch-lomondside.

The founder of the family of Colquhoun of Luss was Humphrey de Kilpatrick or Kirk-patrick, who obtained from Malcolm, Earl of Lennox, during the reign of King Alexander II., a grant of the lands of Colquhoun, "*pro servitio unius militis.*" Ingram, the son of Humphrey Kilpatrick, was the first who assumed the name of Colquhoun.

The lands of Luss were acquired during the reign of King Robert II. by marriage with the " Fair Maid of Luss," heiress of the House of Luss of that Ilk, descending Maldwin, Dean of the Lennox, 1150.

Sir John Colquhoun of Luss was Governor of Dumbarton Castle under James II., and Luss was erected into a barony in 1457 for his grandson, another Sir John, and the old barony of Colquhoun embodied in it.

Sir Humphry Colquhoun, 12th Laird of Luss, acquired the Heritable Coronership of Dumbartonshire in 1583. He died without issue, and was succeeded by his brother, Sir Alexander. His descendant, Sir Humphrey, 17th Laird of Luss, married a daughter of Houston of that Ilk, by whom he had only a daughter, Anne, who in 1702 married James Grant of Pluscardine, second son of Grant of that Ilk ; and being resolved that the young couple should succeed him in his whole estate and honours, in 1704 he resigned his baronetcy to the Crown, and obtained a new grant—to himself in life rent, to his daughter and son-in-law in fee, providing that their heirs should adopt the name and Arms of Colquhoun, and that the estates of Grant and Luss should never be conjoined. Sir Humphry died in 1715. James Grant succeeded as Sir James Colquhoun ; but his elder brother dying without issue in 1719, he succeeded to the estates of Grant, and resuming that name, was succeeded in the chiefship of Colquhoun and the Luss estates by his second son, Sir Ludovick. He, on the death of his elder brother, unmarried, also succeeded to the estates of Grant, and that of Luss went to his younger brother, James, who was officially recognised by Lyon as chief of the name of Colquhoun in 1781. He was created a baronet in 1786, and, dying the same year, was succeeded by his son, Sir James, great-grandfather of Sir James, 5th Baronet of Colquhoun and Luss, who died in 1907, and was succeeded by his cousin, Sir Alan John Colquhoun, 6th Baronet. His son, Sir Iain Colquhoun of Luss, Bt., K.T., was a famous Chief and Lord High Commissioner. He died 1948, and his son, Sir Ivor Colquhoun of Luss, 8th Baronet, is now 29th Chief of Clan Colquhoun, Laird and Baron of Luss. His seat is Rossdhu House, Luss, Dunbartonshire.

There is a Clan Colquhoun Society, with its headquarters in Glasgow. The principal cadet is Campbell Colquhoun of Killermont and Camstradden.

15. COLQUHOUN

CRAWFURD

THIS surname is derived from the Barony of Crawford in the Upper Ward of Clydesdale, and Galfridus de Crawford appears to have flourished about 1179. In 1248, Sir John Crawford of that Ilk died, leaving two daughters, of whom the elder married Archibald de Douglas, and the younger, David Lindsay of Wauchopedale, ancestor of the Earls of Crawford. Sir Archibald de Crawfurd, a cadet of the main line, married about 1200, Margaret, daughter and heiress of James de Loudon, and dying 1229, was succeeded by his son, Hugh Crawfurd of Loudon, Sheriff of Ayr. His son, another Hugh, was father of Sir Archibald, the Sheriff, who was treacherously murdered by the English at a banquet in Ayr, 1297, and a daughter Margaret, who married Sir Malcolm Wallace of Ellerslie and was mother of the patriot. Sir Archibald's granddaughter, Susan Crawfurd, heiress of Loudon, carried that estate into the House of Campbell, and the representation of the Crawfords is understood to have devolved upon Crawfurd of Auchinames (deriving from a brother of Sir Archibald), a house which originated in a grant of Auchinames from Robert the Bruce in 1320. The male line continued unbroken until the death of Archibald Crawford, 14th of Auchinames, when his daughter Jane succeeded and married a kinsman, Patrick Crawfurd of Drumsoy. Their son Patrick succeeded to Auchinames, and his son John Crawfurd, 18th of Auchinames, M.P., was awarded arms and supporters by Lyon Court, 1789. He was succeeded by his cousin, John Crawfurd, 19th of Auchinames, by whose grandson, Hugh R. G. Crawfurd, 21st of Auchinames, this old estate has been sold. He was chief of the Crawfords, and resided in Alberta, Canada, where he died recently.

Craufurd of Craufurdland derives from a younger son of Sir Reginald de Craufurd and Margaret de Loudon, who married Alicia de Dalsalloch. Ardoch, otherwise called Craufurdland, was confirmed to the 6th Laird by Robert III. in 1391, and has continued uninterruptedly in the family, down to the present laird, J. D. Houison-Craufurd, 25th of Craufurdland.

The Craufurds of Kilbirnie are another ancient branch of the clan, whose origin is deduced from Sir John Craufurd of Craufordjohn, living about 1255. Kilbirnie was acquired in 1499. A baronetcy was conferred on this branch in 1781.

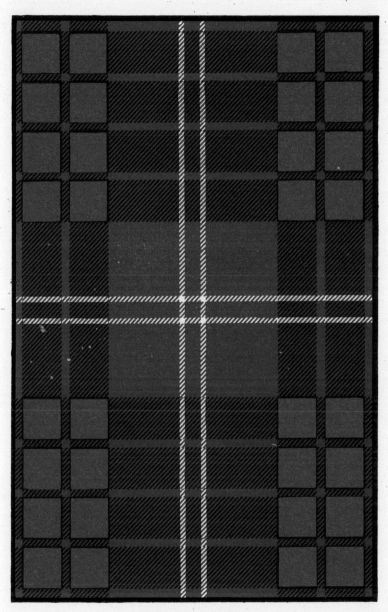

16. CRAWFORD

CUMIN (CUMMING)

Badge :—Lus Mhic Cuimin (Cumin plant)—really Wheat.

ROBERT DE COMYN, a companion of William the Conqueror, and whose name is understood to have been derived from Comines in Flanders, was created Earl of Northumberland 1069. His grandson, Richard Comyn, came to Scotland with King David. He married Hexstilda of Tynedale, whose mother was Bethock, daughter of King Donald Bane, by whom he had a son, William, who in right of his second wife Marjory, became Earl of Buchan. By a previous union the Earl had a son and heir, Richard, who was father of Sir John the Red Comyn, Lord of Badenoch and chief of a clan which then comprised three Earls and thirty-two Knights of the Name. His son, Sir John Comyn of Badenoch, The Black Comyn, was —along with The Bruce—one of the competitors for the Crown of Scotland in 1296, but withdrew his claim and supported John Baliol, by whose sister Alienora, he had a son, John of Badenoch, also styled The Red Comyn, one of the Guardians of Scotland who defeated the English at Roslin 1302. He submitted to King Edward in 1304. His disagreement with Robert the Bruce, and murder in the Church of the Minorite Friars at Dumfries in 1306, opened the way for the Bruce's campaign and Scottish War of Independence, which involved the collapse and extinction of the chief House of Comyn. The House of Altyre, on whom the undifferenced arms and chiefship devolved, claims descent from Robert, younger brother of the Black Comyn, whose son Thomas was exempted from the proscription of the clan in 1320; and his son Sir Richard Cumming, Hereditary Forester of Darnaway, in the days of King David II., established the House of Altyre which has continued to hold that estate for five centuries. Robert Cumming of Altyre, 13th Chief of his line, married Lucy, daughter of Sir Ludovic Gordon of Gordonstown, and his great-grandson, Sir Alexander Cumming of Altyre, was created a Baronet in 1804, and took the name of Gordon-Cumming on succeeding to the estates of Gordon of Gordonstown. The present chief of the clan (excepting for the objection of the double-surname) is Sir William Gordon-Cumming of Altyre, 6th Baronet and 22nd Chief. The cadets of Altyre are the Cummings of Lochtervandich and Auchry, from whom descends Cumming of Rattray in Aberdeenshire, and the Cummings of Logie, Relugas, and Dunphail. From the Earls of Buchan derive the baronial House of Cumming of Inverallochy, springing from Jordan Cumming, apparently brother of Earl Alexander. Sir William Cumming of Inverallochy was Lord Lyon King of Arms to James IV. and conveyed the Flodden challenge to Henry VIII., and the Cumming Baronets of Culter were a branch of Inverallochy. The seat of the present Baronet of Altyre and Chief of the clan is the House of Blair-of-Altyre in Morayshire. The Aberdeenshire house of Buchan of Auchmacoy came off the line of Celtic Earls of Buchan prior to the time of Countess Marjory, and is recognised by Lyon Court as Chief of the Name of Buchan. They wear a darker sett called "Cumming, Ancient," which is regarded as the old Buchan District Tartan.

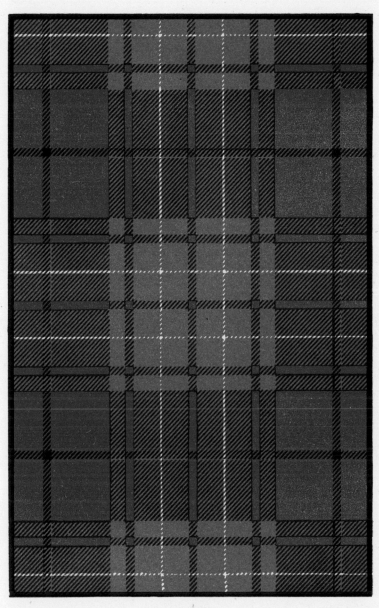

17.   CUMIN

CUNNINGHAM

CUNNINGHAM as a surname is derived from the district of that name in Ayrshire, and the *eponymus* is stated to have been Wernibald, who, it is said, received a grant of Kilmaurs in Cunningham from Hugo de Morville, Constable of Scotland about 1140. Other traditions deduce the descent of the Cunninghams from Malcolm, son of Freskin. Harvey de Cunningham is said to have fought at the Battle of Largs 1263, and to have had a confirmation of Kilmaurs from Alexander II., 1264, and Hugh de Cunningham got the lands of Lamburgton from Robert the Bruce, 1321. His grandson, Sir William, married the heiress of Danielston of that Ilk, by which he acquired Finlaystoun, which became one of the principal seats of the family. His grandson, Sir Alexander, was created Lord Kilmaurs about 1462, and Earl of Glencairn 1488. From his second son derived the Cunninghams of Craigends, Robertland, and Auchinharvie. Robert, 2nd Laird of Kilmaurs, was deprived of his father's earldom, which, however, was revived for his brother and heir, Cuthbert, 3rd Lord Kilmaurs and 2nd Earl of Glencairn. William, 3rd Earl, was captured at the rout of Solway Moss, but released on undertaking to promote a marriage between Edward VI. and Mary, Queen of Scots. Alexander, 4th Earl, was a friend of John Knox, and James, 6th Earl, was notorious for his feud with the Earl of Eglinton. William, 8th Earl, was Lord Justice-General, and after the Restoration, Chancellor of Scotland. James, 13th Earl, sold Kilmaurs in 1786. His brother John, 14th Earl, is celebrated as the friend of the poet Burns, and since his death the Earldom has been dormant. The chiefship is regarded as being in the House of Cunningham of Corsehill, deriving from the Honourable Andrew Cunningham of Corsehill, second son of the 3rd Earl of Glencairn. Sir Alexander, 7th Laird of Corsehill, was created a Baronet 1673, and his representative, Sir William Montgomery Cunninghame, 11th Baronet, is regarded as the present chief of the name of Cunningham, and rightful heir to the Earldom of Glencairn. The Baronets of Robertland, created 1630, derive from the Craigends branch, and Thomas Cunningham of Baidland, great-uncle of the 1st Lord Kilmaurs, was father of Adam Cunningham, 1st Laird of Caprington, about 1425, from whom is descended the present Wallace Cunninghame, 15th of Caprington, which was erected into a feudal barony by Mary, Queen of Scots.

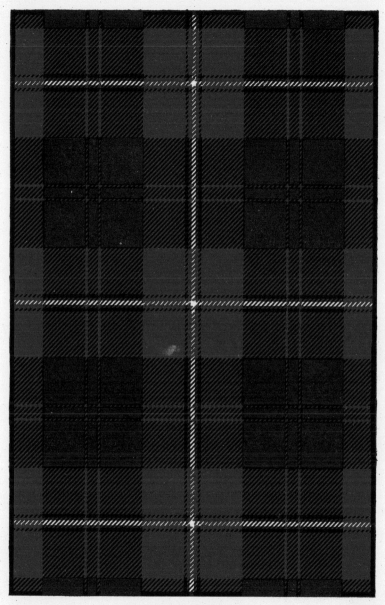

18. CUNNINGHAM

DALZELL

HUGH DE DALZELL was Sheriff of Lanark, 1288, and the territorial Barony of Dalzell is situated in Lanarkshire. Sir William de Dalzell was a celebrated knight, whose successor, Sir John, settled the representation of the family upon his third son Robert. He, in 1446, became Dalzell of that Ilk, from whom descended the Laird of Dalzell who fought for Queen Mary at Langside, whose son and successor, Sir Robert, was created Lord Dalzell in 1633, and Earl of Carnwath in 1649. Robert ruined his estate in supporting King Charles I. and is celebrated for the remark in Parliament 1641 : " Now we have three kings, and by God, two of them (Hamilton and Argyll), behove to want their heads." On the death of John, 5th Earl, last of the direct line, the dignity reverted to Sir Robert Dalzell, 3rd Baronet of Glenae, descended from Sir John of Glenae and Newtown, second son of the 1st Earl. Earl Robert and his brother Sir John both took the field on behalf of the Chevalier, and although the Earl was condemned to death, he ultimately escaped with forfeiture of title and estates, and whilst the estate of Glenae ultimately devolved upon his granddaughter Margaret, whose successors took the style Dalzell of Glenae, the Earldom of Carnwath was in 1826 restored to Robert Alexander Dalzell, his grandson and heir male, through descent from the attainted Earl's fifth son, the Hon. Robert Dalzell. Arthur Edward, 15th Earl of Carnwath, died in 1941, when the Earldom became dormant ; but the estates have all been lost through devotion to the Stewart cause. From John Dalzell, an uncle of the 1st Earl, descends the cadet branch of Dalzell of Binns, founded by the celebrated General Thomas Dalzell, " The Muscovite Devil," who, after service with the Czar, returned to Scotland and in the reign of Charles II. established Scotland's Royal regiment of Dragoons, the Scots Greys. As Commander-in-Chief in Scotland he defeated the Covenanters in 1666 at Rullion Green. The General's son, Sir Thomas, was created a Baronet in 1685, with destination to heirs male and tailzie, and this title has descended through heirs female along with the feudal barony of the Binns in West Lothian.

Dalzell Castle, in Lanarkshire, the ancestral seat of the chiefs of this race, is a picturesque fortress-mansion with courtyard and 15th-century tower overlooking the river Clyde.

19. DALZELL

H

DAVIDSON

Badge :—Lus nan cnàimhseag, or Braoileag (Red Whortleberry).

THIS clan associated themselves and took protection of and under William Mackintosh (VII.) of Mackintosh prior to 1350, and have ever since been regarded as a sept of Clan Chattan.

Kinrara, in his history (1676), says: " The Davidsons, styled of Invernahaven, in Badenoch, were, according to common tradition, originally a branch of the Comyns." After the downfall of the Comyns, Donald Dhu of Invernahaven associated himself with Clan Chattan, married a daughter of Angus (VI.) of Mackintosh, and became a leading member of Clan Chattan. The favour shown to him by the Captain of Clan Chattan roused the jealousy of another tribe, a jealousy which brought about the virtual extinction of the Davidsons.

The Davidsons, called *Clann Dà'idh* from their first known leader, David Dhu of Invernahaven, were chief actors in the two notable battles—Invernahaven (1370) and the North Inch of Perth (1396)—and the losers in both battles.

The leading families are the Davidsons of Cantray, in Inverness, and the Davidsons of Tulloch, in Ross-shire.

About the year 1700 Alexander Davidson of Davidson, in Cromarty, married Miss Bayne of Tulloch, and purchased the estate from his father-in-law. The Baynes of Tulloch were for many generations of great position and influence in Ross-shire. Tulloch Castle is of ancient date, the keep having been built in 1466, and other parts of it in 1665. A branch of this family entered the service of France in the 17th century, having proved their descent to be noble for six generations prior to July 1629, as shown by the *Livre d'Or* in the imperial archives of France.

The Davidsons are said to have been almost annihilated at the Battle of the North Inch, Perth, in 1396.

Davidson of Tulloch was latterly regarded as chief, but his estates have passed in the female line to Mrs Vickers, who has not taken up the name and arms of Davidson, so the representation lies dormant.

There is a Davidson Association entitled *Clan Dhai*, which has recorded arms in Lyon Court.

20. DAVIDSON

DOUGLAS

THIS surname is territorial, from the wild pastoral dale possessed by William de Douglas, living 1174 and 1199. His eldest son, Sir Archibald, left two sons—Sir William, and Andrew, ancestor of the Morton family. Sir William died about 1274. His son was Sir William *le Hardi*, whose son, " the Good Sir James," the greatest of Bruce's captains in the War of Independence, was killed fighting against the Moors in Spain, 1330. Hugh, brother of Lord James, settled the family estates on his nephew, Sir William, in 1343.

In 1357 this Sir William was made Earl of Douglas, and by marriage became Earl of Mar. He died 1384. His son, James, 2nd Earl of Douglas and Mar, fell at Otterburn, 1388. His own natural son became progenitor of the Marquesses of Queensberry, while he was succeeded under entail by Archibald " the Grim," 3rd Earl, natural son of " Good Sir James." The 4th Earl was created Duke of Touraine in France, and married Princess Margaret, daughter of Robert III. The earldom was forfeited when James, 9th Earl, was defeated at Arkinholm, 1455. The chiefship of this great family then devolved upon the Earls of Angus in the person of George, 4th Earl, who received a grant of the ancient inheritance of Douglasdale in reward for having supported the Crown. His son, Archibald, 5th Earl, celebrated as Bell-the-Cat, led the insurgent nobles against James III., and survived Flodden Field. Archibald, 6th Earl, married the widowed Queen Margaret Tudor, but dying without issue the earldom passed subsequently to the Houses of Pittendreich and Glenbervie, and William, 11th Earl, was in 1633 created Marquis of Douglas. Archibald, 3rd Marquis, was created Duke of Douglas, 1703, but dying without issue, 1774, his marquisate and the earldom of Angus devolved on the Duke of Hamilton, whilst the Douglas estates, in consequence of the celebrated lawsuit, " The Douglas Cause," passed to his nephew and heir of line, Archibald Stewart Douglas of Douglas, to whom the armorial bearings and the Douglas chiefship were awarded by Lyon Decree 1771, and he was created Lord Douglas of Douglas 1790. On the death of the 4th Lord Douglas, 1857, the Douglas estates devolved upon his niece, Lucy Elizabeth Douglas of Douglas, Countess of Home, whose grandson, Charles, 13th Earl of Home, is feudal Baron of Douglas. It is difficult to say who is now chief of the name and family of Douglas, as the arms and estate are at present merged in the Earldom of Home, and the Duke of Hamilton, although paternally a Douglas, became by marriage with the Hamilton heiress, on taking her name and arms, by the law and custom of Scotland, chief of the name and house of Hamilton. If Douglasdale were settled, with the name and arms of Douglas, upon a younger son of Lord Home, he would thereupon as next of blood bearing the name be chief of the House of Douglas, failing which that position may pass to the next brother of the House of Hamilton resuming the name and arms of Douglas of Douglas.

21. DOUGLAS

DRUMMOND

Badge :—Lus an Righ (Wild Thyme) or Cuileann (Holly)

THIS clan's name is evidently a territorial one, from the lands of Drummond or Drymen, in Stirlingshire.

Malcolm Beg, so called from his low stature, Steward of the Earldom of Strathearn, 1225, is the first of the line on record and his son Sir Malcolm first assumed the name of Drummond.

Sir Malcolm de Drymen (or Drummond) was one of the chiefs who fought on the side of King Robert the Bruce at Bannockburn, and to his action in strewing the field with the caltrops or spikes, which had the effect of disabling a large proportion of the English cavalry, much of the success of the battle was due. The caltrops, on which the savages (which form the supporters of the arms of the Chief of Clan Drummond) stand, as well as the chief's motto, " Gang warily," allude to this. He was twice captured by the English during the Scottish War of Independence. His son, another Malcolm, was father of Sir John, Baillie of the Abthanery of Dull in 1357 and of Margaret, who married Sir John Logie of that Ilk and afterwards became notorious as the Queen of David II. Sir John married Mary de Montfichet, heiress of Cargill and Stobhall. His daughter Annabella, was Queen of Robert III., and her son, Sir Malcolm Drummond, was ancestor of John, 5th of Cargill and Stobhall who became Lord Drummond in 1487. His eldest daughter became attached to John IV., and she and her twin sisters died in 1502 under tragic circumstances.

James, 4th Lord Drummond, was created Earl of Perth in 1605. James, 4th Earl, was Lord Chancellor of Scotland, and followed the fortunes of James VII., who created him Duke of Perth. He died in 1716. James, his son, 2nd Duke, was married to Lady Jane Gordon. He died in 1720, and was succeeded by his elder son, James, 3rd Duke, who was wounded at Culloden. On the death of Edward, 6th Duke, the direct line expired, and the representation of the earldom passed to James, 10th Earl, whose son James, 11th Earl, was succeeded by his cousin James Lewis, 4th Duc de Melfort, as 12th Earl. This line of earls expired in 1902 with George, 14th Earl and 6th Duc de Melfort, when the succession to the houses of Perth opened to the house of Strathallan.

James, second son of David, 2nd Lord Drummond, was created Lord Maderty in 1610, and in 1686 the 4th Lord was created Viscount of Strathallan. In 1902 William, 11th Viscount, succeeded as 15th Earl of Perth and Chief of the clan. His brother Eric, 16th Earl of Perth, the present chief, is celebrated as First Secretary-General of the League of Nations.

Among the principal cadets are Drummond of Hawthornden, in Midlothian ; Drummond of Concraig ; Drummond of Stanmore, in Middlesex ; and Drummond of Blair Drummond.

The tartan shown is the historic and ancient sett of the clan. In recent times a version of the Grant tartan has sometimes erroneously been used, apparently through a mistake of the Willoughbys, who inherited Drummond Castle.

22. DRUMMOND

DUNBAR

CRINAN the Thane and Seneschal of the Isles, born about 975, was father of King Duncan I., and of Maldred, whose son, Gospatric, was confirmed in the Earldom of Northumbria by William the Conqueror in 1067. In 1072 he was deprived of that Earldom, and, flying to Scotland, was given Dunbar and the adjacent lands by King Malcolm III., thus becoming Earl of Dunbar. His descendant, Patrick, the 8th Earl of Dunbar, was also Earl of March. He was one of the competitors for the Crown of Scotland, but withdrew his claim and submitted to Edward I. in 1291. His son Patrick, 8th Earl, also favoured the English party, and after the Battle of Bannockburn he received King Edward II. in his castle of Dunbar and helped him to escape to England. Patrick, 9th Earl, married Agnes Randolph, daughter of Thomas Randolph, 1st Earl of Moray, and companion of Bruce. She is celebrated in history as "Black Agnes," and when the English forces under Salisbury besieged Dunbar Castle in 1337, she successfully defended it for some months. In 1346, on the death of her brother John, 3rd Earl of Moray, she became Countess of Moray, but dying in 1368 without surviving issue, the Earldom of Dunbar devolved on his grandnephew, George, whose brother, John, became Earl of Moray in 1372, their mother being Isabelle Randolph, sister of "Black Agnes." George, 11th Earl of Dunbar and March, was a faithful supporter of James I., but the King thought him too powerful and forfeited his earldoms in 1435. His son became ancestor of the line of Dunbar of Mochrum, which expired in 1564. John, the Earl of Moray, married Marjorie, daughter of King Robert II., and had a son Thomas, 2nd Earl, who first married the heiress of Frendraught, by whom he had Thomas 3rd, and James, 4th Earl, who was murdered at Frendraught, having by his first wife two daughters successively Countesses of Moray. By Isobel Innes, who died before the dispensation for their marriage arrived from Rome, he left a son, Sir Alexander Dunbar of Westfield, ancestor of the hereditary Sheriffs of Moray.

The Dunbars, Baronets of Mochrum, descend from Sir Alexander Dunbar of Westfield, a son of the last Earl of Moray. They were created Baronets in 1694. Sir James Dunbar of Mochrum, 10th Baronet, whose seat is Mochrum Park, Wigtonshire, is apparently the present chief of the name of Dunbar. The Baronets of Durn, 1698, and of Northfield, 1700, are cadets of Westfield. So also are the Baronets of Hempriggs, in Caithness, whose dignity, like the Baronetcy of Dunbar of Baldoon, passes to heirs female.

Of the Mochrum family was Gavin Dunbar, Archbishop of Glasgow and Lord Chancellor of Scotland in the reign of King James V. William Dunbar, born about 1460, is one of the most celebrated of ancient Scottish poets. Gavin Dunbar, of the Westfield family, was appointed Bishop of Aberdeen in 1518.

23. DUNBAR

DUNDAS

SERLE DE DUNDAS, living in the time of King William the Lion, and traditionally a cadet of the Earls of Dunbar and March, is the founder of the race of Dundas which takes its name from these lands on the southern shore of the Forth. His descendant, Saer de Dundas, submitted to Edward I. in 1296, but his successor, Sir Hugh, fought with Wallace in defence of Scotland, and the next chief, Sir George, was a steady friend of Robert the Bruce, and is said to have fallen fighting for King David II. at the battle of Dupplin, 1332. His grandson, John, acquired Fingask in 1364. James, 11th of Dundas, was forfeited along with his father-in-law, Sir Alexander Livingstone of Callender, Governor of Scotland, and died without issue in Dumbarton Castle, but the estate was restored to his brother and heir Sir Archibald, 12th of Dundas, Sheriff of Linlithgow, whose son John, 13th of Dundas, was to have been created Earl of Forth by James III., but this was prevented by the king's death at Sauchieburn, 1488. James IV., however, gave him the Island of Inchgarvie. Sir Walter, 17th of Dundas, was knighted at the baptism of Henry, Duke of Rothesay, but his son George, 18th of Dundas, supported the Covenant.

The direct line expired with his grandson, Ralph, 20th of Dundas, when the succession devolved upon another of his grandsons, George, 21st of Dundas, M.P. for Linlithgow and Master of the King's Works in Scotland. James, 24th of Dundas, was obliged to sell the ancient barony in 1875, but retained Inchgarvie, which devolved upon his grandson Sir Charles Hope Dundas, 20th Chief and Laird of Inchgarvie, a celebrated admiral whose son Adam Dundas of that Ilk and Inchgarvie, is the 27th and present chief of the name of Dundas.

The Fingask branch descends from Alexander Dundas, half-brother of Sir Archibald, the 12th Laird. Of this line, Thomas Dundas of Fingask, Lyon Depute, was found guilty of falsifying the Lyon Register in order to represent his father as chief. The arms complained of were expunged from Lyon Register, but Dundas's son, being a friend of the Prince Regent, subsequently received, by Royal Warrant, an heraldic augmentation in place of the insignia of chiefship, which had been adjudged to the Laird of Dundas. Sir Laurence of Kerse, cadet of Fingask, was created a Baronet, 1762, and his son, Sir Thomas, Lord Dundas of Aske in 1794, Laurence, 2nd Laird, Earl of Zetland, 1838, and Laurence, 3rd Earl, Marquis, 1892. The 2nd and present Marquis has been Viceroy of India. The House of Dundas of Arniston was founded by Sir James, Governor of Berwick, 3rd son of George, 16th Laird of Dundas. His son, Sir James, 2nd of Arniston, became a Lord of Session, 1662, and five generations in succession sat as judges, an exceptional instance of hereditary legal eminence. Robert, 4th of Arniston, is celebrated as one of the most distinguished Lords President of the Court of Session. Henry Dundas, the Lord President's 5th son, as Lord Advocate, created Viscount Melville 1802, was a celebrated Scottish statesman.

24. DUNDAS

ELLIOT

THE great Border clan of Elliot is mentioned in the 16th century as one of the clans of the Middle March, and as having a chief, and at this period the House of Elliot of Redheugh was recognised as chief of the clan, and the name spelt Elwold. Robert Elwold, chief of the Elliots in the second half of the 15th century, was Captain of Hermitage Castle, and his son, Robert Elliot of Redheugh, fell at Flodden and was father of another Robert, Captain of Hermitage 1531. The last of the line appears to have been Robert Elliot of Redheugh, who was accused of conspiracy against the Earl of Buccleuch 1624. The Elliots of Larriston and of Braidlee were cadets of Redheugh. From Archibald Elliot of Gorrinberry, third son of Robert Elwold of Redheugh, who fell at Flodden, sprang Walter Elliot of Arkleton, now represented by Walter Scott Elliot, 10th of Arkleton. Since the 17th century, the most outstanding branch has been the house of Stobs, deriving from Gawen Eliot of Stobbes 1584. His descent from Elliot of Redheugh and the Captains of Hermitage has now been largely elucidated. The next laird, Gilbert Eliot of Stobs, celebrated as "Gibbie wi' the gowden gartens," married a daughter of Scott of Harden, and his fourth son, Gavin Eliot of Grange, was father of Sir Gilbert Eliot, 1st Baronet of Headshaw and Minto, cr. 1700. Of this line, Sir Gilbert, 4th Baronet, Viceroy of Corsica, and a celebrated ambassador, was created Earl of Minto 1751. This house has distinguished itself in Imperial affairs, and Gilbert, 4th Earl, was a celebrated Viceroy of India. The line is now represented by Victor, 5th Earl, whose seat is Minto House, Hawick. William Eliot of Stobs, M.P. for Roxburgh, the eldest son of "Gibbie wi' the gowden gartens," was father of Sir Gilbert Eliot, 1st Baronet of Stobs, whose descendant, Sir William Francis Eliot, 7th Baronet of Stobs, was regarded as chief of the Eliots, and in 1859 his son, Sir William Eliot, 8th Baronet of Stobs, was recognised in Lyon Court as "head of his family"—a judiciously ambiguous pronouncement, but research indicates that the House of Stobs became the chief line of the Elliot clan. His grandson, Sir Gilbert Alexander Boswell Eliot of Stobs, 10th and present Baronet, resides at Wolfllee, Roxburghshire. George Augustus Eliot, second son of the 3rd Baronet of Stobs, is celebrated for his defence of Gibraltar, 1782, and was created Lord Heathfield.

25. ELLIOT

ERSKINE

THE name is derived from the Barony of Erskine, in Renfrewshire, held by Henry de Erskine, in the reign of Alexander II. Sir Robert Erskine, Chamberlain of Scotland 1350–57, married, first, Beatrix, daughter of Sir Alexander Lindsay of Crawford, by whom he had two sons—Thomas, his heir, and Malcolm, ancestor of the Erskines of Kinnoull. Sir Robert's eldest son, Sir Thomas, married Janet Keith, granddaughter of Lady Elyne of Mar, and had issue—Robert, created Lord Erskine, and John, ancestor of the Erskines of Dun.

Robert, 4th Lord Erskine, was killed at Flodden, and his son, James, 5th Lord, was father of the Regent, John, 6th Lord Erskine, who was restored as 18th Earl of Mar by Queen Mary, and also in 1565—perhaps in case of the Crown ever cancelling the restoration—received a new Earldom of Mar, of which the seat was Alloa. He died in 1572, and was succeeded by his son, John, as 19th and 2nd Earl. This nobleman was twice married, and his great-great-grandson (by his first marriage), John, 23rd and 6th Earl, is celebrated in connection with the Scottish Rising of 1715, wherein he raised the Royal Standard for King James at Braemar, and was created " Duke of Mar." His descendant, John Francis Miller, 28th and 9th Earl, successfully claimed the Earldom of Kellie on the extinction of the junior branch of the family ; but, dying without issue 1866, his cousin, Walter Coningsby, succeeded as 12th Earl of Kellie, and also claimed the Earldom of Mar. This claim was resisted by John Francis Erskine Goodeve, the nephew of the last (28th and 9th) Earl. In 1875 the House of Lords decided that Walter Henry, 13th Earl of Kellie (son of the 12th Earl), had made out his claim to the Earldom of Mar, dated 1565. He died in 1888, and his son, Walter John, now Earl of Mar and Kellie, K.T., and 17th Lord Erskine, Chancellor of the Knights of the Thistle, is chief of the Erskines. His seats are at Alloa, and Kellie Castle, Fife. Branches of Erskines have also inherited the earldom of Buchan, and a Lordship of Erskine of Restormell, and Sir Thomas Erskine of Cambo represents the line of Sir Charles and Sir Alexander Erskine of Cambo, the celebrated Lord Lyon Kings of Arms. The ancient Earldom, originally Mormaership of Mar, was confirmed to John Francis Goodeve-Erskine as 29th Earl, and has devolved on Lionel Young-Erskine, as 35th Earl from Gillocher, Mormaer of Mar in the days of King David I. This ancient Pictish dignity was never " created." By 1014 it had already passed through one heir-female to a scion of the Norse race of Ivar, and has ever since descended to heirs of line of the original Pictish *Righ-Mhair*.

26. ERSKINE

FARQUHARSON

Slogan :—" Càrn na cuimhne " (" Cairn of Remembrance ").

Badge :—Cranberry ; Scots Fir.

Fiðe et Fortitudine

THE Clan Farquharson derives from Farquhar, fourth son of Alexander Ciar, the third Shaw of Rothiemurchus, a branch of Clan Chattan. Taking up their residence in Aberdeenshire, the descendants of this Farquhar were called Farquharsons. Farquhar's son, Donald, married Isobel Stewart, heiress of Invercauld, and their son was Finlay Mòr, 1st of the House of Farquharson of Invercauld. In their early history the name of this Finlay Mòr, royal standard-bearer at Pinkie, where he fell, 1547, stands prominent, and from and after him the Farquharsons are termed *Clann Fhionnlaigh*, or descendants of Finlay.

In the Rising of 1715 John Farquharson of Invercauld, with four officers and 140 men, joined the Clan Chattan Regiment, in which he was Lieutenant-Colonel; and accompanying it to England, was taken prisoner at Preston, where he remained for ten months. At Culloden, the Farquharsons were led by Francis Farquharson of Monaltrie, the " Baron Ban." They mustered 300 men, and were in the centre of the front line.

James Farquharson of Invercauld died in 1750, and was succeeded by his son, also named James, who appears to have been, in 1745, a Captain of Foot in the Hanoverian army. He died in 1806, after having been in possession of the estates for fifty-six years. He left no male issue, and was succeeded in the estates and chiefship by his only surviving child, Catherine Farquharson of Invercauld. She married Captain James Ross, R.N. (second son of Sir John Lockhart-Ross of Balnagowan), who took the name of Farquharson of Invercauld, and died in 1810. She was succeeded by her son, James, who died in 1862, and was succeeded by his eldest son, James Ross Farquharson, 13th of Invercauld, who died 1888. He was succeeded by his son, Alexander Haldane Farquharson of Invercauld who, in virtue of the Lyon Court Decree 1815, assigning the chief arms and supporters, was the head of the central or " stem family " of Farquharson of Invercauld, and so chief of the clan. On his death, the crest, arms, and supporters were by Lyon Court Decree, 3rd December, 1936, confirmed to his daughter, Mrs Myrtle Farquharson of Invercauld. Her nephew, Captain Alwyn Farquharson of Invercauld, is now Chief, by decree of Lyon Court 1949. His seat is Invercauld House, Braemar.

The principal branches of the name and clan of Farquharson have been Monaltrie, Whitehouse, and Haughton, Allargue, Breda, and Finzean. In Aberdeenshire Joseph Farquharson of Finzean, R.A., the celebrated artist, was chieftain of the Finzean branch until his death in 1935, and Colonel Wilson Farquharson of Allargue in Strathdon is the present chieftain of the Allargue branch. The Farquharsons of Inverey were a celebrated Jacobite branch, of whom the " Black Colonel " (John, 3rd Laird of Inverey) lives in Deeside legend and ballads.

27. FARQUHARSON

FERGUSSON

Slogan :—" Clann Fhearghuis gu bràth."
Badge :—(Strachur) Giuthas (Pine) ; (Dunfallandy) Aithean (Poplar).

ARGYLL was the ancient home of the Clann Fhearghuis of Stra-chur, which claims descent from the Royal House of Dalriada, and long held the lands of Glenshellich of Stra-chur on Loch Fyne, and the Celtic office of Hereditary Maors of Stra-chur. Many of the name are still in Cowal and North Argyll. Their representative is Seumas, Chief of Clannfhearghuis of Strachur, C.M., The Explorers' Club, New York, U.S.A., whose arms, standard, and title have been duly established in Lyon Register.

In Carrick the House of Fergusson of Kilkerran, descending from Fergus, son of Fergus, who got a charter from Robert I., may have been the Keepers of the Cross of St. Chiaran. They supported Charles I. Sir John Fergusson of Kilkerran was created a Baronet in 1703. James, 3rd Baronet, was a Judge as Lord Kilkerran.

The Rt. Hon. Sir James Fergusson of Kilkerran, 6th Baronet, G.C.S.I., K.C.M.G., M.P. for Ayrshire, and eminent statesman and Colonial Governor, perished in the Jamaica earthquake, 1907. His son, General Sir Charles Fergusson, G.C.M.G., succeeded him as 7th Baronet of Kilkerran.

In Dumfries and Galloway the name Ferguson is of great antiquity as is the House of Ferguson of Craigdarroch, who claimed descent from Fergus, Prince of Galloway. Annie Laurie of Maxwelton married Alexander Ferguson of Craigdarroch.

The Fergussons of Atholl descend from Adam, son of Fergus—styled *Adam na canabaig*, " Adam of the pavilion "—who had charters of lands in Perthshire from Baliol and Bruce and also claim descent from the Princes of Galloway. Adam acquired the barony of Derculich in Atholl, and then, by murdering the *Baron Maol* of Dunfallandy and his sons at the " bloody stone " of Dunfallandy, acquired that estate by marrying the heiress to his son. John of Dunfallandy became Baron of Douny in 1514 ; on his son's death, 1521, Dunfallandy and Douny reverted to the line of his younger brother, Robert of Derculich, and descended to General Archibald Fergusson of Dunfallandy, who died 1834. Under his settlement Dunfallandy passed to heirs of entail, and, on the death of Margaret Fergusson of Dunfallandy, 1900, to the General's heir at law through his sister Jane, the Baron and Head of the *Clan 'ic Fhearghuis na Derculich-Atholl* being J. K. S. Fergusson of Dunfallandy. They were among the gallant Atholl men who followed the banner of Montrose in the Civil War, and in 1745 were " out " with Prince Charlie.

In Aberdeenshire, where the Fergussons have been landowners since the 14th century, the best-known families are those of Baddifurrow, Kinmundy, and Pitfour, many of whom distinguished themselves on the Bench, at the Bar, and in Parliament.

28. FERGUSSON

FORBES

Slogan:—"Lònach" (A mountain in Strath Don). *Badge*:—Bealaidh (Broom).

THE clan took its name from the Aberdeen-shire parish of Forbes, where the present chief still holds part of the *duthus* or Lordship of Forbes. Quite credible tradition says that the founder of the clan, *Oconachar*, having killed a bear, or bears, which rendered the Braes o' Forbes uninhabitable, took possession as "first occupier" of these lands, and his successors remained *allodial* chiefs "under God" until 1271, when the tenure was made feudal by a charter for Duncan de Forbes, then the reigning chief of the clan.

John de Forbes opposed Edward I., and his son, Sir Christian de Forbes, defended the castle of Urquhart in 1303. He left a son, Sir Alexander, who fell at the Battle of Dupplin in 1332, and founded a Chantry at St Nicholas Kirk, Aberdeen. His son or brother, John, Laird of Forbes, who died 1387, "a gude man, wise, michty, and manly in his tyme," was father of Sir John Forbes of that Ilk, "John with the Black Lip," who died in 1406. He had four sons : (1) Sir Alexander ; (2) Sir William, ancestor of Pitsligo ; (3) Sir John of Tolquhoun ; (4) Alister of Brux, from whom Shellater and Inverarnon. From the Pitsligo branch descended the famous Jacobite, Alexander, Lord Forbes of Pitsligo, and the Forbeses of Newe in Strathdon, erected Baronet 1823.

Alexander, eldest son of Sir John of the Black Lip, was by James I. erected Lord Forbes. James, 2nd Lord Forbes, had three sons—William, the 3rd Lord ; Duncan, ancestor of the Forbeses of Corsindae and Monymusk ; and Patrick of Corse, Squire to James III., ancestor of the Forbes Baronets of Craigievar, of whom Sir William, 8th Baronet, in 1884 succeeded his kins-woman as Lord Sempill. Sir William, 19th Lord Sempill, is 11th Baronet of Craigievar, a celebrated and picturesque Aberdeenshire tower.

The Forbeses of Tolquhoun, a very old branch, acquired that estate in 1420, and were progenitors of the Lairds of Culloden—a cadet branch, of whom Duncan Forbes of Culloden, Lord President of the Court of Session, was famous during the 1745 Rising.

According to what W. Forbes Skene told Mr Elphinstone Dalrymple, the present Forbes tartan was designed for the Pitsligo family in 1822 by adding a white line to the 42nd, and prior to this the Forbeses wore Huntly tartan. Yet the tartan appears older.

James, 16th Lord Forbes, built the present Castle Forbes, and from him descends Atholl, 20th Lord Forbes, who is now chief of the clan ; his seat is Castle Forbes, Donside, Aberdeenshire. The older seat was the fortress of Drumminor on the northern slope of the Braes o' Forbes.

Castle Forbes.

128

29. FORBES

FRASER

Slogan :—" A Mhór-fhaiche " (The Great Field) and later, "Caisteal Dhùni " (Castle Downie).   *Badge* :—Iubhar (Yew).

THE name of this clan is understood to be derived from the Seigneurie of Freseliére in Anjou, and Simon Fraser, who about 1160 gave the Church of Keith to the Abbey of Kelso, was first of the name in Scotland. Udard Fraser established the house of Oliver-castle, by marriage with the sister of Oliver, son of Kylvert, who was succeeded by his nephew Adam Fraser. Sir Gilbert Fraser, another son, was Sheriff of Traquair, and John, the son of Gilbert, was father of two sons, Alexander and Richard, between whose lines the chiefship was disputed. Alexander of Cornton, in Stirling, was ancestor of the Frasers of Muchal-in-Mar, of whom Andrew completed the magnificent house of Castle-Fraser in 1617, and was in 1633 created Lord Fraser, which led to a dispute about the chiefship, but the title was confirmed by statute 1662, and in 1672 Lord Fraser was awarded the chief arms of the family. Charles, 4th Lord Fraser, was out in 1715, and on his death, whilst " lurking," in 1716, the peerage expired. Sir Richard Fraser of Touch-Fraser, Sir Gilbert's other grandson, became progenitor of the Frasers of Philorth. His grandson, Sir Alexander of Touch and Cowie, married Lady Mary Bruce, sister of Robert the patriot King. Their grandson, Alexander of Durris and Cowie, acquired in 1375 by marriage with Joanna, daughter of William, Earl of Ross, the Philorth estates in Buchan, which with the fortress of Cairnbulg, have remained the chief seat of this line. Sir Alexander, 8th of Philorth, founded Fraserburgh, where he contemplated a university town. Alexander, 9th of Philorth, married Margaret Abernethy, daughter of the 7th Lord Saltoun, and their son Alexander, 10th of Philorth, succeeded to the Saltoun dignity which was confirmed to him and his heirs by Act of Parliament 1770. His descendant, Alexander Arthur, 19th Lord Saltoun, is the present chief of Clan Fraser, his seat being Cairnbulg Castle, Aberdeenshire. The Clan Fraser of Lovat in Inverness-shire derives from Hugh Fraser of Lovat and Kinell, whose descent genealogists deduce from Sir Simon Fraser, one of the heroes of Bannockburn, second son of Sir Andrew Fraser of Touch. William Fraser, 4th of Lovat, K.T., is found as Lord Fraser of Lovat, prior to 1464. Hugh, 3rd Lord Lovat, had a charter settling the succession upon his heirs male, and the line continued directly to Hugh, 9th Lord, on whose death his daughter Amelia was adjudged Baroness Lovat, to the chagrin of Simon Fraser of Beaufort, the heir male, who ultimately obtained the dignity in 1730, on the charter of 1539. This Simon, 11th Lord Lovat, notorious in Jacobite intrigue, and a traitor to both parties, was created Duke of Fraser by the Chevalier, but captured and executed after Culloden. The representation later passed to Thomas Fraser of Strichen, who, having in 1837 been recognised in Lyon Court as chief of the Clan Fraser *of Lovat*, was created Lord Lovat, and in 1857 restored to the old Scottish dignity. His great-grandson, Simon, 15th Lord Fraser of Lovat, is now chief of Clan Fraser of Lovat, his seat being **Beaufort Castle, Inverness-shire.**

30. FRASER

GORDON

Slogan :—" A Gordon ! A Gordon ! " *Badge* :—Iadh-shlat, Eitheann (Ivy).

THIS surname is territorial. Richard, who was Baron of Gordon in Berwickshire in 1150 and 1160, granted land to the monks of St. Mary at Kelso.

For services at Slioch' battle King Robert the Bruce gave Sir Adam, Lord of Gordon, the Lordship of Strathbogie in Aberdeenshire. His great-grandson, Sir Adam, was slain in battle, 1402, leaving an heiress, Elizabeth, who married Alexander, second son of Seton of Seton. Her only son, Alexander, was created Earl of Huntly in 1449. He settled the Earldom on his second son, George, who took the name of Gordon and became chief of the clan which was declared by Lyon Court in 1727 to be in the Ducal line of Huntly-Gordon. George, 4th Earl, the most powerful noble in Scotland, fell at Corrichie, 1562.

In 1599 the 6th Earl of Huntly was created Marquis. His son, George, 2nd Marquis, beheaded by the Covenanters, declared " You may take my head from my shoulders, but not my heart from my king." The 4th Marquis was in 1684 created Duke of Gordon by Charles II. On the death of George, 5th Duke, in 1836, the title became extinct, but the Marquisate of Huntly went to the Earl of Aboyne, lineally descended from George, fourth son of George, 2nd Marquis of Huntly, and is now held by Douglas, 12th Marquis, and Chief of the Gordons, whose seat is Aboyne Castle in Aberdeenshire, whilst Huntly Castle is a magnificent ruin. John Gordon of Pitlurg is male representative of the Gordons of Strathbogie ; being descended from a half-brother (by a " hand-fast " marriage) of the heiress, and accordingly ranks as chiefest cadet under the Marquess of Huntly.

The Earls of Aberdeen, so created 1682, are descended from Patrick Gordon of Methlic (cousin of Pitlurg), who fell at the battle of Arbroath in 1445. John, 7th Earl, and 1st Marquess of Aberdeen, K.T., was Lord Lieutenant of Ireland and Governor-General of Canada. His son is George, 2nd Marquess, whose seat is Haddo House, Aberdeenshire.

Two regiments named the " Gordon Highlanders " have been raised from this clan ; the old 81st in 1777, disbanded 1783 : and the 92nd or Gordon Highlanders, by the 4th Duke and Jane, his celebrated Duchess, in 1794. For the " Gay Gordons," a yellow strip was introduced into the Black Watch pattern. Gordons still sometimes use the *Huntly* tartan on full-dress occasions. The original red and green *Gordon* tartan is seen in a portrait at Abergeldie Castle. The Huntly estate and Gordon Castle passed in 1876 to the Duke of Richmond, who in that year was created Duke of Gordon, but Queen Victoria intimated that this should not affect the chiefship, which had already devolved with the dignity of Huntly upon the line of the 11th Marquis who died in 1937 in his ninetieth year. By him much of the Aboyne estate was sold, but Aboyne Castle remains the seat of the 12th Marquis.

Huntly Castle.

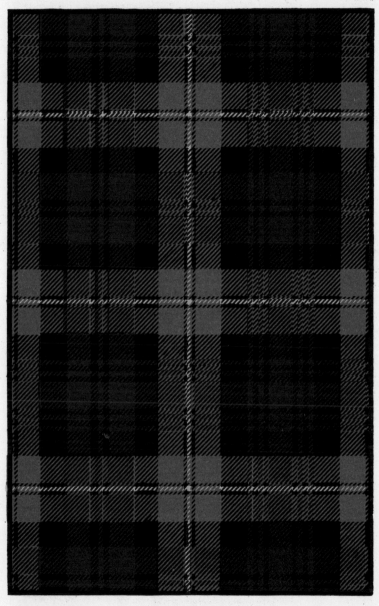

31. GORDON

GRAHAM

Badge :—Buaidh-chraobh, na Labhras (Laurel).

THE first of this great Scottish house on record is William de Graham, who lived in the reign of David I., and from his elder son Peter, descend the Grahams of Dalkeith and Eskdale, of which the direct line ended with Sir John Graham of Dalkeith, who resigned the estates to Sir William Douglas in 1341. From Alan de Graham, the younger brother, derives the great House of Montrose, of which his great-grandson, Sir David Graham of Dundaff, was the real founder. His successor, Sir Patrick, was Keeper of Stirling Castle, and fell at Dunbar 1296. His descendant, Sir William de Graham of Mugdock and Kincardine, acquired Old Montrose from the Duke of Albany 1405, and his grandson was a peer as Lord Graham prior to 1445. William, 3rd Lord Graham, was created Earl of Montrose 1505, and fell at Flodden. William, 2nd Earl, supported Mary, Queen of Scots, and James, 5th Earl, celebrated as the Marquis of Montrose, created 1644, was the illustrious Royalist general of Charles I. whose campaigns are famous in Scottish history, and who was executed by the Covenanting Parliament in 1650. His great-grandson, the 4th Marquis, was created Duke of Montrose in 1707, and his descendant, James, 6th Duke of Montrose, is the present chief of the clan. To James, Marquis of Graham, afterwards 3rd Duke of Montrose, highlanders are indebted for carrying through Parliament in 1782 the Act repealing the disgraceful Act of 1747, which proscribed the use of the highland garb. Amongst the distinguished cadets of the great House of Graham, were the Earls of Airth, Menteith, and Strathearn, but the most celebrated branch is Graham of Claverhouse, whose chieftain, John Graham of Claverhouse, the great Jacobite general who fell at Killiecrankie, was created Viscount of Dundee, 1688. From this line are descended the Grahams of Duntrune. Another ancient cadet, Graham of Fintry, is still represented in South Africa by Robert, 16th Chieftain of Fintry. Graham of Aberuthven and Inchbraikie, descending from Patrick, younger son of the 1st Earl of Montrose, has stood for sixteen generations. Graeme of Garvock is represented by Agnes Graham, 16th Chieftainess of Garvock. Graham of Duchray, and Cunningham-Graham of Ardoch, are cadets of the Earls of Menteith. Graham of Auchincloich and Tamrawer claims to be the eldest cadet of Montrose, descending from the third son of Sir David Graham of Dundaff. The Clan Graham has been one of the most famous, loyal, and patriotic supporters of Scotland and her Royal House.

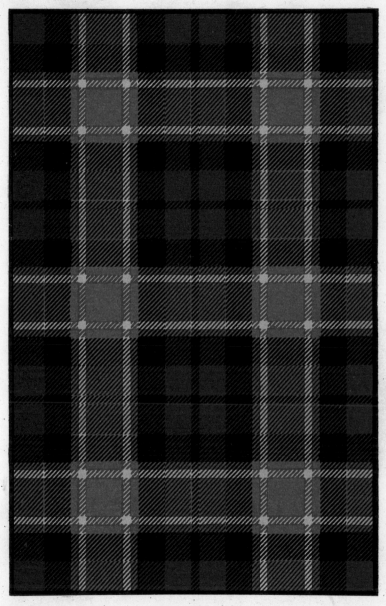

32. GRAHAM

GRANT

Slogan :—" Stand fast, Craigellachie."   *Badge* :—Giuthas (Pine Tree).

THE Grants are said to derive their origin from Gregor Mor MacGregor, who lived in the 12th century. The territory of Clan Grant is Strathspey, where an extensive moor called *Griantach*, otherwise *Sliabh-Griantais*, or "Plain of the Sun," may be the origin of the clan name. Sir Lawrence Grant, Sheriff of Inverness, 1263, is the first authentic ancestor, and whilst a number of others of the name, such as Patrick Grant of Stratherrick and Inverallan, and Sir John le Grant, Forester of Darnaway, are mentioned 1331–71, *Ian Ruadh* Grant, Knight, and Sheriff of Inverness in 1434, is the 1st Chief from whom an uninterrupted succession is deducible. He married Matilda, daughter of Gilbert of Glencairnie, a descendant of the Earls of Strathearn, and whilst his younger son is claimed as ancestor of *Clan Phadruig* (Tullochgorum), the elder became Sir Duncan Le Grant of Freuchie, first chief so designated, and this was in 1494 erected into a Barony for his grandson John Grant, *Am Bard Ruadh*, Keeper of the Castle of Urquhart. His son and successor, *Sheumas nan Creach*, was an adherent of Mary, Queen of Scots. His son and successor, John " the Gentle," was with the Queen at Holyrood when Rizzio was murdered, and his grandson, John Grant of that Ilk, 5th Baron of Freuchie, at whose marriage with Lady Lilias Murray of Tullibardine the King and Queen were present, is said to have been offered a peerage of Strathspey by James VI. but politely declined it with the query : "And wha'll be Laird o' Grant ? " James, 7th of Freuchie, was to have been created Earl of Strathspey in 1663, but died before the warrant was signed. In 1694 his grandson, Ludovic, the 8th Baron, had his whole lands erected into a Regality of Grant, and the *Ballachastil* of Freuchie named Castle Grant. His eldest son, Brigadier Alexander Grant of Grant, died without issue, and James, the second son (who had married the heiress of Luss, and by tanistry succeeded his father-in-law as Chief of the Clan Colquhoun), on the Brigadier's death, resumed the name and took up the succession as Laird of Grant, when the Colquhoun chiefship passed with Luss to his second son, Ludovick. But, Humphrey, the eldest son, dying, Sir Ludovick also had to resume the name of Grant, becoming 11th Baron of Freuchie and 20th Chief, when Luss and the Colquhoun chiefship passed to a younger brother, James. The proceedings well illustrate the principles of inheritance of chiefship. This Sir Ludovick, 20th Chief, married Lady Margaret Ogilvie, eldest daughter of James, Earl of Findlater and Seafield. Their grandson, Sir Lewis, succeeded as 5th Earl of Seafield in 1811. The Chiefs of Grant have since borne the name Ogilvie-Grant. Ian Charles, 8th Earl, died without issue, and was succeeded by his uncle, James, 9th Earl, created Lord Strathspey 1884. His grandson, James, 11th Earl, was killed in action 1915, when his Ogilvie honours were inherited by his only child, Nina, now Countess of Seafield in her own right, whilst his brother, Trevor, succeeded as 4th Lord of Strathspey. His son, Sir Patrick Grant of Grant, 5th Lord of Strathspey, is now 32nd Chief of Clan Grant.

Castle Grant.

33. GRANT

GUNN.

Badge :—Aitionn (Juniper) or Lus nan laoch (Roseroot).

THIS clan is of Norse origin. The Gunns were a warlike clan of Caithness and Sutherland; the name is derived from the Norse word *gunnr*—war.

The Gunns and the Keiths were for ever at enmity. Lachlan Gunn of Braemor had an only daughter, Helen, who was famous for her beauty, and the day of her marriage with her cousin Alexander was fixed; but Dugald Keith, a retainer of Keith of Ackergill, whose advances she had repelled, surrounded her father's house with a body of armed Keiths, slew many of the Gunns, who were unprepared for an attack, and carried off the girl to Ackergill, where she became the victim of her abductor, and eventually threw herself from the summit of the tower.

Raid upon raid now ensued, and during one of these, in 1426, a desperate battle was fought between the two clans at Harpsdale, eight miles from Thurso. The conflict was rancorous and bloody, but indecisive.

About the middle of the 15th century the chief of the clan was George, who lived with barbaric pomp in his castle at Clyth. From the office he held he was known as Crouner Gunn, but by the natives as "*Am Bràisteach Mór*," from a large silver brooch which fastened his plaid. Weary of the feud, he and the chief of the Keiths agreed to meet with twelve horsemen a-side at the Chapel of St. Tears and settle it amicably. This was in 1464. The Keiths came with twenty-four men—two on each horse—and attacked the Gunns; the latter fought desperately, and were cut to pieces. George Gunn was slain and stripped of his arms, armour and brooch. Soon after William MacKames, a kinsman of the Gunns, killed George Keith of Ackergill and his son, with ten men, at Drummoy.

The patronymic of Gunn of Kilearnan is *Mac-Sheumais-Chataich*.

The chiefship is considered to be now in the family of Gunn of Rhives, who are descended from a son of the 5th Chief, but has not been adjudicated on in Lyon Court. It was also claimed by Gunn-Munro of Newmore.

Feilebeg and full plaid.

34. GUNN

HAMILTON

THE illustrious family of Hamilton is stated to derive its name from the lands of Hamildoun in Northumberland. Gilbert de Hamilton, in the reign of Alexander III., is said to have married Isabella, sister of Thomas Randolph, Earl of Moray, the companion of King Robert the Bruce. Their son, Walter FitzGilbert Hamilton, became Lord of Cadzow, the famous park and forest where Scotland's native wild cattle still survive, and where the ruins of Cadzow Castle on a lofty crag still overhang the River Clyde. His descendant, Sir James Hamilton, 6th of Cadzow, was created a peer as Lord Hamilton in 1445. He married first Lady Euphemia Graham, daughter of the Earl of Strathearn, and secondly Princess Mary, eldest daughter of King James II. His son James, 2nd Lord Hamilton and 1st Earl of Arran, was Regent of Scotland 1517 and was succeeded by his son James, 2nd Earl of Arran, who on the death of James V. in 1542 was chosen Regent of Scotland and Guardian of Mary, Queen of Scots, and should she leave no issue, was declared heir to the throne through his grandmother. Created Duke of Chatelherault in France, he married Lady Margaret Douglas, daughter of the 3rd Earl of Morton, and was father of John, created Marquess of Hamilton in 1599, whose grandson, James, 3rd Marquess, was created Duke of Hamilton in 1643 and Hereditary Keeper of the Palace of Holyroodhouse. An active Royalist, he was beheaded in 1649, and was succeeded by his brother, William, 2nd Duke of Hamilton, whose campaign on behalf of Charles II. ended with his death in 1651 at the Battle of Worcester. The Dukedom reverted to his niece, Anne, 3rd Duchess of Hamilton, who married Lord William Douglas, Earl of Selkirk; they were created Duke and Duchess of Hamilton in 1663, the Earldom of Selkirk being transferred to their second son. Their eldest son, James, 4th Duke of Hamilton, had two sons, James, 5th Duke, and Lord Anne Hamilton, called after Queen Anne, whose great-great-grandson, Alfred Douglas, became 13th Duke in 1895. The 5th Duke and his descendants maintained great state at Hamilton Palace, recently demolished on account of coalmining. The 13th Duke inherited the Hamilton estates along with the historic castle of Cadzow, and at his death in 1940 was succeeded by his son, Douglas, 14th Duke of Hamilton, G.C.V.O., Premier Peer of Scotland, feudal Lord of Cadzow, and Hereditary Keeper of Holyroodhouse, who, as heir-male of the Douglas Earls of Angus is, as Earl of Angus, the peer who had the first vote in the Scottish Parliament, and the leading of the vanguard in battle.

The Duke of Abercorn, created in 1868, descends from Lord Claud Hamilton, Commendator of the Abbey of Paisley, youngest son of the 2nd Earl of Arran. He commanded the vanguard of Queen Mary's army at Langside, 1568, and his son was created Earl of Abercorn in 1603. In 1651 the Abercorn line became heirs-male of the House of Hamilton, but since the ducal line continued to bear the name and inherited the Chiefship, the arms of Abercorn have never in Scotland been allowed the Hamilton arms without a label for cadency.

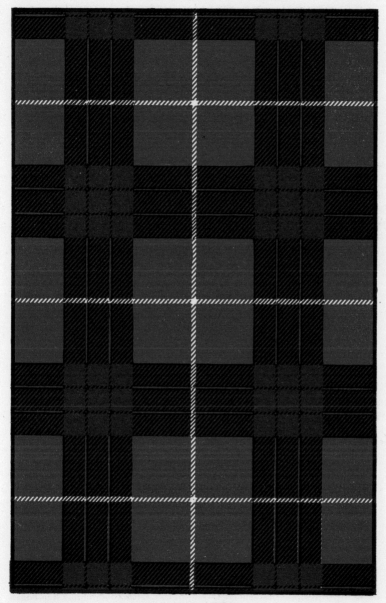

35. HAMILTON

HAY

Slogan :—" A Hay, A Hay, A Hay ! "   *Badge* :—Mistletoe.

WILLIAM DE HAYA, progenitor of this celebrated Clan, was cupbearer to Malcolm IV. and married Eva, Lady of Pet-mulin. About 1178, he received the Barony of Erroll. Tradition associates the Hays with a victory over the Danes at a battle of Luncarty, on which history is silent. Sir Gilbert, 5th of Errol, a faithful adherent of the Bruce, was created Hereditary Constable of Scotland. Sir Thomas, 4th High Constable, married Princess Elizabeth, daughter of Robert II., and from their second son, Sir Gilbert of Dronlaw, descend the Hays of Delgaty, of whom Sir Arthur, 10th Baronet of Park, seems heir male of the race. Sir William, 5th Lord High Constable, was grandfather of William, created Earl of Errol 1452 ; his descendant William, 6th Earl, had an only daughter, Jean, wife of the 8th Earl, the honours meantime passed by entail to her cousin and father-in-law, George Hay of Logie. Francis, 9th Earl, joined Lord Huntly and defeated Argyll at Glenlivet, 1594. Gilbert, 11th Earl, having no issue, executed an entail on his cousin, Sir John Hay of Kellour, 12th Earl. Charles, 13th Earl, imprisoned as a Jacobite, dying unmarried, was succeeded by his sister Mary, Countess of Erroll, an ardent Jacobite, whose obituary notice describes her as Chief of the Noble Family of Hay. Her sister Margaret, Countess of Linlithgow, had a daughter married to the Jacobite Earl of Kilmarnock, who was executed 1746, but her son James succeeded his great-aunt as 15th Earl of Erroll and Constable, and took the name of Hay. William George, 18th Earl's magnificence as Lord High Constable to George IV. in 1822 nearly ruined the family. Josslyn Victor, 22nd Earl, was succeeded by his only daughter, Diana Denyse, Countess of Erroll. She is now Hereditary High Constable of Scotland and Chief of the Hays. Her home is Delgaty Castle, Aberdeenshire. From Hay of Locherwort and Yester—with its " Goblin Ha "—derive the Marquises of Tweeddale ; from another branch (cadet of Erroll) the Hays of Megginch and Kinfauns, descends the Earl of Kinnoull, whose seat is Balhousie Castle, Perthshire. Hay of Megginch was declared by Lyon Court to be chief of the ancient branch of Hays of Lennoch and Concraig. Slains Castle, the now ruined seat of the Earls of Erroll, is situated on a lofty cliff on the Aberdeen-shire coast. On the terrace was the " Falcon Stone," brought from Erroll, and reputed to be that on which the " falcon of Luncarty " re-alighted after circling the barony of Erroll when this was, by a falcon's flight, demarcated for the founder of the race.

36. HAY

HENDERSON

(MACKENDRICK)

Badge :—Canach (Cotton Grass).

THE Hendersons claim descent from *Eanruig Mór Mac Righ Neachtan*—Big Henry, son of King Nectan. Naturally there is no evidence substantiating this, and it is likewise impossible to explain when or how the alleged descendants of *Eanruig Mór* became possessed of that tract of country embracing Glencoe, both sides of Loch Leven and Ardnamurchan. According to tradition, the chiefs of the clan held their seats at Callart, on the north side of Loch Leven, and as late as the 15th century a chieftain of the clan held the lands of Callart. The direct line of the Hendersons of Glencoe is understood to have terminated in an heiress, who, as " Heretrix of the clan," carried, according to Scottish clan-law, the chiefship of the descendants of her predecessors to her issue—a son, *Iain Fraoch*, from whom the Glencoe Hendersons became intituled the Clan Ian of Glencoe. He was brother of John, 1st Lord of the Isles, and son, presumably by a handfast connection, of Angus Og of Islay. Gregory says : " Angus Og had a natural son, known as *Iain Fraoch*, or Heather John, on whom his brother, John, Lord of the Isles, bestowed Glencoe." *Iain Fraoch's* mother is said to have been a daughter of one Dugald MacHendry—*i.e.* Dugald Henderson—chief or headman of Glencoe. They lived at Inverlochy for a time, where their first son and heir was born, who in due time became the first MacIain of Glencoe, or, as the Glencoe people called him, *Iain Abrach* (John of Lochaber). *Iain Fraoch*, although a MacDonald, appointed Hendersons as his bodyguard, and until the death of the last MacIain Chief they were accorded the honour of the first " lift " of the remains when borne forth for burial.

The Hendersons of Caithness have no connection with those of Glencoe. They are descendants of Hendry, son of George Gunn, Crouner of that county. There are also Hendersons of Fordell, Fifeshire. They derive from James Henderson, 1st of Fordell, Lord Advocate in 1494, and they claim as a cadet of their family Alexander Henderson, the great divine and leader of the Reformation. The Fordell line came from Dumfriesshire to Fife, and are now represented as heir of line by the Earl of Buckinghamshire, who bears the name of Mercer-Henderson, and if he records the relative arms in Lyon Court, will presumably be regarded as representing the chief family of the name of Henderson in Scotland. Lord Faringdon is descended from another branch of the Dumfriesshire race.

37.   HENDERSON

HOME

Slogan :—" A Home, A Home, A Home ! "   *Badge* :—Broom.

PATRICK, second son of Cospatrick, Earl of Dunbar, is said to be the founder of this family. Aldan de Home (1172–78), who derived his name from the lands of Home in Berwickshire, is the first recorded ancestor. His descendant, Sir Thomas Home, married the heiress of Douglas, and had with other issue two sons, Sir Alexander and David Home of Wedderburn, ancestor of the Earls of Marchmont. Sir Alexander, a great soldier, fought as an ally of the Earl of Douglas at Homildon in 1402, and fell with him at the great battle of Verneuil in 1424. He had three sons, from the youngest came Home of Spott, and from the second the Homes of Tyninghame and Ninewells. Sir Alexander, the eldest son, carried on the family, and his son, Sir Alexander, was created Lord Home in 1473, and died 1491. His eldest son, Alexander, Master of Home, died in his father's lifetime, but left two sons, Alexander, 2nd Lord Home, and John Home of Whiterigs and Ersilton, of whom later. The 2nd Lord led the van of the army which defeated James III. at Sauchieburn and he was much in favour with James IV. Alexander, 3rd Lord, was Royal Cap-bearer, Great Chamberlain of Scotland and Warden of the Marches. He survived Flodden and was executed by the Regent Albany 1516. His grandson, Alexander, 5th, had supported the marriage of Queen Mary with Bothwell but later was one of the nobles who imprisoned her in Lochleven. His son Alexander, 6th Lord, was created Earl of Home in 1605, and his son James, 2nd Earl, dying without issue in 1633, the titles went to his distant cousin, a descendant of the John Home of Whiterigs and Ersilton referred to above. Sir James Home of Coldingknows, who thus became 3rd Earl of Home, is the ancestor of the present 13th Earl, whose seat is the Hirsel, Berwickshire.

Sir David Home of Wedderburn, mentioned above, left two grandsons, George of Wedderburn and Sir Patrick of Polwarth. Sir Patrick's descendant, Sir Patrick Home, was created Lord Polwarth in 1690, with the remainder to the heirs male of his body and the heirs of these heirs male. In 1697 he was made Earl of Marchmont with remainder to his heirs male whatsoever. His grandson, the 3rd Earl, died in 1794, when the Earldom of Marchmont became dormant, and the Barony of Polwarth went to the elder daughter of the 3rd Earl, but she, dying without issue in 1822, was succeeded by her younger sister Diana, who married Walter Scott of Harden, and from this marriage descends the present Lord Polwarth.

Sir David Home, third of Wedderburn, had a family of sons celebrated as " The Seven Spears of Wedderburn," from whom sprung the houses of Manderston, Blackadder, Simprin and Broomhouse.

Home of Blackadder was created a baronet 1671, and this title is still extant.

George Home, son of Sir John Home of North Berwick, a descendant of the House of Polwarth, was also created a Baronet in 1671, but his title came to an end with the death of the 4th Baronet about 1750.

38. HOME

INNES

THE Clan Innes derives from Berowald, to whom in 1160, Malcolm IV. granted the Barony of Innes in Moray—being all the land along the seashore between Spey and Lossie ; and in 1579 the Privy Council recognised the Inneses as a " clan." " Good Sir Robert," 8th Laird of Innes 1364–81, had a son, Sir Alexander Innes, 9th of that Ilk, who married Jenet, the heiress of the thane of Aberchirder. Their son, Sir Walter, was chief of the clan for forty-two years, and died 1454. His son, " Ill Sir Robert," 11th Laird, fought under Huntly at the Battle of Brechin, 1452, was Sheriff-depute of Moray, and after a wicked life expiated his sins by founding the Greyfriars of Elgin. His eldest son, Sir James, 12th Chief, was Esquire to James III. and entertained James IV. with much state at the Castle of Innes, 1490. He and his son Alexander, 13th Laird, were patrons of art and architecture ; his great-grandson William, 15th Chief, on 1st Jan. 1554 at the " Bloody Vespers," attempted to slay the Prior of Pluscarden on the altar steps in Elgin Cathedral ; he sat in the Reformation Parliament, 1560 ; his son, Alexander " the Proud," 16th Chief, was beheaded by the Regent Morton, and John, 17th, resigned his chiefship to Alexander Innes of Crommey, grand-nephew of the 13th. This laird, the 18th Chief, was murdered in romantic circumstances by the 3rd Laird of Invermarkie. His son, Robert, 19th of that Ilk, founded the burgh of Garmouth 1587, dabbled in witchcraft, and harboured the " Queen of Elphin." His son, Sir Robert, 20th Chief, P.C. and M.P. for Moray, a prominent Covenanter, was created a Baronet 1625. and welcomed Charles II. at Garmoch 1650. He built Innes House 1640–53 and raised a regiment for Charles II. Sir James, 6th Baronet and 25th Chief, succeeded as 5th Duke of Roxburghe, 1805. His son was created Earl Innes in 1836. George, 9th Duke, is 4th Earl, 10th Baronet, and 29th Chief.

The Baronets of Balveny (created 1628), descend from Walter of Innermarkie, 2nd son of Sir Robert, 11th Chief. Robert, 2nd of Innermarkie, was Hereditary Constable of Redcastle in Ross and married Lady Elizabeth Stewart of Atholl, niece of James II. His grandson, Robert, 3rd Laird, who supported Queen Mary, was slain in his own castle, betrayed by his son, Robert, 4th of Innermarkie, who was beheaded 1595, for assisting to murder the " Bonnie Earl o' Moray." Sir Robert, 5th of Innermarkie, and 1st Baronet of Balveny, completed the magnificent castle on Speyside ; but his son, Sir Walter, lost all in support of Charles I. Sir Robert, 6th Baronet, enlisted in the Scots Greys, and romantically married the Colonel's daughter. Sir William, 8th Baronet, was succeeded by Sir John Innes, 9th Baronet, and 9th Laird of Edingight, whose father was " out " with Prince Charlie. Sir James Innes, 14th Baronet of Balveny and Edingight, in Banffshire, represents this branch.

The Baronets of Coxton (*cr.* 1686), branch off the 1st Laird of Innermarkie. They were " out " in all the Jacobite Risings, and built Coxton Tower, a celebrated old Scots fortalice, about 1574. Sir Alexander, 1st Baronet of Coxton, fought under Dundee 1689 and organised a rising in 1708. His son, George, died after Sheriffmuir.

Father Lewis Innes, Lord Almoner to the Chevalier, and Jacobite Secretary of State for Scotland, 1690, his brother, Father Thomas, the historian, and James Innes of Balnacraig, officer in Prince Charlie's Lifeguards, were descended from Robert of Drainie, 3rd son of the 11th Chief.

From Innes of Benwall sprang Robert of Blairton, Lyon Depute in 1672, when the present Lyon Register was instituted ; and George of Stow, the millionaire banker, whose fortune passed to the Mitchell-Inneses, now represented by Ian Mitchell-Innes of Stow.

Professor Cosmo Innes, the famous antiquary, was of the family of Luchars and Dunkinty, Hereditary Keepers of the Castle of Spynie, a branch of Innes of Cromey. John, Bishop of Moray, 1407–14, who rebuilt Elgin Cathedral after the " Wolf of Badenoch " burnt it, and Cardinal George Innes, 1412–18, who sat in the Council of Constance, were sons of " Good Sir Robert," 8th Chief.

39. INNES

JOHNSTON

Badge :—Red Hawthorn.

THIS is one of the Border clans, whose origin goes back to the 13th century in the person of Sir Gilbert de Johnstoun, son of John, who lived about 1200. He had a son, Gilbert, who was father of Sir John, living 1296. Sir John was father of John and Gilbert de Johnstoun ; the latter was succeeded by his son, Sir John. The last named had one son, Adam, who was ancestor of the Johnstons of Newbie, Mylnefield, and Galabank. The above-named Adam Johnston was twice married, and had by his first wife a son, John, ancestor of the Johnstons of Westerhall, and by his second wife he had Sir Gilbert, ancestor of the Johnstons of Elphinstone. Sir James of Johnstone was created Lord Johnstone 1633 and Earl of Hartfell 1643. The Earl was succeeded by his son, James, created Earl of Annandale and Hartfell 1661. The 2nd Earl was succeeded by his son, William, who was created Marquess of Annandale 1701. He was twice married. By his first marriage he had James, 2nd Marquess, who died without issue 1730, and Henrietta, who married Charles, 1st Earl of Hopetoun ; she is now represented by the Hope-Johnstones of Annandale. By his second marriage, the 1st Marquess, who died 1792, had George, 3rd Marquis, at whose death the peerages became dormant and the estates devolved upon the next of line, James, 3rd Earl of Hopetoun, and passed to his daughter Lady Anne Hope-Johnstone of Annandale, and her descendant, E. W. Hope-Johnstone of Annandale, is chief of the Border Johnstones (or would be, if he took the name of Johnstone alone and matriculated the appropriate arms). From Matthew, first of Westerhall, descended Sir James, who died 1699. He left two sons, Sir John, who died without issue, and his brother, Sir William, who left two sons, Sir James, 3rd Baronet of Westerhall, and John, whose son, Richard, was created a Baronet in 1795, whose grandson, Harcourt, 3rd Baronet, was created Baron Derwent 1881. The 3rd Baronet of Westerhall left six sons. John, fifth son, was the ancestor of the Johnstones of Alva. The North-Country Johnstons descend from Stephen, the clerk, who married Margaret, daughter and heiress of Sir Andrew Garioch, with whom he obtained lands of Johnston, which gave the name to his descendants. He is now represented by Sir Thomas Alexander Johnston (11th Baronet) of that Ilk, Hilton and Caskieben, whose arms are illustrated. Having been allowed the title " of that Ilk " by the Lord Lyon, he is the received Chief of the Name of Johnston of the North, but these are evidently quite a different race from the Border clan of Johnston of Annandale.

40. JOHNSTON

KEITH

AMONGST the most romantic names in Scottish history, is that of Keith, Marischal of Scotland, and a Celtic ancestry is claimed for the race. The first authentic ancestor is Hervey Keith, who held the office of Marischal under Malcolm IV. His descendant succeeded to the office of Marischal in 1294, was imprisoned by the English until 1304, and in 1305 was one of King Edward's four Deputy Wardens of Scotland, but at Christmas 1308 he joined the cause of Robert the Bruce and was rewarded with a grant of the Royal Forest of Kintore. As Commander of the Scots cavalry at Bannockburn, his attack materially contributed to the annihilation of the English army, for which he was rewarded with many of the forfeited Comyn estates in Buchan. He signed the letter to the Pope in 1320. His great-grandson, Sir William, founded the tower of Dunottar Castle. His son, Sir Robert, was elevated to the peerage as Lord Keith. William, 2nd Lord, was created Earl Marischal 1458, and a mistake in the *Scots Peerage* has involved the misnumbering of the successive earls. William, 2nd Earl, fought at Flodden, and his standard is preserved in the Advocates' Library.

The 3rd Earl, "William of the Tower," a distinguished statesman, lived long in seclusion at Dunottar. His estates lay in so many counties that he could travel from Berwick to John o' Groats eating every meal and sleeping every night on his own lands. His grandson, George, 4th Earl, Ambassador Extraordinary to Denmark, in 1593 founded Marischal College, Aberdeen. William, 5th Earl, was created Admiral of Scotland, but "my Lord wold never boate." He appeared as Marischal at the Coronation of Charles I.

William, 6th Earl, was a Covenanter, but in 1651 rescued the Regalia and carried it to Dunottar. His brother, George, 7th Earl, was a Royalist whose grandson George, 9th and last Earl Marischal, joined the Earl of Mar in 1715, and with his celebrated brother, Field-Marshal James Keith, retired to the Continent where their exploits rendered the name of Keith famous throughout the world. The Earl was Frederick the Great's closest friend, and the Field-Marshal, who fell at Hochkirsch 1758, his greatest General. On the Earl's death in 1778, the chiefship was understood to have passed to Keith of Ravelston, who acted as Knight Marischal to George IV. Since the expiry of this line the Earls of Kintore represent the House of Keith-Marischal, and descend from Sir John Keith, third son of the 5th Earl, who helped to save the "Honours of Scotland" from falling into Cromwell's hands, and was consequently created in 1677 Earl of Kintore, with the motto : *Quae Amissa Salva.*

William, 2nd Earl, fought with Dundee, and in the Rising of 1715. On the death of William, 4th Earl, the dignity and representation passed to the grandson of his sister, Lady Catherine Keith, Antony Adrian Keith-Falconer, 5th Earl and 8th Lord Falconer of Halkerton. Arthur George, 10th Earl of Kintore, now Chief of the Name of Keith (apart from the objection of the double-surname), has his seat at Keith Hall, Aberdeenshire.

Inverugie.

41. KEITH

KENNEDY

THE Kennedys apparently spring from a branch of the Pictish Lords of Galloway, deriving from Gilbert, father of Duncan, 1st Earl of Carrick, whose son Neil, 2nd Earl, settled the chiefship in favour of his kinsman (perhaps nephew) Roland de Carrick, who appears to have married one of the Earl's daughters and died before 1275. From his grandson, Gilbert de Carrick, this *kenkynol* (chiefship), which by Crown charter was settled on heirs female, passed (apparently in right of his wife) to John Kennedy of Dunure, Captain of the Clan Muintircasduff, his heiress-wife being Mary de Carrick. He had acquired Cassillis, by purchase or marriage, from Marjory Montgomery, a marriage previous to that with Mary de Carrick with whom his descendants inherited the *kenkynol*. His son, Sir Gilbert Kennedy of Dunure, was father of James of Dunure, who married Princess Mary, daughter of Robert III. Their son, Gilbert, was one of the six Regents of Scotland during the minority of James III. He was made Lord Kennedy, 1457, and David, 3rd Lord Kennedy, was created Earl of Cassillis, 1509. He fell at Flodden. Gilbert, 2nd Earl, was assassinated 1527 by Sir Hew Campbell of Loudon. Gilbert, 3rd Earl, was one of the ambassadors poisoned at Dieppe for protecting the Scottish Royal succession in Mary, Queen of Scots', marriage contract. John, 4th Earl, " a very greedy man," was celebrated for " roasting the Abbot of Crossraguel." His son John, 5th Earl, had no issue, and was succeeded by his nephew the 6th Earl, whose Countess, Lady Jean Hamilton, was the reputed lover of Sir John Faa, the gipsy. On the death of John, 8th Earl, the honours passed to the heir male, Sir Thomas Kennedy, 4th Baronet, of Culzean, a descendant of the Hon. Sir Thomas Kennedy, second son of the 3rd Earl. Archibald, 11th Earl was a distinguished naval officer, closely concerned in the American War of Independence, and owned part of New York City. His son, Archibald, 12th Earl, was created Marquis of Ailsa 1806. Archibald, 4th Marquis, was a distinguished authority on Celtic matters and President of the Royal Celtic Society. His brother, the present chief, is Charles, 5th Marquis, whose seats are Culzean Castle, and Cassillis, in Ayrshire.

James Kennedy, a younger brother of the 1st Lord Kennedy, was Bishop of St. Andrews, Chancellor of Scotland, and one of the greatest statesmen of his time. He founded the University of St. Andrews.

42. KENNEDY

KERR

THE Border Kerrs claim a Norman descent, and John Ker, the hunter of Swinhope, is the first of the name on record in Scotland. He lived in the reign of William the Lion. They are divided into two branches, whom tradition derives from the brothers Ralph and John, who settled near Jedburgh about 1330. The Kerrs of Ferniehurst claim to be descended from Ralph, the elder brother, and to have inherited the chiefship of the Kerrs through the marriage of Thomas (third son of Andrew Kerr of Altonburn) with Margaret Kerr, heiress of the house descending from Ralph. They apparently satisfied the Lord Lyon of this, as they were awarded the undifferenced arms of the race. Thomas Kerr and the heiress of Ferniehurst and Smailholm had a son, Sir Andrew, Warden of the Middle March in 1502. In the siege of his castle in 1523, the English alleged it was defended by " spirits and fearful sights," including the devil in person. Sir John, the next laird, recovered Ferniehurst from the English, and his successor, Sir Thomas, was a supporter of Mary, Queen of Scots. His son Andrew was created Lord Jedburgh in 1662. This dignity eventually devolved upon the Marquesses of Lothian, who derive from Robert Kerr of Woodhead and Ancrum (second son of Sir Andrew Kerr of Ferniehurst) whose grandson Robert was created Earl of Ancrum 1633. His eldest son was created Earl of Lothian 1631, on his marriage with Lady Anne Kerr, daughter of Robert, 2nd Earl of Lothian, who was descended from Mark Kerr, Commendator and Abbot of Newbattle, second son of Sir Andrew Kerr of Cessford. His son, Robert, Earl of Lothian and Ancrum, Lord Justice-General, was created Marquess of Lothian 1701, and the present chief is Peter Francis, 12th Marquess, whose seat is Mount Teviot, Ancrum. The other great branch of the Kerrs derives from John Kerr of Altonburn, 1357. His descendant, another Andrew, of Altonburn, became Baron of Cessford in 1467, and his descendant, Sir Andrew Kerr of Cessford, was Warden of the Middle March 1515. It was his second son, Mark, who founded the first comital line of Lothian, whilst his elder son, Sir Walter, was grandfather of Robert, 1st Earl of Roxburghe, creation 1616. Of this line, John, 5th Earl, was created Duke of Roxburghe in 1707, a dignity which in 1805 devolved upon Sir James Innes of that Ilk, whilst Major-General Walter Kerr of Littledean became the heir male of the Kerrs of Cessford. Other celebrated branches were the Kerrs of Fawdonsyde, and Riddell-Carre of Cavers-Carre.

43. KERR

LAMONT

Badge:—Craobh-ubhal fhiadhain (Crab-apple tree) or Machall-monaidh (Dryas).

Ne parcas nec spernas

THE first chief of the Clan Lamont of whom there is definite historical evidence is Ferchar, who flourished about 1200. Ferchar's grandson, Laumun, was the first to use the name which has since become hereditary. About 1238, Duncan, son of Ferchar, and this Laumun, son of Malcolm, son of Ferchar, granted certain lands at Kilmun, etc., to the monks of Paisley.

About 1646 the Lamont country was ravaged by the Campbells, who carried about two hundred prisoners to Dunoon and massacred them at the Gallowhill. A memorial to commemorate the event was erected by the Clan Lamont Society in 1906.

From the 13th to the 17th century the chiefs used the barony title of "Inveryne," with Toward Castle for part of that time as principal residence. In 1646 Ardlamont became the seat of the chief, and so remained until its sale in the 19th century.

The Lamonts of Knockdow claim descent from Geoffrey (or Gorre), son of John Lamont, alive in 1431, and are now represented by Sir Norman Lamont, 2nd Baronet and 15th Laird of Knockdow.

The families of Auchagoyll (now Otter) and Auchinshellich (or Willowfield) both descended from Walter, son of Sir John Lamont of Inveryne; Cowston from Patrick Lamont, Crowner of Cowal in 1450. Silvercrags family was descended from Robert, lawful son of Sir John (X.). Stilaig was held by Archibald, second son of Sir John, and his successors till about 1643, when Sir James (XIV.) granted it to his brother Archibald.

In the 18th century the chiefship passed through Margaret, daughter and heiress of Dugald Lamont of Lamont, to the heir of line, her son Archibald Lamont of Lamont, from whom descended John Henry Lamont of Lamont, who was awarded the chief arms as heir of line and was also awarded supporters by the Lord Lyon in 1909.

The present chief is Ronald Coll Lamont of Lamont (24th Chief) who lives in Australia.

There is a Clan Lamont Society, founded in 1895. Its headquarters are in Glasgow.

44. LAMONT

LESLIE

Badge :—Rue.

THIS surname is derived from the lands of Leslie, in Aberdeenshire. The first on record was Bartholf of Leslie and "Malcolm, son of Bartolf," had a charter of Leslie in the reign of William the Lion. The Leslies of that Ilk were Constables of the Royal Castle of Inverurie in the Garioch.

George Leslie of Ballinbreich, a great-great-grandson of Sir Andrew Leslie, 6th of that Ilk, was the 1st Earl of Rothes, so created by James II. William, 3rd Earl, fell with his Royal master at Flodden. George, 4th Earl, accompanied James V. to France. His son, Norman, Master of Rothes, after being engaged in the murder of Cardinal Beaton, was slain in battle in Picardy in 1554. The Earl died at Dieppe in 1558. John, 7th Earl of Rothes, carried the Sword of State at the Coronation of Charles II. at Scone in 1651. In 1680 he was created Duke of Rothes, but died the following year, leaving a daughter, the Countess, whose eldest son, John, succeeded to the Earldom of Rothes, while Thomas, her second son, carried on the honours of Haddington. Malcolm, 20th Earl of Rothes, is the present chief of the clan. He still owns the Castle-hill of Rothes in Strathspey, and his brother, the Hon. John Leslie, is Keeper of the ancient Castle of Leslie-in-the-Garioch.

Sir Alexander Leslie (1st Earl of Leven, *cr.* 1641) was a famous General during the Civil War. His title is now united with that of Melville, and Ronald, 11th Earl, founded the Chapel of the Thistle at St. Giles' Cathedral, Edinburgh. His second son, Archibald, is now 13th Earl.

Sir Patrick Leslie of Pitcairlie, second son of the 5th Earl of Rothes, was created Lord Lindores in 1600, a title dormant since 1775.

A famous branch are the Leslies of Balquhain, in Aberdeenshire. Sir George, the founder, got a grant of that estate from David II. in 1340. Of this line came Walter, Count Leslie, who assassinated Wallenstein. He was fourth son of John, 10th Baron of Balquhain.

Sir Andrew, 3rd of Balquhain, slain 1420, had a bitter feud with the Forbeses, by whom his castle was burnt. Sir William, 7th of Balquhain, rebuilt it, and died in 1545. This house is now represented by Allan Leslie, 29th Baron of Balquhain. Leslie of Wardis, Balquhain's most important cadet, is now represented by Sir Henry Leslie, 9th Baronet of Wardis. Leslie of Warthill, cadet of Wardis, has held that estate in the Garioch since 1518 and William, brother of the 5th Laird of Warthill, was Prince Bishop of Laibach in Austria and Privy Councillor of the Empire.

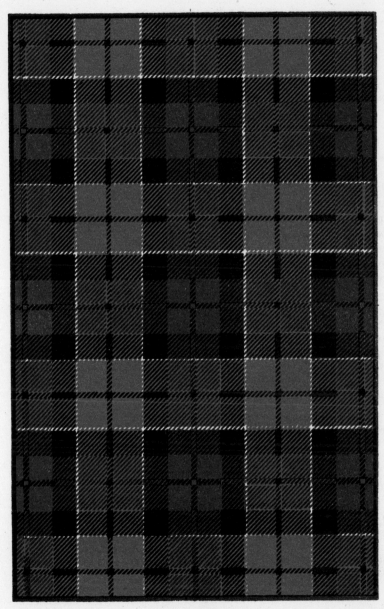

45. LESLIE

LINDSAY

Badges :—Rue, and Lime Tree.

BALDRIC DE LINDESAY, a Norman, is the first recorded member of this illustrious race. In 1120 Sir Walter Lindsay was a member of the Council of Prince David, and in 1180 William de Lindsay was Baron of Luffness and Laird of Crawford in which he was succeeded by a son, Sir David. A subsequent Laird, Sir David Lindsay of Crawford, living about 1340, acquired Glenesk, in Angus, by marriage with Maria Abernethy, one of the heiresses of the Earldom of Angus.

He had two sons : (1) Alexander of Glenesk, father of David, a celebrated knight, who was created Earl of Crawford 1398 ; and (2) Sir William of the Byres. The grandson of the 1st Earl—David, 3rd Earl—left two sons—Alexander, 4th Earl, and Walter of Edzell. On the death of the 16th Earl the title went by settlement to the Lindsays of the Byres, passing over the Edzell family.

The 4th, or " Tiger Earl," or " Earl Beardie," made a " deal " with the Earl of Douglas which imperilled the Crown, but Crawford was defeated by Huntly at Brechin in 1452, and eventually pardoned. Alexander, " The Wicked Master," son and heir of the 8th Earl, was so evil that, having been convicted of attempt to kill his father, the Earl, he was disinherited, and the dignity devolved on his cousin, the Laird of Edzell as David, 9th Earl of Crawford (at whose death the dignity reverted to the son of the Wicked Master). He left two sons ; (1) Sir David of Edzell, whose line failed in 1744 ; and (2) John of Balcarres, father of David, created Lord Lindsay of Balcarres 1633, whose son, Alexander, was created Earl of Balcarres 1651. This Earl's grandson, James, 5th Earl of Balcarres, left two sons : (1) Alexander, 6th Earl, who became 23rd Earl of Crawford 1808, on the failure of the direct line of Lindsay of Byres on whom the Earldom of Crawford had devolved under a regrant obtained by the 16th Earl. The present (27th) Earl of Crawford and Balcarres is David Alexander Edward Lindsay, K.T., P.C., whose seat is Balcarres, in Fife.

The Lindsays, known as " The Lightsome Lindsays," are practically the only Lowland clan who have formed a Clan Association. This they did in October 1897, under the presidency of the Right Hon. The Earl of Crawford, K.T., chief of the clan.

Sir William, fourth son of the 6th Baron of Crawford, was created Lord Lindsay of the Byres 1366, and John, 10th Lord, was created Earl of Lindsay 1633. Sir David Lindsay of the Mount, poet and Lord Lyon King of Arms, was a cadet of this line. This house was celebrated in the heraldic annals of Scotland as it produced three Kings of Arms—two Sir Davids of the Mount and Sir David Lindsay of Rathillet.

To the Clan Lindsay we are indebted for the well-known song, " Auld Robin Gray," which is the composition of Lady Anne Lindsay, eldest daughter of James Lindsay, 5th Earl of Balcarres. She was born 1750.

The headquarters of the Clan Society are in Edinburgh, with a branch in Glasgow.

46. LINDSAY

LIVINGSTON

THE surname Livingston or Livingstone is of territorial origin from the lands, now a parish of the same name, in West Lothian. A Saxon named Leving or Leuing appears to have settled in Scotland under Edgar. He certainly obtained a grant of lands, which he called Levingestun. His grandson is designated in a charter of William the Lion (1165–1214) as of Livingston. Sir Archibald de Livingstone, *del counte de Edenburk*, rendered homage in 1296. His grandson, Sir William Livingston, accompanied King David II. in his expedition to England in 1346, and was taken prisoner at the battle of Durham, 1346. He had a grant from David II. of the barony of Callander, Stirlingshire, on the forfeiture of Patrick Callander, whose only daughter and heiress he married. His younger son, Sir William, had a son, Sir John Livingstone of Callander, killed at the Battle of Homildon 1402, leaving four sons : Sir Alexander, who succeeded ; Robert, ancestor of the Livingstones of Westquarter and Kinnaird ; John, of the Livingstones, Bonton ; and William, of the Viscount of Kilsyth. Sir Alexander, who died about 1450, was succeeded by his eldest son, Sir James Livingstone of Callander, 1st Lord Livingstone, who died about 1467.

Alexander, 5th Lord, was one of the guardians of Mary, Queen of Scots, during her childhood, and his daughter, Mary, was one of the celebrated "Four Marys." His son William, 6th Lord, fought for her at Langside, and dying 1592, was succeeded by his eldest son, Alexander, 7th Lord, who was created Earl of Linlithgow in 1600.

James, 4th Earl, joined the Jacobite rising of 1715 and was forfeited. The Hon. James Livingston, younger son of the 1st Earl, served in the Earl of Leven's army during the Civil War and was created Earl of Callander with remainder to his nephew, and James, 4th Earl, was, like his chief, forfeited for his share in the 1715.

What have been termed the " Highland Livingstones " have quite a different origin. A member of this section of the Livingstones is called in Gaelic *Mac-an-leigh*, " son of the physician." From this we have the surname MacLeay, and the MacLeay's of the north-west are said to be descended from *Ferchar Leighiche* who got land in Assynt in 1386. He was one of the famous family of Beatons who were physicians to Lords of the Isles. The " Mac-an-léighs " of Appin, who were followers of the Stewarts of Appin, Englished their name as Livingstone, of whom was the celebrated Dr David Livingstone, the famous African missionary and traveller.

This family of Livingstone, styled the Barons of the Bachull, received in early times a grant of lands in Lismore, which they long held as keepers of the Bishop of Lismore's crozier, or *baculum*, called in Gaelic " Bachull Mor." This is an interesting instance of a Celtic " Barony " attaching to the inheritance of the office of Keepers of the Crozier of Lismore. The Baronage of " Argyll and the Isles " was recognised as an Order by the old Scots Parliament.

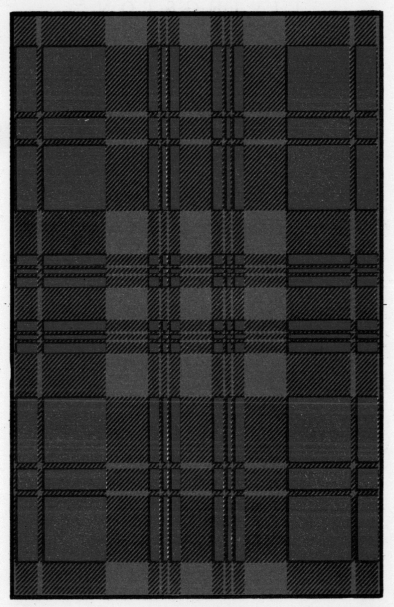

47. LIVINGSTON

LOGAN

(MACLENNAN)

Slogan :—" Druim nan deur " (" The Ridge of Tears ").

Badge :—Conasg (Furze).

THE traditional account of the origin of the Maclennans is as follows : In a feud between the Frasers and the Lobans (or Logans), the latter were defeated at the Battle of Drumderfit, near Kessock Ferry, and their leader, called Gilligorm, slain. Gilligorm left a posthumous son, born among the Frasers, by whom tradition says his back was broken to prevent him from growing up strong and warlike enough to avenge the death of his father. This son was called Crotair MacGilligorm (the humph-back son of Gilligorm). He was educated at Beauly Priory, took Holy Orders, and eventually moved to the West Coast, where he founded and built two churches— one at Kilmuir in Skye, and the other in Glenelg. This was about the beginning of the 13th century. Crotair married, as priests in the High- lands frequently did in those days—for the Celtic Church, unlike that of Rome, did not ordain celibacy of the clergy—and had, with other issue, a son, whom he called *Gille Fhinnein*, in honour of St. Finnan, and whose descendants became known as the Maclennans.

The Maclennans were at one time numerous in Kintail, in Ross-shire, and tradition has preserved the name of a renowned warrior, Donald Maclennan, who took a prominent part in the great feud between Kintail and Glengarry about 1600. The Maclennans appear to have been, on some occasions, the standard-bearers of Kintail, and at the Battle of Auldearn, in 1645, a certain Roderick Maclennan and his brother, Donald, were killed while bravely defending the banner of their chief.

Loban, or Lobban, is a Morayshire name. William Lobane appears in 1564 as tenant in Drumderfit, in the Black Isle, where the family were so long tenants that the local proverb says, " As old as the Lobans of Drumderfit." A wooden effigy of Gilligorm, the clan-hero, and possibly that off his tomb, was long preserved and venerated in the House of Drumderfit, but it was destroyed when this was burnt after the Rising of 1715. It seems likely that the Morayshire and Banffshire Lobbans are of different origin, and that they derive their name from peat-creels.

The arms shown are recorded for Logan of that Ilk, but no one has meantime established right to the chief arms and chiefship of either the Logans or the Maclennans.

48. LOGAN or MACLENNAN

MACALISTER

Badge :—Fraoch gorm (Common Heath).

IT is generally understood that this clan branched off from the main Clan Donald stem early in the 13th century. They are supposed to be descended from Alastair Mor, second son of Donald, Lord of the Isles, and younger brother of Angus Mor.

In 1366 Ranald, son of Alexander, appears as chief of the Clan Alister. Ranald had his residence in Kintyre, where the Clan Alister at a later time are found in large numbers. In 1481 Charles MacAlister was appointed by James III. to the Stewartry of Kintyre, and at the same time received a charter for a considerable grant of lands in that peninsula. Charles was succeeded by his son, John, who is styled "John of the Lowb," now rendered Loup, from the Gaelic *lùb*, a curve or bend, this being the configuration of the shore which bounded the ancient patrimony of the Clan Alister.

During the 15th and 16th centuries members of the clan obtained settlements in Bute and Arran, and their descendants are there to this day.

In the latter half of the 16th century a new branch of Clan Alister of Kintyre sprang into existence—namely, the family of Tarbert. The heads of the House became hereditary Constables of Tarbert Castle. To this branch belonged Sir Donald MacAlister, Principal of Glasgow University.

Angus-Vic-Ian-Dhu-M'Alastair of the Loup was chief of Clan Alastair in 1515.

Gory MacAlester, 7th of Loup, had a son, Alexander, who succeeded him as 8th of Loup. He was an active Jacobite. He fought at Killiecrankie, under Viscount Dundee, and afterwards served with the Royal army in Ireland against William of Orange.

His son died without issue, so he was succeeded by his brother, Charles, 10th of Loup, who married a daughter of Lamont of that Ilk. His grandson, the 12th Laird, Charles, born in 1765, married the heiress of Somerville of Kennox, in Ayrshire, and in 1846 his son, Charles MacAlester of Loup and Kennox, was awarded arms as chief of the clan by decree of Lyon Court.

The present chief of the clan is Lieut.-Col. Charles Godfrey Somerville MacAlester of the Loup and Kennox, who succeeded to the chiefship of Clan Alastair in 1903. His seat is Kennox, in Ayrshire.

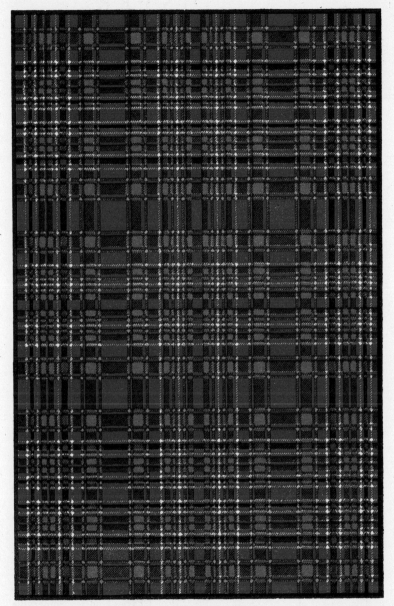

49. MACALISTER

MACARTHUR

Slogan :—" Eisd ! O Eisd ! " (" Listen ! O Listen ! ").

Badge :—Roid (Wild Myrtle) or Garbhag an t-sléibhe (Fir Club Moss).

THE Clan Arthur is one of the oldest of the clans of Argyll ; and its *duthus* was on the shores of Loch Awe, where its chief also held Innestrarynich. This particular clan was known from others of the name of Arthur as the *Clann-Artair-na-tir-a-chladich ile*—" of the shore-land." So long had they been seated there that even in Celtic days they gave rise to a celebrated couplet :

" *Cruic 'is uillt 'is Ailpeinich*
Ach cuin a thaing Artairich ? "

" The hills and streams and MacAlpine—
But whence came forth MacArthur ? "

The title *Mac-ic-Artair* suggests that the Clan Arthur of Tirracladich were originally a branch of a major line (which of course would be the case if their ancestor was a son of the " King Arthur " of Romance, as they duly claim !) Their slogan was *O eisd ! O eisd !* (Listen ! Listen !)

Staunch supporters of the Bruce, *Mac-ic-Artair* was rewarded with grants of lands forfeited by the Macdougalls, but a century later their influential position was lost. Ian, Chief of the Clan Artair of Tirracladich was one of the chiefs of Argyll put to death by James I. ; and from this disaster they never recovered.

There has been a good deal of confusion between the fore-going Clan Arthur, and another of the same patronymic, the MacArthur-Campbells, one of the branches of the Clan Campbell.

A family of MacArthurs were hereditary pipers to the MacDonalds of Sleat. The most celebrated of the family was Charles, whose musical education was perfected by Patrick Og MacCrimmon.

It is maintained that the chiefship of the clan rests in the family of the MacArthurs of Proaig, Islay, some of whose ancestors were armourers to the MacDonalds of Islay. The arms shown are those of MacArthur of Milton, whose line still holds the Milton-of-Dunoon.

Born near Glasgow, the grandfather of General Douglas MacArthur, the conqueror of Japan in the Second World War, emigrated to the United States about 1840.

50. MACARTHUR

MACAULAY

Badge :—Muileag (Cranberry) or Giuthas (Pine Tree).

THERE were two Clans MacAulay. The best known were the MacAulays of Ardincaple, in Dumbartonshire, a property disposed of by the 12th Chief in the 18th century to the Campbells of Argyll. They have no connection with the Lewis Clan MacAulay. The MacAulays of Ardincaple are believed to be of the family of Lennox, for in a charter granted by Maldowen, Earl of Lennox, to Sir Patrick Grahame, is Aulay, the Earl's brother, as also in another charter by the same Earl to William, son of Arthur Galbraith, the witnesses are Duncan and Aulay, the Earl's brothers.

Sir Aulay MacAulay of Ardincaple appears in 1587 in the Roll of the Landlords and Bailies in the Highlands and Isles as one of the principal vassals of the Earl of Lennox.

The last portion of the clan territory passed out of the hands of the 12th Chief in 1767, when Ardincaple was sold to the Duke of Argyll.

The first MacAulay of Lewis on record is Donald *Cam*, mentioned in 1610, who is said to have been captured along with Torquil Dubh in 1597, but escaped. Donald Cam's son, Angus of Brenish, was killed at Auldearn Battle, 1645. His son, Dugald, succeeded him as *Fear Bhrenis*, and his son was Rev. Aulay Macaulay, minister of Harris, married to Rev. Kenneth Morrison's daughter, of Stornoway. His son was the Rev. John Macaulay, Minister of Inveraray, whose son, Zachary, was father of the famous Thomas, Lord Macaulay, poet, essayist, and historian. An M.P. from 1830-56, he was raised to the peerage in 1857, but died unmarried.

The Lewis MacAulays had namesakes, no doubt kinsmen, on the mainland, vassals to the MacKenzies. Lochbroom is said to have been their original possession, a district which the heiress of Duncan MacAulay is said to have given with her hand to the chief of the MacKenzies in the 14th century. The MacAulays of the mainland are coupled with the Macleays and MacIvors in the 15th century as giving trouble to the Earl of Ross and his tenants.

51. MACAULAY

M

MACCALLUM

(MALCOLM)

In ardua tendit

Deus refugium nostrum

THE district of Lorn, Argyllshire, is generally regarded as the country of the MacCallums; and Colgin, about three and a half miles from Oban, has long been considered the headquarters of the Mac-Callums. Tradition states that the chief family of Colgin—consisting at the time of three sons—resolved to leave the parental roof. Their father prepared horses with panniers and gave one to each of the lads. He then sent them away with the direction to take up their residence in whatever place the panniers would fall off the horses. The panniers of the horse of one of them having fallen within the boundaries of the farm, he remained at home. The other two went on their journey, going in different directions. The panniers of the one having fallen in Glenetive, he settled there, and the panniers of the other having fallen at Kilmartin, he made his home in that district. That at least is the tradition—and one found in many parts of the world. Some more definite account of the MacCallums from documentary sources would be preferable. In later years the name was, it is said, changed to Malcolm. Of this surname there is, however, more definite historical fact; in 1562 Donald M'Gillespie vic O'Challum was seized in the lands of Poltalloch. He was the lineal ancestor of Neil Malcolm of Poltalloch, who succeeded his cousin, Dugald, in 1787 and died in 1802. John Wingfield, 15th Laird, was created Lord Malcolm of Poltalloch in 1896, and died in 1902. He was succeeded in the estate by his brother, whose son, Sir Ian Malcolm of Poltalloch, K.C.M.G., the 17th Laird and Chieftain, was succeeded by his son, Lieut.-Col. George Ian Malcolm of Poltalloch.

The tartan here shown was approved as correct by the late Sir Ian Malcolm of Poltalloch.

The general impression (according to recent works on clan tartans) is, that this family, having lost trace of the original sett, endeavoured to have it prepared from the recollection of aged natives of Argyllshire, but, as might be expected, the recovery of the old sett shows that deviations in detail had, as usual, occurred. It has to be kept in mind, however, that such deviations in detail was quite normal in olden times.

G. Seton, Advocate, says :—

" Armorial bearings afford us invaluable assistance in authenticating genealogies, and in distinguishing the numerous branches of a widely-extended clan." (*Law and Practice of Heraldry*, p. 9).

52. MACCALLUM

MACDONALD

Slogan :—Fraoch Eilean (" The Heathery Isle "). *Badge* :—Heather.

THIS, the oldest and most famous of Scottish clans, is descended from Donald, grandson of Somerled of the Isles. The Sennachies claim for them descent from *Colla Uais*, High King of Ireland, and through Somerled's marriage with Ragnhild, daughter of Olaf, the Kingdom of Man ultimately came to the House of Somerled. He died in 1164, and was buried in Saddel Monastery, leaving three sons—Dugall, Reginald, and Angus. The Southern Isles and part of Argyll were divided among them : Lorn, Mull, and Jura were given to Dugall ; Kintyre and Islay to Reginald ; Bute, with part of Arran and other lands from Ardnamurchan to Glenelg, to Angus.

Reginald, the son of Somerled, died in 1207. By Fonia, daughter of the house of Moray, he had three sons. Donald succeeded his father in the lordship of South Kintyre, Islay, and other islands ; Roderick got North Kintyre, Bute, and Garmoran from Ardnamurchan to Glenelg ; Lochaber passed to the Comyns.

From Donald, son of Reginald, the clan takes its name. Angus Mor Macdonald of the Isles, great-grandson of Somerled, held state as an independent Prince of the Isles. His son, Angus Og, supported The Bruce, but maintained independent principality. John, 7th of the Isles, had by his first marriage with Amy MacRuairidh, a son, Archibald, ancestor of Clanranald, and by his second wife, Princess Margaret, daughter of King Robert II., Donald, on whom he settled his Lordship of the Isles and Chiefship of Clan Donald. This Donald claimed the Earldom of Ross, and fought at Harlaw in 1411. His son, Alexander, was acknowledged Earl of Ross, and John, 10th of the Isles, maintained royal state with his own Parliament at Ardtornish. He was created a Peer of Scotland as Lord of the Isles, 1476, but in 1494 was compelled to surrender his position and Lordship of the Isles to the King of Scots and died in 1498. Though his son Donald endeavoured to re-establish the Sovereign Lordship of the Isles in 1545, and was supported by his vassals, the Barons of *Inchegallie*, he did not succeed. Clan Donald then remained divided into some nine more or less independent branches which the Scottish Crown regarded as independent clans, until in 1660 King Charles II. restored the Name and Chiefship to Æneas Macdonald of Glengarry, heir of line of Celestine of Lochalsh, as Lord Macdonald and Aros, limited to the heirs male of his body. This expired 1680 ; and soon after Sir James Macdonald of Sleate, Bt., Chief of Clan Huistean, was received by Parliament as Laird of Macdonald, and his heir, Sir Alexander Macdonald of Macdonald (7th Bt.) had the chiefship restored in his person by erection of the Sleate estates into the Barony of Macdonald. His son was in 1776 created Lord Macdonald, and under entail and Act of Parliament, 1847, their estates in Skye (with the fairy castle of Dunscaith) have descended to Alexander Godfrey, 7th Lord Macdonald, who has been officially recognised by the Lord Lyon as Macdonald of Macdonald, Chief of the Name, and got restoration of the undifferenced arms of the old Macdonald chiefs. His seat is Armadale Castle in Skye.

53. MACDONALD, CLAN

MACDONALD OF CLANRANALD

Slogan :—" Dh'aindeoin co theiradh e " (" Gainsay who dare ").

Badge :—Fraoch (Common Heath).

BY his marriage with Amy MacRuari, John, 7th Lord of the Isles, left three sons. From the second, named Ranald, are descended the Houses of Glengarry and Clanranald. He had five sons, Allan of Clanranald, Donald of Glengarry, John Dall, Angus of Morar, and Dugal of Sunart.

Dugall, 6th Chief of Clanranald, made himself so odious by cruelties that the tribe slew him, and elected his uncle Alistair Allanson, Captain of Clan Ranald. Alistair died in 1530, when his eldest natural son, John of Moydart, styled *Mac Mhic Ailein*, was invested in the family stronghold Castle Tirrim and other lands, 1531, but on account of unruly conduct he was imprisoned by James V. in 1540. The Frasers now attempted to reduce the rights he had acquired in favour of Ranald Gallda, son of Alan MacRuari, 5th Chief of Clanranald, 1481–1509. This ended in the Battle of Blarnaleine, 1544, where Ranald fell, and John of Moydart became eventually the firm friend of Lovat and secured recognition from the Crown as Chief of Clan Ranald. He died in 1584.

His son Alan married a daughter of MacLeod of MacLeod and died in 1593. Alan's son Sir Donald, 10th Chief, was knighted by James VI.

The MacVurichs were the hereditary Sennachies to Clanranald and kept the *Leabhar Dearg*, or Red Book of Clanranald.

John, 11th of Clanranald, served under Montrose in 1644, and in the march to Argyll penetrated as far as Lochcreran, and, according to the Red Book, killed about 900 men. He died in Uist 1670. His son John, 12th Chief, served with him under Montrose : and in 1650 he appears as one of the " Colonells of the clans in the Isles and Heighelands." He died in 1686.

Alan, 13th Clanranald, adhered to James VIII., and was killed at Sheriffmuir. He had married Penelope Erskine, daughter of the Lord Lyon King of Arms, but having no issue, was succeeded by his brother Ranald, who died at the Jacobite Court of St. Germain, 1725, when the succession passed to his cousin and brother-in-law, Donald, 15th Clan Ranald and 3rd of Benbecula, who, according to the Clan Chattan principle, was chief *jure uxoris*, from his marriage to the sister and heiress of line. Their grandson, " Young Clanranald," afterwards 17th Chief, supported Prince Charles and only escaped afterwards by misdescription. His descendant, Reginald George Macdonald, was in 1810 recognised in Lyon Court as Chief and Captain of Clanranald. His son, Admiral Sir Reginald MacDonald, 20th of Clanranald, K.C.S.I., died 1899, leaving two sons, of whom the second, Angus Roderick, 23rd Chief of Clanranald died 1944 without issue.

Eilean Tirrim.

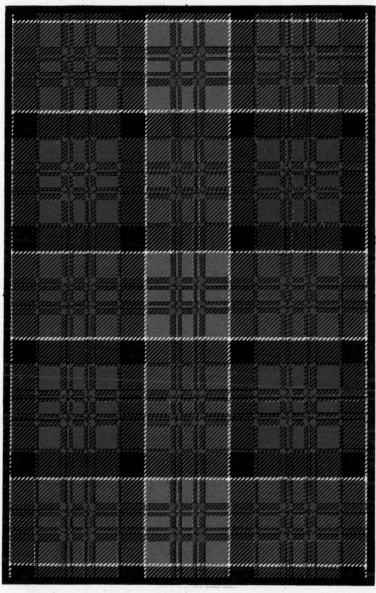

54.   MACDONALD OF CLANRANALD

MACDONALD OF SLEATE

Badge :—Heath.

THE MacDonalds of Sleate are descended from Hugh, son of Alexander, Earl of Ross and Lord of the Isles—hence their patronymic of *Clann Uisdein*, or Children of Hugh. The earliest residence connected with the Barony of Sleate in occupation of *Clann Uisdein* was the fortalice of Dunskaich, lying south of Sleate.

Hugh, 1st of Sleate, was thrice married. He died in 1498, and was succeeded by his son, John, who died in 1502. He was succeeded by his brother, Donald Gallach, whose mother was Elizabeth Gunn, a daughter of the Coroner of Caithness, hence the appellation *Gallach*—*i.e.* a native of Caithness. Donald was murdered by his half-brother in 1506, when he was succeeded by his eldest son, Donald Gruamach, who died 1534. He was succeeded by his eldest son, Donald Gorm, who claimed the Lordship of the Isles, and was killed in 1539 at the siege of Eilandonan Castle. He was succeeded by his son, Donald, who was known in history as " *Dómhnull Gorm Sasunnach*," on account of his having spent part of his minority in England. His son and successor, Donald Gorm Mór, died without issue, and was succeeded by his nephew, Sir Donald MacDonald, 1st Baronet of Sleate (*cr.* 1625). Sir Donald, 4th Baronet, supported the Chevalier in 1715.

Sir Alexander, 9th Baronet of Sleate, was created Lord MacDonald in 1796. He married a daughter of Bosville of Thorpe, Yorkshire, to which the Macdonald line became heirs. Godfrey, 3rd Lord Macdonald, died in 1832, and Alexander, his firstborn son, took the name *Bosville* in 1832, in accordance with the requirements for succession to the Bosville estates, whilst the peerage and Macdonald estates devolved, along with the name *Macdonald* and chiefship of Macdonald, on the eldest son born after the 1803 marriage, Godfrey, 4th Lord Macdonald, 19th Chief of Sleate and Macdonald of Macdonald. The arrangement was confirmed by Act of Parliament, 1847. The chiefship (and also, as supposed—but without procedure—the Baronetcy) descended to Godfrey, 6th Lord Macdonald, until in 1910 Alexander, Bosville's grandson, got a Declarator of Legitimacy, and (after being 78 years *Bosville*) took the name Bosville-Macdonald and was declared by Lyon Court 14th Baronet and Chief of the Family of Macdonald of Sleate. He then became 22nd Chief of Clan Huistean. His son, Sir Godfrey, 15th Baronet, is 23rd Chief of Sleate and Clan Huistean. (Lord Macdonald remained Chief of the Name, and his grandson is now 7th Lord Macdonald and The Macdonald of Macdonald.) The Chiefs of Sleate have latterly assumed the style " of the Isles," but this has not been officially recognised by Lyon Court. The seat of Sir Godfrey Macdonald of Sleate, Bt., Chief of Clan Huistean, is Thorpe Hall, Yorks.

55. MACDONALD OF SLEATE

MACDONELL OF GLENGARRY

Slogan :—" Creagan-an-fhithich " (" The Raven's Rock ").

Badge :—Fraoch gorm (Common Heath).

THIS branch of the Clan Donald derives from Archibald, second son of John, 7th Lord of the Isles. Alistair Macdonell, 6th of Glengarry, married Margaret, daughter and co-heiress of Sir Alexander Macdonald of Lochalsh, and he and his wife had a Crown Charter of Castle Strone, and half the lands of Lochalsh. According to *The Loyall Dissuasive*, p. 118, this marriage gives Glengarry the best claim to the chiefship of the Clan Donald—so unheard of was " Salic Law " in pre-18th-century Scotland. He died in 1560, and his son, Angus Macalister Macdonell, 7th of Glengarry, had a Crown confirmation of Glengarry in 1574, and Glengarry was erected into a barony in 1627 for his son, Donald, 8th Chief of Glengarry. Angus, 9th of Glengarry, was a Royalist who supported Montrose, and at the Restoration was (from the Crown and Privy Council holding the same view as Macpherson of Invershie) created a peer as Lord Macdonell and Aros, but, dying without issue, the peerage (and apparently confirmation of chiefship to this line) expired, and the chiefship of Glengarry passed to the son of his uncle (Donald Gorm Macdonell of Scotus), Archibald, 2nd of Scotus and 10th of Glengarry. Alistair Macdonell, 11th of Glengarry was created a peer by the Jacobite King, James VIII., in 1716, and Field-Marshall Wade reported in 1746 that John, 12th Chief of Glengarry, could put five hundred clansmen in the field. Alistair, 13th of Glengarry, was imprisoned in the Tower as a Jacobite, and succeeded by his nephew, Duncan, 14th of Glengarry and fourth Jacobite " Lord Macdonell," whose son and successor, Alistair Macdonell, 15th of Glengarry, is celebrated as the friend of Sir Walter Scott and the subject of Raeburn's portrait. He was the last Highland chief who maintained complete Celtic magnificence, wore the Highland dress on all occasions, and was invariably accompanied by a body of retainers in full Highland costume. Dying in 1828, his son Æneas Ranaldson Macdonell, 16th of Glengarry, was obliged to sell the whole estate except the ruined castle, and his sons, successively 17th and 18th Chiefs, emigrated to New Zealand. On the death of the younger Charles Ranaldson, 18th of Glengarry, the chiefship devolved upon his cousin, Æneas Ranald, 7th of Scotus and 19th Chief of Glengarry, whose great-grandson is the present Ranald Macdonell, 21st Chief of Glengarry.

56. MACDONELL OF GLENGARRY

MACDONELL OF KEPPOCH

Slogan :—" Dia is Naomh Aindrea " (" God and St. Andrew ").

Badge :—Heath.

THE Macdonells of Keppoch derive from Alistair Carrach Macdonell, third son of Ian, 7th Lord of the Isles, by his second wife, Lady Margaret, daughter of King Robert II. He burnt Elgin in 1402 and fought under his brother Donald, 8th Lord of the Isles, at Harlaw, 1411. His son, Angus, 2nd of Keppoch, supported the 10th Lord of the Isles in his Rising of 1452, and in consequence of his loyalty to the chief of Clan Donald, the Lordship of Lochaber was forfeited to the Crown. Donald Glas Macdonell, 6th Chief, built the old castle of Keppoch, and his son, Ranald, 7th of Keppoch, supported John Moidertach against Lord Lovat at the Battle of *Blarleine* in 1544, and three years later was seized by the Earl of Huntly and beheaded. His sons, Alexander and Ranald Og, were successively 8th and 9th Chiefs of Keppoch. Alistair nan Cleas, son of the latter, became 10th Chief of Keppoch, and from one of his sons derive the Canadian line of Macdonells *Seigneurs de Rigaud* in Canada. The third son, *Alistair Buidhe*, eventually, upon the murder of his nephew the 12th Chief, became 13th Chief of Keppoch, and from him descended Colonel Macdonell, 15th of Keppoch, who fought for the Jacobites at Sheriffmuir in 1715. His son and successor, Alistair, 16th of Keppoch, was amongst the earliest adherents of Prince Charles and prevented the Hanoverian forces from reaching Glenfinnan at the momentous gathering of the clans and raising of the Standard. Keppoch fell at Culloden, when his natural son, Angus, became Captain of the branch until the majority of his half-brother Ranald, who vainly endeavoured to recover the forfeited estates of Keppoch. His great-grandson, Donald Nicholas Macdonell, last Chief of Keppoch in the direct line, died in 1889. His sister, Alice Bardess of Clan Donald. There is a Canadian branch of Keppoch, represented by a Canadian *Seigneur*, Charles de Bellefeuille *Macdonell de Rigaud*, Quebec.

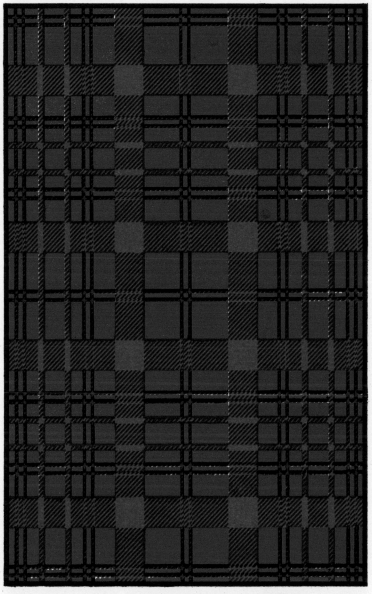

57. MACDONELL OF KEPPOCH

MACDOUGALL

Slogan :—" Buaidh no bàs " (" Victory or Death ").

Badge :—Fraoch dearg (Bell Heath) ; also Cypress.

THIS clan is descended from Dugall, the eldest son of Somerled of the Isles by Raghnild, sister of Godfred of Man and the Isles. Dugall's son was Duncan of Argyll or Ergadia. From his father Duncan got the cradle of the clan—Lorn—and " Duncan of Argyll " appears on record as early as 1244. Duncan's son was Ewin, Lord of Lorn, who refused to join Haco in 1263.

Ewin Macdougall's son was Alexander of Lorn, who died about 1310. He was succeeded by his son, John (*Ian Bacach*), the obstinate opponent of Robert the Bruce, who gained possession of the " Brooch of Lorn." John was seized in 1318 and imprisoned in Dumbarton for his opposition to Bruce. His son, Ewen, 5th of Lorn, married Joanna MacIssak, a grand-daughter of the Bruce, and got his property restored 1344.

Lorn, having passed to the Stewarts of Durrisdeer and Innermeath by marriage with the two co-heiresses of Ewen, the representation of the name and clan of Macdougall passed to their cousin, Ian, son of Duncan Macdougall, as 7th of Dunollie, and in 1457 his great-grandson, Sir John MacAllan MacDougall, 10th Chief, had a charter of Kerraray and Dunollie.

John MacAllan's descendants held the lands of Dunolly undisturbed till 1715, when they were forfeited on account of the 21st Chief, Iain Ciar, having been present, with 200 of his clansmen, at Sheriffmuir. Iain Ciar died 1737, and was succeeded by his son, Alexander, whose grandson was Vice Admiral Sir John MacDougall of Dunollie, K.C.B., 24th Chief. The Admiral died in 1864, and was succeeded by his son, Alexander, a captain in the army, who was succeeded in 1867 by his brother, Lt.-Col. Charles Allan MacDougall of Dunollie, who died in 1896. His brother, Henry Robert MacDougall, 27th of Dunollie, Deputy Surgeon-General, Bombay Army, was succeeded by his son, Alexander James MacDougall of MacDougall and Dunollie, C.M.G., Lt.-Col., R.A.M.C., 28th Laird of Dunollie and Chief of the clan, to whom the arms and supporters were confirmed in Lyon Court, 1927.

There is a Clan MacDougall Society in Lorn, with branches in Edinburgh and Glasgow.

58.   MACDOUGALL

MACDUFF (DUFF)

MACDUFF is the patronymic of the first or Celtic Earls of Fife. Ethelred, son of King Malcolm Canmore, is the first recorded Earl of Fife. He was also Abbot of Dunkeld. Constantine was Earl of Fife in the early days of David's reign, and, dying about 1129, was succeeded by Gillimichel Mak-duf, or Son of Duff or Dufagan, probably his brother. The origin of these three Earls is unknown, but it is a significant fact that the genealogies given for King Lulach and King Macbeth are headed " Genealogy of Clan Duff."

Certain privileges known as the " Law Clan Macduff " are referred to in an Act of 1384. These privileges were : First, that they should seat the king in his Royal chair on his coronation day ; second, that they should lead the vanguard in every Royal battle ; and third, a remission for homicide on a fixed payment, with sanctuary at Cross MacDuff, which stood to the north of Newburgh.

Gillimichel MacDuff was succeeded by his son, Duncan, and he again by his son, Duncan, 5th Earl. Duncan's son, Malcolm, was succeeded by his nephew, Malcolm, who left two sons—his successor, Colban, and MacDuff—his Christian name is not given—who was the primary cause of John Baliol's rebellion against Edward I. Duncan, the 11th Earl, died about 1353, leaving an only daughter, and the line of the Celtic Earls of Fife came to an end, the Earl of Wemyss being declared their representer by the Lord Lyon in 1757.

The Duffs of Banffshire claim descent from the Earls of Fife. It is possible that David Duff of Muldavit, in Banffshire (1401), was a descendant of the Earls of Fife, as was claimed, but there is no actual evidence. After the direct line of Craighead-Muldavit expired, Duff of Keithmore, descendant of Adam Duff of Clunybeg, assumed the chiefship and acquired vast estates in north-eastern Scotland during the 17th and 18th centuries. The representer of this line, William Duff of Braco, was created Lord Braco in 1725, and received in 1759 the titles of Viscount MacDuff and Earl of Fife in the Peerage of Ireland. James Duff, the 4th Earl, was created Baron Fife in the British Peerage in 1827, and Alexander, 6th Earl, was created Duke of Fife, 1889, on his marriage to Princess Louise, daughter of King Edward VII.

The present representative of the House of Braco is H.R.H. Princess Alexandra, who succeeded her father as Duchess of Fife in 1912. Duff of Drummuir was adjudged heir of line of Craighead in 1731 by Lyon Court. Duff of Hatton and Duff of Fetteresso are the other prominent Branches.

59. MACDUFF

N

MACEWEN

THIS clan was of considerable importance at one time. Its country was in Cowal. The MacEwens were known as *Clann Eóghain na h-Oitrich*—the MacEwens of Otter—and as late as 1750 there stood on a rocky point on the coast of Lochfyne, about a mile below the church at Kilfinnan, the vestige of a building called *Caisteal Mhic Eóghain*—MacEwen's Castle. The MacEwens were closely allied to the MacLachlans and the MacNeills. In the 12th century the Lamonts, the MacLachlans, and the MacEwens were in possession of the greater part of Cowal. The earliest chief of whom there is any account is understood to have flourished about the 13th century, and to have been succeeded by Severn (II.) of Otter. About 1315 Gillespie (V.) of Otter held the chiefship. From this date there were four chiefs—Ewen (VI.), John (VII.), Walter (VIII.), and Swene (IX.), the last of the Otter Chiefs.

In 1431–32 this Swene granted a charter of certain lands of Otter to Duncan, son of Alexander Campbell. In 1432 he resigned the Barony of Otter to James I., but received it anew from the king, with remainder to Celestine Campbell, son and heir of Duncan Campbell of Lochow. After Swene's death, King James in 1493 confirmed the grant to Archibald, Earl of Argyll, as heir to his father, Colin. In 1575 another Archibald Campbell appears in a charter as " of the Otter," and in the Act of 1587 a Campbell is entered as " the Laird of Otter."

After the middle of the 15th century the barony and estates of Otter having thus passed into the hands of a branch of the Campbells, the MacEwens became a scattered clan. As a necessity of the times some of them sought new alliances. Some appear to have followed MacLachlan of MacLachlan, and others sought protection as " men " of the Earl of Argyll. Some joined the Campbells of Craignish, while colonies were formed in the Lennox country in Dumbartonshire, and in Galloway.

The MacEwens were hereditary bards to the Campbells.

The only landed branch of the clan at present extant is M'Ewen of Bardrochat, in Ayrshire, and of Marchmont, in Berwick, descending from the Rev. John M'Ewen, and now represented by Captain John H. F. M'Ewen of Bardrochat, M.P., sometime Under-Secretary of State for Scotland, whose arms are here illustrated.

60. MACEWEN

MACFARLANE

Slogan :—" Loch Slòigh " (Loch Sloy).

Badge :—Muileag (Cranberry), Oireag or Foighreag (Cloudberry).

THE Clan Macfarlane is a branch of the ancient Celtic Earls of Lennox, deriving from Gilchrist, younger brother of Malduin, Earl of Lennox, who gave him the lands of Arrochar on the western shore of Loch Lomond about 1230, and in 1280 they were confirmed to his son and successor, Duncan MacGilchrist. Malduin, the 3rd Chief, was a supporter of The Bruce. The " wild Macfarlane's plaided clan " derives it's patronymic from the 4th Chief, Bartholomew, which in Gaelic is *Parlan*, and the slogan, " Loch Sloy," from a small loch near the foot of Ben Voirlich. John, 7th Chief, had a confirmation of Arrochar 1420, and Walter, 9th Chief, apparently fell at Sauchieburn. He was succeeded by his son, Andrew, 10th Chief, whose son, Sir John, 11th Captain of the Clan Macfarlane, fell in battle at Flodden, as did his grandson, Duncan, 13th of Macfarlane, at Pinkie, 1547. Andrew, 14th Chief, supported the Regent Murray at Langsyde, and this, it was said, turned the fate of war against Mary, Queen of Scots, that day. Walter, 16th Chief, 1624–64, was a Royalist who fought for the king under Montrose, and received confirmation of his coat of arms and a slogan from Lord Lyon Balfour. Walter Macfarlane of that Ilk, 20th Chief, was a celebrated antiquary who obtained a re-matriculation of the armorial achievement of the chiefs, with a destination to " his heirs," a term which, in Scots Law, and in the " Law of Arms " as applied in the 15th century Court of Chivalry, includes heirs female. Dying without issue 1767, he was succeeded by his brother, Andrew, who sold Arrochar 1785, and the direct male line expired with William Macfarlane, 25th of that Ilk, in 1866. His sister, Jane Macfarlane, Mrs Scott, was mother of Walter Macfarlane-Scott of Farmfield, Ayrshire, who succeeded to the heirlooms of the race, and in whom seems vested the right to the arms and chiefship, under the destination awarded to the 20th Chief, so that if he dropped the name of Scott and re-matriculated as *Macfarlane of that Ilk*, he would be the 27th and present chief. Among the most prominent cadets of the clan have been Macfarlane of Gartartan, and Macfarlane of Huntstown in Ireland.

A Macfarlane Society was established in Glasgow in 1912.

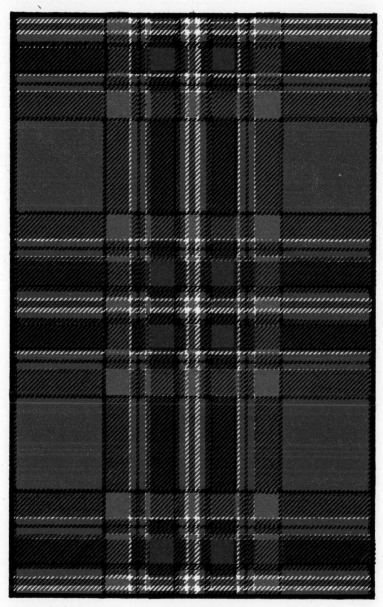

61. MACFARLANE

MACFIE

(MACPHEE)

Badge :—Darag (Oak) or Dearca fithich (Crowberry).

THE oldest form of this surname is MacDuffie (*MacDubh-sìthe*), and it is so written in a charter of 1463. The original home of the clan was Colonsay, of which they were in possession till about the middle of the 17th century. MacDuffie of Colonsay was Hereditary Keeper of the Records of the Lords of the Isles.

Murroch was the name of the MacDuffie Chief in 1531. In 1609 Donald Macfie of Colonsay was one of the twelve chiefs and gentlemen who met the Bishop of the Isles, the king's representative, at Iona, when the celebrated " Statutes of Icolmkill " were enacted, for the purpose of abrogating so far as the Lowlanders could, the ancient Celtic customary laws of the Lordship of the Isles. In 1615 Malcolm Macfie of Colonsay joined Sir James MacDonald of Islay after his escape from the Castle of Edinburgh, and was one of the principal leaders in his subsequent rebellions. He and eighteen others were delivered by Coll Kitto Mac-Donald (*Colla Ciotach*) to the Earl of Argyll, by whom he was brought before the Privy Council—for we learn that in 1623 Coll Kitto was delated for the murder of the umquhile Malcolm Macfee. From this period Colonsay seems to have gone into the possession of the Mac-Donalds, and afterwards to the Duke of Argyll, who exchanged Colonsay and Oronsay for Crerar, in South Knapdale, with Donald MacNeill, two of whose descendants have shed great lustre upon Colonsay—in law and in diplomacy—Lord Colonsay and his brother, the Right Hon. Sir John MacNeill, G.C.B.

On the death of Sir John Carstairs Macneill, V.C., K.C.M.G., in 1904, the Island was purchased by Lord Strathcona.

When the Macphees were dispossessed of their original inheritance they became a " broken clan," lost their independence, and so were obliged to rank under more powerful clans. The greater part followed the MacDonalds of Islay, while others settled in the country of the Camerons under Lochiel, where they were distinguished for their bravery.

Andrew Macfie of Langhouse, Renfrewshire, is now the most prominent landholder of this clan, and of this line Macfie of Dreghorn is a cadet. The arms shown are those recorded for Macfie of Dreghorn in 1864.

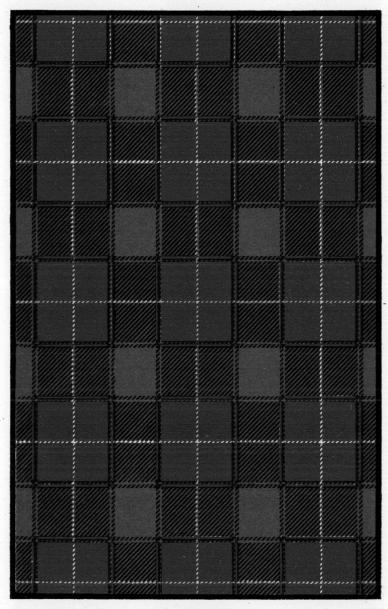

62.   MACFIE

MACGILLIVRAY

Slogan :—" Dunmaglass."

Badge :—Lus nam braoileag (Red Whortleberry).

THE MacGillivrays, one of the oldest septs of Clan Chattan, are known in Gaelic as *Clann Mhic Gillebhràth*, and, according to the Croy MS. history, it is said that about the year 1268 " Gillivray, the progenitor of Clan vic Gillivray, took protection and dependence for himself and posterity of this Farquhard Mackintosh (5th of Mackintosh, who was killed in 1274, aged thirty-six)." He was thus, by a process of adoption known to Celtic Law, indigenated into the Clan Mackintosh, and subsequently by Mackintosh's inheritance into the Clan Chattan.

It is more than likely that the MacGillivrays came originally from the West Coast—probably from Mull—where we find them centuries ago, and where they are still to be found in considerable numbers. Those of them who came northward must have settled at Dunmaglass many centuries ago.

Duncan MacGillivray, who flourished about 1500, is regarded as 1st of Dunmaglass. In 1609, when the famous Clan Chattan Bond of Union was signed, the MacGillivray Chief was a minor, and so the Bond was signed by three representatives of the clan on behalf of the heir.

The MacGillivrays took an active part in the Rising of 1715. The Laird and his brother, William, were Captain and Lieutenant respectively in the Clan Chattan Regiment. The clan was also " out " in " the '45," and were led at Culloden by Alexander, their chief, who fell, fighting, at a well on the battlefield, which still bears his name.

About the end of the 18th century the estate was in a very embarrassed condition, and the chief (William) got a captaincy in the Gordon Regiment. He died in 1783, and was succeeded by his son, John Lachlan MacGillivray of Dunmaglass, who possessed the estate for nearly seventy years. He died in 1852, " possessed of some £40,000 of money, which was destined by will, including a year's rent, to all his tenants ; also the heritable estates undisposed of, but free and unburdened." A legal competition arose as to all the estates except one, with the result that the patrimonial estates were dispersed. Since then no one has established his right to the chiefly arms and insignia.

The burial place of the chiefs of Dunmaglass, with many armorial tombstones, is in the picturesque kirkyard of Dunlichity. The arms shown above are those of a cadet, and differ considerably from those of the old chiefs carved in the burial ground of the MacGillivrays of Dunmaglass.

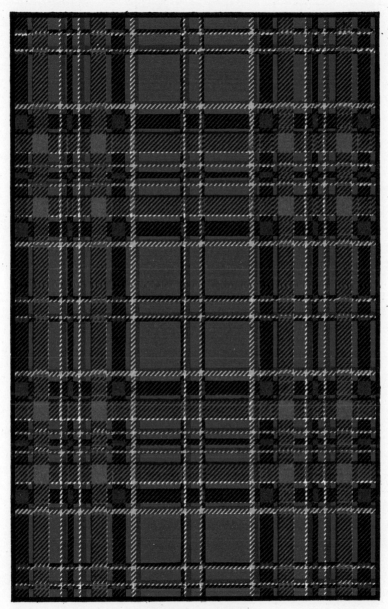

63. MACGILLIVRAY

MACGREGOR

Slogan :—" Ard Choille " (" High Wood ").

Badge :—Giuthas (Pine Tree).

THE ancient motto of this clan, " 'S Rioghail Mo Dream," claims for them a Royal descent, the clan tradition being that their founder was Gregor, brother of Kenneth Macalpine. Their earliest possessions were in Glenorchy, and the other motto of the family, " E'en do and spare nocht," is attributed to Sir Malcolm Macgregor of Glenorchy, who lived in the reign of David I. and is said to have been made a peer, but more probably received a feudal charter and juris-diction, presumably by actual investiture and without a charter, since the clan had subsequently to defend their lands *coira chlaidheimh*. Very likely the " dignity " was really a *Ken Kynol* such as those conferred or confirmed under the Great Seal by David II., and it is still more likely that it was *this* king and *not David I.* who made the " creation " ! Malcolm, Laird of Macgregor, was an adherent of The Bruce, whom he is said to have lodged in the King's Cave near Craigroyston, and his successor had several sons, of whom the fourth was ancestor of the Macgregors of Roro in Glenlyon, a great house which had many cadets, amongst them the Macgregor-Drummonds of Balhadie, one of whom. for political reasons, obtained himself to be elected chief of the clan in 1707. The second son, John Macgregor of Breachsliabh, succeeded his brother Malcolm in the chiefship, and the next chief, also Malcolm, lost many of the clan lands in the 15th century. Alexander Macgregor of that Ilk fought the celebrated Battle of Glenfruin in 1602, in which two hundred Colquhouns were slain, and other circumstances led to the prosecution of the clan, and the Laird of Macgregor was executed with many of his fol-lowers in 1604. Leaving no lawful issue, the chiefship was long disputed, the immediate claimant being his bastard son Gregor. Montrose recognised Patrick, Chief of the House of Brachsliabh, as Laird of Macgregor, and in the time of his son John, proscription of the name of Macgregor was renewed, and the chief was obliged to assume the name of Murray. John Macgregor Murray of Glencarnock assisted the Chevalier, but to prevent forfeiture of the remaining lands, the active support was conducted by Rob Roy Macgregor, the most-celebrated freebooter in Scottish history. The next chief, Robert of Glencarnoch, joined Prince Charles and fought at Culloden, but was pardoned and fell in the American Civil War. His nephew, John Murray-Macgregor, made a fortune in London, secured in November 1774 an Act in favour of the *Members of Clan Gregor* repealing the suppression of the name, and was created a Baronet in 1795, in which year, having (in consequence of the chief-ship being *de jure* and *de facto* vacant) been elected chief-designate, he was recognised by the Lord Lyon and granted the plain arms of the chief with heritable destination as Chief of the Macgregors. The present chief, Sir Malcolm Macgregor of Macgregor and Balquhidder, 5th Baronet, has his seat at Edinchip, Lochearnhead.

64.   MACGREGOR

MACINNES
(CLAN AONGHAIS)

THE clan Aonghais (Macinnes) is of Celtic origin, and formed, along with the MacGillivrays, a branch of the Siol Gillebride, the original inhabitants of Ardnamurchan and Morvern, but suffered in the conquest of Argyll by Alexander II. Tradition says that, after an expedition in which the Macinneses had distinguished themselves, their chief was addressed by the Lord of the Isles:

"*Mo bheannachd ort Fhir Ch'inn-Lochalainn! Fh'ad's a bhios MacDhomnuill a stigh, cha bhi MacAonghais a muigh.*" (My blessing on you, Chieftain of Kinlochaline! whilst Macdonald is in power, Macinnes shall be in favour.) The saying is an apt illustration of the use of the territorial title in Gaelic, as the appropriate style for a chief, or chieftain. Their last chief is said to have been murdered at Ardtornish in 1390, when the traditional tenure (whatever its nature) presumably terminated. Part of the clan became identified with the Macdougall-Campbells of Craignish, and another is said to have founded the hereditary bowmen of the Mackinnons in Skye. The Macinneses appear to have been Constables of the Castle of Kinlochaline, one of the most picturesque ruins of the Western mainland, whose massive walls and battlements overhang the rocky estuary of the Gearrabhrainn, and probably a Macinnes was its governor on behalf of the "Tutor of Kintail," during the siege by "young Colkitto" in 1645. If so, descendants of the race of the chief murdered in 1390 may have recovered possession as keepers of the castle, on which there are carvings of a stag hunt, and which is said to have been built by a dark-haired lady.

In the 17th and 18th centuries, the Kinlochaline branch appear to have been under the patronage of the House of Argyll, and to have supported the Covenanting and Hanoverian interests, but in 1745 one section of the clan followed Stewart of Ardsheal.

A family of Macinneses, descending from one "Neil an Bogha," were hereditary bowmen of the Clan Mackinnon.

The crest illustrated as a badge forms the crest of a coat of arms (unlawfully) assumed by the Rev. Niel Macinnes, Minister of Crathie, Aberdeenshire, in the 18th century, who was, however, a native of Argyll. No one of this clan has yet established his claim to to the arms in Lyon Court, or to the chiefship of the Clan Aonghais.

Kinlochaline.

65. MACINNES

MACINTYRE

Slogan :—" Cruachan " (A mountain near Loch Awe).

Badge :—Fraoch gorm (Common Heath).

IT is generally agreed that the Macintyres are an offshoot from Clan Donald. It is a well-known fact that the Macintyres of Glen Noe, Lochetive, occupied these lands for a period of 500 or 600 years prior to 1806. The tenure by which they held Glen Noe from the Campbells of Glenorchy, afterwards of Breadalbane, was a payment annually in summer of a snowball and a white fatted calf. The snowball could easily be got at the back of Cruachan, and as they always kept a white cow or two, a white calf was also procurable. This arrangement continued till about the beginning of the 18th century, when the tenant of Glen Noe, at the time, foolishly agreed to the payment being commuted into money, which then became rent, and was increased to so large a sum that the Macintryes could not pay it and make a comfortable living, and in 1806 they were under the necessity of parting with the home of their fathers—at least that is the story.

There was a strong colony of Macintyres resident for many generations at the village of Cladich, Loch Awe, where they carried on an extensive weaving industry.

A branch of the clan were dependents of the Campbells of Craignish, and are mentioned in 1612 as having given a bond of manrent to Campbell of Barrichbyan.

There were Macintyres in Badenoch who were attached to the Clan Chattan. In 1496 these Macintyres were, by William, 13th Chief of Mackintosh, admitted as a sept of the Clan Chattan. A family of Macintyres were hereditary pipers to Menzies of Menzies, while another family were hereditary pipers to MacDonald of Clan Ranald.

The Macintyres fought under the banner of the Stewarts of Appin in 1745.

MacIntyre of Sorn is at present the only laird in this clan. His seat is Sorn Castle, Ayrshire. The present laird, being a Senator of the College of Justice, is the Hon. Lord Sorn.

Modern Highland Dress (day dress).

66. MACINTYRE

MACKAY

Slogan :—" Bratach bhàn Chlann Aoidh " (" The White Banner of the Mackays "). *Badge* :—Seasgan or Cuilc (Reed Grass), and Great Bulrush.

THIS clan, anciently called *Clan-mhic-Morgainn*, derives through a cadet of Morgund of Pluscarden, from the royal house of MacEth, Mormaors of Moray. The old *Bratach bhàn Chlann Aoidh* bore the same arms as Innes, differenced by a hand, and as both bore *segs* for badge/crest, it seems probable that, whilst a daughter was " given " to the grantee of Innes 1160, the line of Malcolm MacEth became Earls of Ross under the Morayshire re-settlement of King Malcolm IV., but ere long, being deprived of this, retired farther north, and the immediate ancestor of *Clan Aoidh* was *Iye MacEth*, Chamberlain of the Bishopric of Caithness, whose son *Iye Mor MacIye* got 12 davachs of land in Durness from the Bishop, and the House of Tongue in Strathnaver became the seat of the Mackay chiefs. In 1427 Angus Dhu Mackay was chief of 4000 clansmen and his second son, Ian, was ancestor of the Aberach Mackays. In 1529 Donald Mackay of Strathnaver had his lands erected into a barony of Farr. His son, the next chief, Iye Dhu Mackay, lost this barony in the turmoil of Queen Mary's reign, but it was recovered by his son, Huistean Dhu, who married Lady Jane, daughter of Alexander, Earl of Sutherland, and claimed kinship with Clan Forbes. His son, Sir Donald Mackay of Strathnaver, royalist and soldier of fortune in the wars of Gustavus Adolphus, was in 1628 created a Baronet, and was also created Lord Reay with remainder to his heirs-male bearing the name and arms of Mackay, thus tailziing the chiefship. Strathnaver was sold to meet the debts of the 1st Lord Reay in 1642, and the " Reay country " was sold to the house of Sutherland in 1829. John, 2nd Lord, was an ardent supporter of Charles I. His third son, General The Hon. Aeneas Mackay, settled in Holland where his great-grandson, Barthold, was created Baron Mackay of Ophemert, and his son, Sir Donald James, 11th Baronet of Strathnaver, K.T., was created Lord Reay in the United Kingdom peerage 1881. His cousin Sir Aeneas Mackay, 13th Lord Reay, matriculated arms as Chief of the Clan Mackay.

Whilst the chiefs were distinguished as royalists, General Mackay of Scourie, defeated by Viscount Dundee at Killiecrankie, was an adherent of William of Orange and subsequently defeated the Jacobite army at the Haughs of Cromdale in 1690.

To another race of Mackays, in the South, belonged Brian Vicar Mackay, to whom the Lord of the Isles granted the celebrated Gaelic charter in 1408.

The Clan Mackay Society was founded in 1806 and resuscitated in 1888. Its headquarters are in Glasgow.

67. MACKAY

MACKENZIE

Slogan :—" Tulach Ard " (A mountain in Kintail).

Badge :—Cuileann (Holly).

THERE is little definite evidence regarding the early history of the chiefs of this clan—

" MacKenneth, great Earl of the North,
The Lord of Loch Carron, Glenshiel,
and Seaforth "—

but in 1450 " Murdoch, son of Kenneth, son of John, son of Kenneth, son of Angus, son of Christian, son of Adam, son of Gilleoin-Oig of the Aird," is the genealogy given.

Alexander, " Ionraech," 7th Chief of Kintail, the first for whom there is authentic evidence, was a young man in 1427 when he was summoned to meet James I. He lived until 1488. His grandson, John, followed James IV. to Flodden with a body of his clan, and narrowly escaped being made prisoner. He was faithful to Mary of Guise, Queen-Regent, fought in his old age at Pinkie, and died in 1561. His grandson, Colin, is said to have fought for Queen Mary at Langside, but having acknowledged James VI. in 1569 he was pardoned by the Regent Moray.

Kenneth, his eldest son by Barbara Grant of that Ilk, was raised to the Peerage in 1609 as Lord Mackenzie of Kintail. From these descended the Mackenzies of Pluscarden and Lochslinn. Colin, their eldest son, was created Earl of Seaforth in 1623. Dying without issue, 1633, the title devolved on his half-brother, George, 2nd Earl, who went to Holland after the murder of Charles I., and was subsequently Secretary of State for Scotland.

Kenneth, 3rd Earl of Seaforth, was a loyal Cavalier excepted from pardon by Cromwell ; his estates were seized, but an allowance was given to his Countess, Isabel Mackenzie of Tarbat.

His son, Kenneth, 4th Earl, was an original K.T. in 1687. He followed James VII. to Ireland and France, and was created Marquis of Seaforth in the Jacobite peerage 1690. In his time was pronounced the celebrated prophecy of " the Brahan Seer," foretelling the doom of the family.

He died in 1701, and was succeeded by William, 5th Earl, who was attainted in 1715, and with the Marquis of Tullibardine and the Earl Marischal, was at the battle of Glenshiel in 1719. The Jacobites were dispersed, and the Earl of Seaforth fell severely wounded, but made his escape to France, where he remained till pardoned in 1726, after which he returned to Scotland and spent the remainder of his life in peace and retirement. He died in 1740, and would have been succeeded by his son Kenneth, Lord Fortrose, as 6th Earl, but for the attainder.

The fighting force of the Mackenzies is given by Forbes at 2500 men.

Kenneth, son of Lord Fortrose, having repurchased the property from the Crown, was created an Irish Peer as Viscount Fortrose, and in 1771 Earl of Seaforth. In gratitude, therefore, he and the clan of the " Caberfeidh," as the Mackenzies are called, in 1778 raised the old Seaforth Highlanders (the 72nd), 1000 strong, for service in India.

On his death the chiefship passed to his cousin, Thomas, who died in 1783, when his younger brother, Francis Humberston Mackenzie, succeeded and

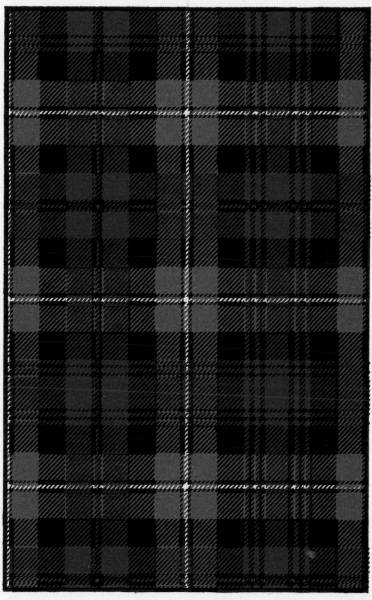

68. MACKENZIE

was created Lord Seaforth 1797. He died 1815, when his peerage expired, and the arms of the Mackenzie chiefs were by decree of the Lyon Court confirmed to his daughter and heiress, Mary, Lady Hood-Mackenzie of Seaforth. By her second husband, the Hon. James A. Stewart, she was grandmother of James, 12th Laird of Seaforth and Chief of the Clan Mackenzie, created Lord Seaforth of Brahan 1921. In 1890, "as present chief of the clan," he successfully interceded with the Crown to prevent the title "of Kintail" being awarded to a cadet. Lord Seaforth dying without issue, his grandnephew, the Hon. Francis Allan Stewart-Mackenzie of Seaforth succeeded, and, falling in action without issue, was succeeded by his cousin, Madam Helena Stewart-Mackenzie of Seaforth, now (saving objection to the double-surname) Chief of the Mackenzies, who holds their ancient seat, Brahan Castle. In 1829, the chiefship was claimed by Mackenzie of Allangrange as heir male, but in 1817 he only received the arms of a cadet. In 1904 his line expired. Rory Mackenzie of Cogeauch, uncle of the 1st Lord Mackenzie of Kintail, was ancestor of the Earls of Cromartie, created 1703. George, 3rd Earl, was forfeited for his share in the Rising of 1745, but the estates were restored and have descended, along with a new Earldom, created 1861, to Sibell, Countess of Cromartie, whose seat is Castle Leod, Strathpeffer.

The Mackenzies have also several Baronetcies—those of Gairloch, 1703 ; Coul, 1673 ; Tarbet, 1628 ; and Scatwell, 1703 ; Glenmuick.

MACKINLAY

THERE can be little doubt the county of this clan was in the Lennox district, where we find them yet in considerable numbers. The oldest account of them is given by Buchanan of Auchmar, 1723. He asserts that the chief sept of the Lennox Mackinlays were descended from Buchanan of Drumikill. After mentioning that the Risks are the first cadets of the Drumikill family, he says : " The second cadets of this kin are the Mackinlays, so named from a son of Drumikill called Finlay ; those lately in Blairnyle and about Balloch are of this sort, as also those in Bamachra and above the Water of Finn, in Luss parish. The Mackinlays in some other parts of these parishes are MacFarlanes."

Like so many Lennox clans, notably their far-off cousins of the Clan MacAuslane, some of the Mackinlays no doubt went over to Ireland at the time of the " plantations " in the 17th century. Hence come the Mackinlays and Macginlays of Ireland, and latterly of America.

It is a common mistake to regard the clan ancestor as *Fionnlagh Mor*, progenitor of the Farquharsons of Braemar. The Farquharsons as a clan are called in Gaelic *Clann Fhionnlaigh*, but the surname *MacFhionnlaigh* has never come to be used in English form. In fact, the surname has been constantly Farquharson, and there were no Mackinlays at all in Braemar or its vicinity. The small Clan Finlayson of Lochalsh are known in Gaelic as *Clann Fhionnlaigh*, and they, too, claim a traditional descent from the Clan Finlay of Braemar. It is probable the name Mackinlay embraces some of the Macleay clan. Some of the modern Mackinlays insist on accenting the "lay" of the name.

69. MACKINLAY

MACKINNON

Slogan :—" Cuimhnich bàs Ailpein " (" Remember the death of Alpin ").

Badge :—Giuthas (Pine Tree).

THE older forms of this clan surname show it to be Fingon, and they claim descent from Fingon, younger son of Alpin, King of Scots, who was slain by Bruch, King of the Picts, in 837. In 1409 Lachlan MacFingon, *vir nobilis* (*i.e.* a gentleman), witnessed a charter of the Lord of the Isles to Hector Maclean of Duart. The original country of the clan was Mull, where they held lands under the Lords of the Isles. They had also possessions in Strathardal, Skye, as early as 1594. The Mackinnons were associated with Iona, and a John Mackinnon was the last Abbot. In 1503 Mackinnon of that Ilk is mentioned to take action against Lachlan Maclean of Duart and Lochiel.

Ewen, who was chief of the clan in the 16th century, received from the king a charter of the twenty merklands of Meysness (Mishnish), in Mull, and the twenty merklands of Strathardal, in Skye.

Sir Lachlan Mackinnon of Strathard, 28th Chief, was a Royalist, and was created Knight-Banneret by Charles II. on the field at Worcester, 1651.

The clan was " out " in 1745, and fought at Culloden ; their old chief was taken, and, after long imprisonment, died in 1756.

Charles, his son, found the estates so burdened with debt that he had to part with them, and Strathaird, the last of the clan lands, held in unbroken succession for 450 years, passed from the clan in 1791. Charles left an only son, John, the last of his line, who succeeded to nothing but the chiefship. He died in 1808, whereupon William A. Mackinnon, M.P. for Dunwich in 1811, got a Lyon Court decree recognising him as Chief of Mackinnon. He was descended from William Mackinnon of Antigua, who in 1756 got arms as a cadet of the main line. Mackinnon of Corry, in Skye, asserts a claim to the chiefship, and the heir of line of John (*d.* 1808) had a better claim, but neither of them opposed, or timeously reduced, the matriculation of 1811, on which prescription has now passed, so the present line is definitely established in the honours according to the Law of Arms. Accordingly Mackinnon of Corry and Pitminster was in 1947 recognised by Lyon Court only as Chieftain of Corrycatachan.

Francis Mackinnon of Mackinnon, 35th Chief, who resided at Drumduan, near Forres, died 1947, aged 95, and his son Arthur A. Mackinnon of Mackinnon, is the present chief.

There is a Clan Mackinnon Society in Glasgow, with a branch in London. *Memoirs of Clan Fingon* was published in 1899.

70. MACKINNON

MACKINTOSH

Slogan :—" Loch Mòigh " (Loch of the Plain), with Chief's castle-island.
Badge :—Lus nam braoileag (Red Whortleberry).

THE name Mackintosh—*i.e. Mac-an-Tosach*—means " son of the Chief," and the Chiefship of Mackintosh is by their old historians treated as passing with the *duthus*. The founder of the clan was, according to tradition which, both on the arms and Wemyss genealogy, has received official sanction, a younger son of MacDuff, ancestor of the Earls of Fife, who was settled in the Laigh o' Moray after the subjection of that Province. The Mackintoshes, since their marriage with the heiress, form the " stem family " of Clan Chattan. Ferquhard, 9th Chief, abdicated, and from him descended the first house of Kyllachy and the Slioch Ferquhar vich Lachlan, amongst which is the heir male of the race. The first really powerful chief was Malcolm (1430–64). The clan lands stretched from Petty to Lochaber, but none were held directly from the Crown. His relations with the Lord of the Isles, or Earls of Ross, were cordial, and his son, Duncan, married Flora, the Earl's daughter.

William, 16th Chief, was the first Mackintosh Chief to get into difficulties with Huntly, Lord-Lieutenant of the North and Sheriff of Inverness-shire. He was tried in Aberdeen for conspiring against Huntly's life, and by a packed jury found guilty. He was executed at Strathbogie, 1550. The estates, with compensation for the murder, were held for his heir through the powerful influence of the Earl of Moray and other relatives.

For the next two hundred years the clan was engaged in feuds with the Gordons, the Camerons, and the Macdonells of Keppoch. In 1678 Mackintosh got the usual " fire and sword " commission, but it was not till 1688 that he could get his friends and clansmen to help him. These, with a company of Regulars under MacKenzie of Suddie, fought with the Macdonells at Mulroy and were defeated. This was the last clan battle. Lachlan, who was chief from 1660, was formally declared Chief of Clan Chattan by the Lord Lyon King of Arms in 1672. He died in 1704, and was succeeded by his son, Lachlan, who took a gallant part in the 1715 and was created " Lord Mackintosh." He died, childless, in 1731, and for a hundred years thereafter no son succeeded a father among the Mackintosh chiefs. His successor was William of Daviot, 22nd Chief, whose brother Angus, 23rd Chief, during " the '45 " gave half-hearted support of King George ; while his wife, " Colonel Anne," and the clan took the field for Prince Charlie, when her strategy won for the Jacobites the engagement named the " Rout of Moy." His successor, Sir Æneas, created a Baronet 1812, died without issue, having entailed the chiefship and estates, which so descended until the succession, 1876, of Alfred Donald, 28th Chief of the Name of Mackintosh and 29th Chief of Clan Chattan.

The Mackintosh died 1938, having by tanistry settled the *duthus* and chiefship on his cousin, Rear-Admiral Lachlan Mackintosh of Mackintosh, C.B., to whom, as *The Mackintosh*, the arms and chiefship were confirmed by Lyon Court in 1947. The chiefship of Clan Chattan passed in 1938 to Alfred Donald's granddaughter, Arbell (who became Mrs Anthony Warre, 1942), when (she no longer bearing the officially recognised " name " of the stem-family of Clan Chattan) the Chiefship of Clan Chattan and the galley arms were held by Lyon Court to have passed to Duncan Alexander Mackintosh of Mackintosh—Torcastle and Clan Chattan, 31st Chief, who resides in Southern Rhodesia. The seat of Rear-Admiral Lachlan Mackintosh of Mackintosh, C.B., 29th Chief of Mackintosh, is Moy Hall, Inverness-shire—the home of the chiefs for over 600 years.

71. MACKINTOSH

MACLACHLAN

Badge: Caorunn (Mountain Ash or Rowan).

THE Maclachlans are believed to have been in possession of Strathlachan, in Argyllshire, since the 11th century. At one time they owned extensive lands in Argyllshire, which are now reduced to the Barony of Maclachlan or Strathlachlan. Their intermarriages are given in the MS. of 1450, and are with such families as those of the Lords of the Isles, the King of Kerry, etc. Lachlan Mor is the chief from whom those succeeding are enumerated. His successor was Gilespic and in 1292 the lands of Gilespic Maclachlan were included in the Sheriffdom of Argyll or Lorn, erected in that year by King John Baliol. From Gilespic there is no difficulty in tracing the direct line down to the present day. Strathlachlan was erected into a feudal barony for Archibald Maclachlan of that Ilk in 1680.

The Maclachlans threw in their fate with Prince Charles, and it says much for the popularity of Lachlan Maclachlan of that Ilk, 17th Chief, that he was able to make his way with his men from the very centre of Argyll and join the Prince in the North, despite the fact that he was surrounded by Campbells and other keen partisans of the House of Hanover. Maclachlan was appointed A.D.C. to the Prince, and was killed at Culloden. The lands were confiscated after "the '45," but his son and heir, Robert, was granted possession by a judgment of the Court, dated 28th November, 1749, and from him the later chiefs are descended.

The three original tribes of Cowal are said to have been the Lamonts, the MacEwens, and the Maclachlans. The Lamonts and Maclachlans intermarried several times.

The eldest cadet of the clan is Maclachlan of Coruanan, in Lochaber, who held the position of hereditary standard-bearer to the Camerons of Lochiel. Another important branch was Maclachlan of Kilchoan.

The 23rd Chief, John Maclachlan of that Ilk, Vice-Lieutenant of Argyll, died in 1942, and was succeeded by his eldest daughter, Madam Marjorie MacLachlan of MacLachlan, 24th Chief of the Clan, to whom the undifferenced arms have been confirmed, in the words of Lord Advocate Mackenzie "as Representative of the Family and in Gaelic Head of the Clan," and whose seat is Castle Lachlan, Strathlachlan, Loch Fyne.

72. MACLACHLAN

MACLAREN

Slogan :—" Creag an Tuirc " (" The Boar's Rock ").

Badge :—Buaidh-chraobh, na Labhras (Laurel).

ACCORDING to the Official Record in Lyon Court the chiefs of this clan were understood to have been for generations proprietors of the Island of Tiree. The MacLarens, in Gaelic, are called *Clann mhic Labhrainn*, and in English the surname is sometimes written MacLaurin. The clan is an ancient one, and in the earlier period of their history were possessed of considerable influence. From various causes they gradually declined in importance and strength.

It has been asserted that they signed the Ragman Roll of 1296, compelled for the time, like many other clans, to swear fealty to King Edward I., and they did so under three branches, represented by Maurice of Tiree, Conan of Balquhidder, and Laurin of Ardveche (Lochearnside). It appears, however, that Maurice of Tyrie belonged to a different and Perthshire family.

An interesting and romantic episode in their history is their alliance —offensive and defensive, it may be called—with the Stewarts of Appin. It arose out of the love-at-first-sight attachment of the third last of the " Stewart " Lords of Lorn in the 15th century for the beautiful daughter of MacLaurin of Ardveche, and their subsequent marriage and legitimation of their son, Dugald, who became the founder of the famous Stewarts of Appin. Chieftains of the line of Ardveche occupied that holding until 1888 when Donald MacLaren in Ardveche was the last of that line.

In local history the clan had their full share of clan feuds with their neighbours—the Buchanans, Campbells, and MacGregors. On one occasion, in the 12th century, a pitched battle took place in Strathyre over an insult to a MacLaren, when they practically annihilated the Buchanans of Leny.

It is interesting to note that it was in connection with some legal proceedings anent the MacLaurins of Invernentie that Sir Walter Scott made his first acquaintance with the Highlands. In 1781 John Mac-Laurin, Lord Dreghorn, son of Professor Colin MacLaurin, established in Lyon Court his claim to chiefship of this clan. He adduced evidence of his representation of the line of MacLaren which possessed Tiree.

The clan is at present landless and chiefless.

73. MACLAREN

MACLAINE OF LOCHBUIE

Badge :—Blaeberry.

THE Lochbuie Maclaines are descended from Hector Reaganach, brother of Lachlan Lùbanach, the progenitor of the Macleans of Duart. Hector Reaganach received the lands of Lochbuie from John, 1st Lord of the Isles. According to tradition, these lands were held in possession by a chieftain named MacFadyen. Hector founded the Lochbuie branch of the Macleans. He had several sons. Tearlach (Charles) was the progenitor of *Clan Thearlaich* of Dochgarroch, or the Macleans of the North. The 2nd Chief of Lochbuie was Murdoch Roy, son of Hector Reaganach.

A quite unnecessary dispute raged in the 19th century regarding the seniority of Hector and Lachlan—with supposed relation to the chiefship of the Clan Maclean. The point is immaterial, as under tanistry a chief could nominate his successor, and Duart was certainly the chief family of the clan. A large clan may have branch clans, and Maclaine of Lochbuie is such within the Clan Maclean.

When John Og (V.) of Lochbuie died he was succeeded by his son, Murchadh Geàrr, or Short Murdoch, about 1494. His uncle, Murdoch of Scallasdale, seized the estate and tried to keep possession of it. Murdoch Gearr fled to Ireland but soon returned, supported by a strong bodyguard. He made himself known to his nurse, who helped him to gain possession of the Castle of Lochbuie. Shortly afterwards he defeated Murdoch of Scallasdale at Grulin.

The Maclaines served with Graham of Claverhouse, Viscount Dundee, and also under Montrose with their kinsmen, the Macleans of Duart. Hector Maclaine of Lochbuie, with 300 men, on his march to join Dundee, was attacked by five troops of horse sent by the enemy to intercept him. The parties met, and, after a severe fight, Lochbuie put the horse to flight and killed the commander.

Donald (20th) of Lochbuie was born in 1816. He went to Batavia in Java, entered into business as a merchant, and amassed quite a fortune. He purchased the estate of Lochbuie from the creditors who held it for debt, and thus, fortunately, saved it from passing out of the hands of the descendants of Hector Reaganach. From his grandson, Kenneth Douglas Lorne Maclaine of Lochbuie, the estate was recently seized by an English bondholder. His son, Gillean Robert, is the present and 23rd Chief of the Maclaines of Lochbuie, and has, it is understood, the real right to the old tower of Lochbuie.

74. MACLAINE OF LOCHBUIE

MACLEAN OF DUART

Slogan :—" Beatha no Bàs " (" Life or Death ") and " Fear eil' airson Eachainn " (" Another for Hector "). Used alternately.

Badges :—Dearca fithich (Crowberry), used by Duart, Brolas, Pennycross, Drimnin ; Cuileann (Holly), used by Ardgour, Coll, Dochgarroch.

THE progenitor of this clan was *Gilleain-na-Tuaighe*, or Gillean of the Battle Axe, who flourished in the reign of Alexander III. The axe which rendered him famous is represented in the Maclean crest. In 1294 " Gillemoir Mackilyn " signed Ragman Roll. His son, Malise, supported the Bruce and was father of Gillicullum who fought at Bannockburn. In the reign of Robert II. this chief's son, Ian Dhu Maclean, settled in Mull. He had two sons, Lachlan Lùbanach, progenitor of the Macleans of Duart, and Eachann Reaganach, the progenitor of the Maclaines of Lochbuie. These brothers appear first as followers of the Lord of Lorn ; but some dispute having arisen, they left him and followed Macdonald, Lord of the Isles, who received them with great favour. Lachlan Lùbanach afterwards married Margaret, daughter of the Lord of the Isles, and was appointed his Lieutenant-General in war. His son, *Eachan Ruadh nan Cath* (" Red Hector of the Battles ") fell at Harlaw 1411, where he and Irvine of Drum killed each other.

The Clan Maclean acquired extensive possessions in Mull, Tiree, Coll, Islay, Morvern, and Lochaber. On the forfeiture of the last Lord of the Isles, the Macleans appear to have gradually risen on the ruins of that great clan. Towards the close of the 16th century the MacDonalds appear to have united for the purpose of effectively crushing the rising power of the Macleans.

In 1632 Lachlan Maclean of Morven, brother and heir of Hector Maclean of Duart, was created a Baronet. He was a zealous Royalist, and died in 1649. Sir Hector, the 2nd Baronet, fell at Inverkeithing, and Sir John, 4th Baronet, raised the clan for James VII. in 1689 and fought under Viscount Dundee. The direct line of Duart became extinct in 1750, on the death of Sir Hector, 5th Baronet, and the honours and chiefship then devolved upon Alan Maclean of Brolas, next cadet in succession. Sir Fitzroy Maclean, 10th Baronet, succeeded in repurchasing Duart Castle, a magnificent Highland stronghold occupying the verge of a lofty cliff on the coast of Mull. A building of great antiquity, it includes a square tower with walls of enormous thickness, and there he lived to be a hundred and one. His grandson, Sir Charles Hector Fitzroy Maclean of Duart, is 11th Baronet, and present chief of the clan. There is a Clan Maclean Society in Glasgow.

Duart.

220

75. MACLEAN OF DUART

MACLEOD OF THE LEWES

(BRANCH OF THE LEWES AND RAASAY)

THE Clan Macleod consists of two great branches descending from Tormod and Torquil, the sons of Leod who got the island of Lewis from his father Olaf, King of Man, and acquired Dunvegan and Trotternish by marriage with the daughter and heiress of Macrailt, the Norse *Armuin* in Skye. From Tormod, the elder son, sprang the Macleods of Macleod, whilst Torquil, the younger, became 2nd Baron of the Lewes. The line continued directly to Torquil, 8th Baron of the Lewes, upon whose forfeiture, 1506, the Crown conferred the estates upon his brother Malcolm, 9th Baron, whose son, Roderick, 10th Baron of the Lewes, nominated his youngest son, *Torquil Dhu*, as 11th Chief of the Lewes. He was killed by his eldest brother, the disinherited *Torquil Conanach*. Margaret, Torquil's daughter, having married Sir Rory Mackenzie of Cogeach, the Lewes passed to the Mackenzie Earls of Cromartie, who, according to Lord Royston, the 18th-century judge, also inherited the chiefship of the Clan Macleod of Lewis and as such bore as their second title *Lord Macleod*. The male representation of the *Siol Torquil* devolved upon the Macleods of Raasay, descending from *Malcolm Garbh*, younger brother of Roderick, 10th of the Lewes. Malcolm received the Isle of Raasay from his father early in the 16th century. His grandson, Malcolm, 3rd of Raasay, had a Great Seal Charter 1571. On the death of John Macleod, 6th of Raasay, the estate passed to his sisters, of whom Janet the elder married Macrae of Inverinate, but neither carrying on the race of Macleod they, in 1692, resigned the estate to their cousin and " heir of expectance," Alexander Macleod, a grandson of the 4th Laird. He became 7th of Raasay. Malcolm, 8th of Raasay, joined Prince Charles Edward in 1745. His son, John Macleod, 9th of Raasay, established in Lyon Court 1779, his being heir male of the house of Macleod of the Lewes, and his descendant, Captain Torquil Bright Macleod, 14th Chieftain of Raasay, is the male representative, with arms as " chiefest cadet " of the *Siol Torquil* (*i.e.* differenced by two crosses). Raasay was sold by the 11th Laird in 1846, and the 14th Chieftain resides in Tasmania. Macleod of Cadboll, a cadet of Macleod of Assynt, is another existing cadet of the *Siol Torquil* descending from the 5th Baron of the Lewes. Of this house Captain Robert D. B. Macleod of Cadboll still holds the ruined fortress of his ancestors on the Ross-shire coast.

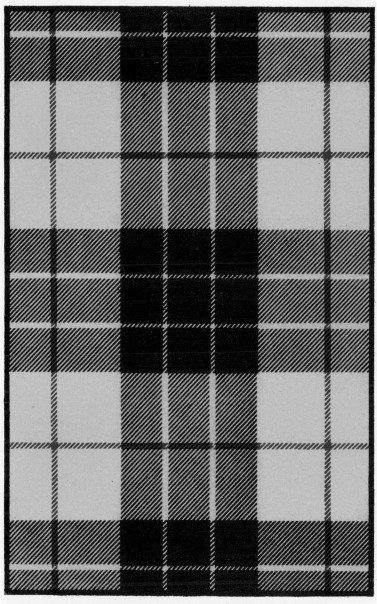

76. MACLEOD OF LEWIS AND RAASAY

MACLEOD OF MACLEOD

(HOUSE OF HARRIS AND DUNVEGAN)

Badge : Juniper.

Murus aheneus esto

LEOD, son of Olaf the Black, King of Man, acquired Dunvegan by marriage with the heiress of MacRailt, the Norwegian *Armuin* of Dunvegan, and his two sons became respectively progenitors of the Siol Tormod, or Macleods of Harris and Dunvegan, and the Siol Torquil, or Macleods of Lewis. Tormod is reckoned the elder, and his descendants subsequently held the chiefly style, Macleod of Macleod. Ian, 4th Chief, who flourished in the 14th century, received the Fairy Flag still preserved at Dunvegan, said to be the gift of a fairy princess to whom, by some accounts, he was married. William, 7th Chief, was killed in a feud with the Macdonalds at the "Battle of the Bloody Bay," and was succeeded by Alastair Crotach, 8th Chief, who captured Duntulm Castle, acquired Trotternish, and entertained James V. at a mountain feast on Macleod's Table, 1536. He also built the "Fairy Tower" at Dunvegan Castle. Being hump-backed, he married Lochiel's tenth daughter, the other nine having refused him, and the succession eventually devolved on his third son, Tormod, 13th Chief, father of William, 14th Chief, and Sir Rory Mor, 16th Chief, who settled the feud with the Macdonalds, enlarged Dunvegan Castle, and is the most celebrated of his line. Roderick, 18th Chief, was a Royalist, and was made a Colonel in the Army of Charles II. His brother, Ian Breack, 19th Chief, further embellished the castle in 1689, and there in 1773 Norman, 22nd Chief, entertained Boswell and Johnson. His portrait in plaid and trews is a valuable example of an 18th-century chief's garb. Much of the extensive MacLeod estates have passed from the race, but the 27th Chief (who d. 1935), Sir Reginald Macleod of Macleod, K.C.B., sometime Under-Secretary for Scotland, and Registrar-General, held their ancient seat, Dunvegan Castle. His elder daughter has, under the settlement of the Macleod estates, succeeded him, and has been officially recognised by the Lord Lyon as Flora, Mrs Macleod of Macleod, with confirmation of the chief arms and supporters, and has consequently become 28th Chief of the Clan Macleod in accordance with the old Celto-Scottish order of succession. Her seat is Dunvegan Castle in Skye. There is a Clan Macleod Society in Edinburgh.

Dunvegan.

77. MACLEOD OF HARRIS

MACMILLAN

Badge :—Cuileann (Holly).

THE origin of this clan is difficult to determine. It is pretty generally believed that they are of ecclesiastical origin. In the Highlands an individual member of the clan is referred to by Gaelic-speaking people as *MacMhaoilein* or *Mac-Gillemhaoil*—*maol* being the Gaelic for bald or tonsured.

A branch of the clan is found at Loch Arkaig, in Lochaber, at an early period. They were among the loyal followers of Lochiel. From Loch Arkaig the clan, as tradition says, were removed by Malcolm IV. (1153–65) and placed on the Crown lands of Loch Tay in Perthshire. The estate of Lawers belonged to them. From Lawers they were driven in the 14th century. Some of them migrated southward to Knapdale on the Argyllshire coast, and others to Galloway. The Knapdale branch soon attained to considerable power and influence. Their chief was Macmillan of Knap, a person of acknowledged importance in the district. The lands were held under a charter from the Lord of the Isles to endure " so long as the waves beat on the rock," but alas, circumstances have struck at that " fixity of tenure " so dear to the Celt, and Macmillan of Knap is no more. In course of time the direct line of the Knap family became extinct, and the chiefship went to Macmillan of Dunmore, an estate lying on the south side of Loch Tarbert. Duncan Macmillan of Dunmore had Arms registered in 1742, and he is described as " representative of the ancient family of Macmillan of Knap." After a while this branch also died out, when the MacNeills, by right of their intermarriage with the Macmillans, claimed the property. They were opposed by the Campbells ; but the dispute was amicably adjusted by the estate passing by purchase into the hands of Sir Archibald Campbell of Inverneil in 1775.

The Macmillans of Galloway are a well-known branch of the clan. Hugh P. Macmillan, a distinguished lawyer and judge, was created Lord Macmillan of Aberfeldy, in 1930—a life peerage.

In some parts of Argyllshire the Macmillans are known as " *Na Belich* "—the Bells.

There is a Clan Macmillan Society in Glasgow.

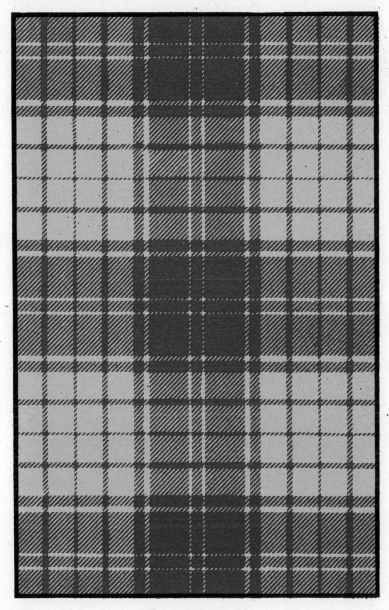

78. MACMILLAN

MACNAB

Badge :—Roebuckberry (Stone Bramble), also *Dearca fithich* (Crowberry).

LIKE several other Highland clans, the Macnabs are of ecclesiastical origin. In Gaelic they are called "*Clann-an-Aba*" Children of the Abbot—and are descended from the Abbots of Glendochart. The clan lands were situated at the side of Loch Tay, and stretched along the course of the Dochart to the head of Strathfillan. The residence of the chief was at Kinnel, on the banks of the Dochart, and although himself chief of a clan, Macnab acknowledged himself a branch of the Clan Mackinnon.

The Macnabs suffered much in the early decades of the 14th century. They took arms against Bruce, and after Bannockburn their estates were forfeited and granted by Bruce to his loyal supporters. In 1336 Gilbert Macnab made peace with King David II., and obtained a charter for the Barony of Bovain, in Glendochart.

In 1612 the sons of Macnab stormed the stronghold of the Neishes, with whom Macnab was at feud, and put all save two to the sword. The old chief gave the hint by observing, " Gin the nicht were the nicht, and the lads were the lads." On returning with the heads of their foes young Macnab observed, "The nicht *wis* the nicht, and the lads *were* the lads."

Iain Mìn, or Smooth John (VIII.), led the clan under Montrose in 1645. In 1745 the family of the chief fought for the House of Hanover ; but the clan was " out " for the Stewarts under Acharn, Inchewen, and Dundurn. John Macnab (XI.) died in 1788, and Francis became 12th Chief. He is the subject of Raeburn's famous portrait, " The Macnab." On this death, at Callander, in 1815, his nephew, Archibald, son of Dr. Robert Macnab, became chief. Owing to financial difficulties, Archibald (XIII.) was obliged to sell his estates. He went to Canada in 1821, but returned in 1853. He obtained a grant of territory and took steps to found a clan community in Canada, which in spite of arduous conditions almost established itself. The chief, however, inspired by desire to repurchase the old clan country in Scotland, overtaxed the resources of the clansmen, and his great plans were brought to nought by the machinations of a traitorous dominie. He died in France in 1860, aged eighty-three, having nominated his cousin, Sir Allan Macnab, Baronet, of Montreal, heir to the chiefship. The 13th Chief was survived by a widow and one daughter, out of a family of eight. His daughter, Sophia Frances Macnab of Macnab, died at Florence in 1894. Sir Allan, 14th Chief, died in 1862, since when the chiefship has been dormant, and it is not meantime precisely known what was the destination beyond Sir Allan.

A family of Macnabs were, for a period of four hundred years, hereditary armourers and jewellers to the Campbells of Loch Awe, whose seat was at Kilchurn Castle.

There is a Clan Society, with its headquarters in Edinburgh.

79. MACNAB

MACNAGHTEN

Slogan :—" Fraoch Eilean " (" The Heathery Isle," Loch Awe).

Badge :—Lus Albanach (Trailing Azalea).

THE earliest authentic reference to the Clan MacNaghten connects them with Strathtay and Argyllshire. The name Nectan is Pictish, and in the 12th century the Clan MacNaghten were proprietors of Strathtay, and were styled *Tòiseachs* or Thanes of Lochtay. In the 13th century we find them possessing land in Argyllshire. These possessions extended over the upper part of Lochawe, Glenara, Glenshira, and Loch Fyne. Their strongholds were " Fraoch Eilean " Castle, Loch Awe, Castle " Dubh-Loch " in Glenshira, and the picturesque Castle of Dundarave on Loch Fyne, the " Castle of the Two Oars."

Alexander III. in 1267 granted to *Gillichrist MacNachdan* the keeping of his castle of *Fraoch Eilean* (Heathery Isle), Loch Awe, so that they should cause it to be built and repaired at the king's expense, as often as needful, and keep it safely for the king's necessity ; and that as often as he should come to it, the castle, well furnished, should be delivered to him to lodge and dwell there at his pleasure. Between the years 1390 and 1406 Robert III. confirmed Maurice MacNaughtane a grant by Colin Campbell of Lochow, in heritage, of various lands in Over-Lochow.

Sir Alexander MacNaghten of that Ilk fell with James IV. at Flodden. In 1689 Alexander, Laird of MacNaghten, fought under Dundee at Killiecrankie and his estates were forfeited in 1691. His son, John MacNaghten of that Ilk and Dunderave, was the last of the direct line. He married about 1700 a daughter of Sir James Campbell, the last of the Campbells of Ardkinglas in the direct male line. Ardkinglas, Laban-like, deceived MacNaghten, who took too much pre-nuptial refreshment, and found himself married to the eldest daughter instead of the second. The following day MacNaghten and the second daughter fled to Ireland, leaving his wife lamenting. Ardkinglas got him " condemned " for incest, and got " gift of his forfeited property." The chiefship became dormant and the succession indeterminate. According to the genealogy addressed in Lyon Court, John Dhu MacNaghten, brother to the Laird of Dundarave, settled in Antrim about 1580 and from him is Bescended the present line of chiefs. In 1818 Edmund A. MacNaghten of dushmills, W. Antrim, in these circumstances, and on the attestation of 400 MacNaghtens, was, on petition to Lyon Court, confirmed judicially in the chief arms of MacNaghten by decree of 13th Jan. 1818. Dying without issue, his brother and heir, Sir Francis MacNaghten of Dunderave, created Baronet 1836, succeeded. Sir Francis MacNaghten of Dunderave, Bushmills, Antrim, 8th Baronet, is the present chief.

Dundarave.

80. MACNAGHTEN

MACNEIL OF BARRA

Slogan :—" Buaidh no Bàs " (" Victory or Death ").

Badge :—Machall-monaidh (Dryas) or Feamainn (Algæ).

THE chiefs of the Clan MacNeil (who are also designated " of that Ilk " as chiefs of the whole name of MacNeil) claim descent from Eoghan of Aileach, one of the sons of " Neil of the Nine Hostages," King of Ireland, and the tradition states that Niall, a grandson of the last King of Aileach, and 21st in descent from that *Oir-Righ-Eireann*, settled in Barra about 1040, and thus founded the clan in Scotland. Neil Og was reckoned 6th Chief of the Clan from *Niall-na*-Barra ; tradition says that he supported Robert the Bruce. In the reign of David II. they came to hold the island under the Lord of the Isles, by whom a charter was granted 1427, to Gilleonan MacNeil, 9th of Barra, and the MacNeils thus rank as barons in the Lordship of the Isles and as such were members of the Council of the Isles. After the forfeiture of the Macdonalds, Gilleonan Mac Roderick MacNeil, 11th of Barra, received a Crown Confirmation of Barra in 1495.

In 1531 Torkill MacNeil was " chief and principal man of the clan and surname of MacNeil," but as he represented none of the leading families, it would seem he was really a chief-wardatour during the minority or incapacity of one of the Gilleonan MacNeils of Barra of whom three succeeded one another. During the 16th century the chiefs kept magnificent state in their island fortress of Kismull. Rory " the Turbulent," 15th Chief, was arrested for piracy of an English ship towards the close of the 16th century, but successfully excused himself to James VI. by stating that he thought it would be deemed good service to harass the subjects of the woman who had killed his sovereign's mother ! His descendant, Roderick, 18th of Barra, got a charter of Barra as a Crown Barony in 1688. He was " out " with Dundee in 1689, and with the Chevalier in 1715. He had three sons : (1) Gilleonan of Brevaig, according to tradition the eldest, and passed over by tanistry as weak ; (2) Roderick, the heir ; (3) James of Ersary. Roderick the Dove of the West, succeeded as 19th Chief and Baron of Barra. He was imprisoned for his share in the 1745, released 1747, and died 1763. His eldest son, " Roderick the Peaceful," younger of Barra, having fallen at Quebec, 1759, he was succeeded by his grandson, " Roderick the Gentle ", 20th Chief, who died 1822, and the direct line ended with his son, General Roderick MacNeil of Barra, who died 1863, having had to sell Barra in 1838. The chiefship devolved upon the MacNeils of Ersary, descending from James, third son of Roderick the Dove, in the person of Hugh Edward, 22nd Chief. His grandson, Roderick Ambrose MacNeil of Barra, 24th Chief, died 1914, having, under the law of tanistry, settled the chiefship on his second son, Robert Lister MacNeil of Barra, the present 25th chief—who established his position by decree of Lyon Court 1915. He and his wife, Mariė, Mrs. MacNeil of Barra, re-acquired the greater part of Barra, including the fortress of Kismull Castle, situated on a rocky island at Castlebay.

Kismull.

81. MACNEIL OF BARRA

MCNEILL OF COLONSAY

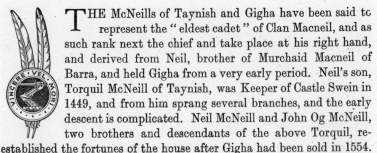

THE McNeills of Taynish and Gigha have been said to represent the " eldest cadet " of Clan Macneil, and as such rank next the chief and take place at his right hand, and derived from Neil, brother of Murchaid Macneil of Barra, and held Gigha from a very early period. Neil's son, Torquil McNeill of Taynish, was Keeper of Castle Swein in 1449, and from him sprang several branches, and the early descent is complicated. Neil McNeill and John Og McNeill, two brothers and descendants of the above Torquil, re-established the fortunes of the house after Gigha had been sold in 1554.

Hector, of the Taynish line, repurchased Gigha from Campbell of Cawdor in 1590, but early in the 19th century the estates were sold by Roger Hamilton McNeill of Taynish (Gigha having been sold to McNeill of Colonsay in 1780). He married Elizabeth Price, eventual heiress of the Hamiltons of Raploch. Their grandson, Daniel McNeill Hamilton, became Laird of Raploch, and his descendants continue to bear that designation—their lands being situated in Lanarkshire.

Donald McNeill of Crear, a descendant of the above-mentioned John Og McNeill, acquired Colonsay and Oronsay from the Duke of Argyll in 1700 in exchange for Crear, etc. Alexander McNeill, 6th of Colonsay, acquired Gigha from his kinsman and sold Colonsay to his brother Duncan, the celebrated Lord Justice-General, created Lord Colonsay, 1867. After his death without issue, his estates were eventually re-united in his nephew, Major-General Sir John Carstairs McNeill of Colonsay and Oronsay, G.C.V.O., Bath King of Arms, whose brother and successor, Alexander McNeill of Colonsay, became representative of the family, but the island was sold to Lord Strathcona. Alexander died in 1915 and was succeeded in the representation of the family by his son, Alexander Carstairs McNeill, who resides in New Zealand.

The illustration shows the crest of McNeill of Colonsay within the plain circlet, appropriate to an *armiger* using his *own* crest (*i.e.* without the " belt and buckle " of the following), and accompanied by the two feathers of a chieftain in the Clan McNeill. The clan McNeill of Gigha now claims an independent Norse descent, as does its branch of Colonsay.

The children of the McNeills of Colonsay were made repeat their genealogy backwards in Gaelic, on Sundays; being a survival of the manner in which old Clan genealogies were preserved—the form noticeably similar to that declaimed at the Scots Coronation by the High Sennachie.

82. McNEILL OF COLONSAY

MACPHERSON

Slogan :—Creag Dhubh (The Black Craig—a hill near Cluny).

Badge :—Lus nan cràimhseag (Red Whortleberry) ; White Heather.

THIS clan is a branch of the Clan Chattan, deriving from Ewen Ban, traditionally second son of Muriach, Chief of Clan Chattan, and Prior of Kingussie, 1173, who married a daughter of the Thane of Cawdor, under an alleged Dispensation from the Pope, which, in view of the Celtic custom of a married clergy, was most likely never obtained, and had two sons. The elder son became *Gilli-Chattan Mhor*, and had a son *Dugal Doul*, 6th Chief of Clan Chattan, whose only daughter, Eva, " heretrix of the Clan Chattan," married Angus Mackintosh of that Ilk, and from them descend the subsequent chiefs of Clan Chattan. *Ewen Ban*, second son of Muriach, had three sons (from whom the Macphersons are also styled " the clan of the three brothers "), viz. : Kenneth, ancestor of Cluny ; Ian (Pitmean) ; and Gillies (Invereshie). Two generations, however, can hardly cover the period between Muriach and Kenneth, who fought at Invernahaven, 1370, and left Duncan, Parson of Laggan, 1438. His son, Donald Mhor Macpherson (first to bear *Macpherson* as a surname), was ancestor of Andrew, who held the " three pleuches " of Cluny-in-Badenoch. Andrew, reckoned 8th Chief, acquired the abbey-castle of Grange in Strathisla, 1618. His son Ewen, a great Royalist under Montrose, had Andrew, of Cluny Macpherson, who died unmarried, and Duncan, 10th Chief, the Macpherson of Cluny who was in 1672 the unsuccessful claimant for the Chiefship of Clan Chattan which the Lord Lyon King of Arms on 10th Sept., 1672, officially declared to have passed, through Eva, to Mackintosh. Duncan had no male issue, and proposed settling (as by tanistry he was entitled) the chiefship of the Macphersons on his daughter Anne, and her husband Sir Duncan Campbell. William of Nuid, the heir male, and others, bound themselves to dissuade him—in which they succeeded—so upon Cluny's death, 1722, Lachlan, 4th of Nuid, succeeded as chief, dying 1746. His son Ewen Macpherson of Cluny (son-in-law of the notorious Lord Lovat) became a famous Highland leader in the Rising of 1745. Cluny-Macpherson hid in Badenoch, after Culloden, for nine years, during which he was faithfully supported by his clan and tenantry, and to his son Duncan, Cluny was restored in 1784. His son, Ewen Macpherson of Cluny, recognised in Lyon Court as chief of the Clan Macpherson in 1873, picturesquely maintained the state of a Highland Chief until his death in 1885. On the death of his youngest son, Albert Cameron Macpherson of Cluny (by tanistry 17th Chief), the estate was sold, whilst the arms and chiefship devolved on his nephew, Ewen George Macpherson of Cluny-Macpherson, 18th and present chief of the Clan Macpherson, who resides at Adelaide in South Australia.

The Macphersons have a red tartan, and two " grey " ones, of which Cluny (born 1804, died 1885) wrote acidly in 1850 : " The design was known as the *Breacan Glas* long before John (Sobieski) Stuart was heard of in this country. . . . At all events the tartan is an old Macpherson." The tartan now used by, and beloved of, the Macpherson Clan, and marketed as " Hunting Macpherson," is the celebrated *Breacan Glas*—" the grey plaid of Badenoch," whereof the exact sett used was copied in 1745 from an old plaid then at Cluny, by the Jacobite Chief's wife, the Hon. Jean Fraser of Lovat, Lady

83. MACPHERSON, HUNTING.

Q

Cluny-Macpherson. Found in the earliest collections, this sett is, with white ground, the dress tartan of the clan, and with grey ground (as used since the middle of the 18th century) the " hunting " sett. It is the sett which is here illustrated. The Chief's tartan of black and white includes narrow red and yellow lines.

The " Green Banner " and " Black Chanter," with other treasures, were saved by the Clan Trust, which holds several acres of the Clan Macpherson "country" in Badenoch. The Chief has (in accordance with the same principle as that on which the King of Scots appoints a Lord High Commissioner) appointed Tom Macpherson, M.P., " Commander of the Clan " in Scotland, Duncan Macpherson, a cadet of Breckachie, as Commander of the Clan in U.S.A., Douglas, also a Breckachie, in Canada, and Duncan F. Macpherson as Commissioner in Australia.

MACQUARRIE

Slogan:—"An t-Arm Breac Dearg" ("The Army of the Checkered Red tartan ").

Badge :—Giuthas (Pine Tree).

THE name Macquarrie comes from the Gaelic *Guaire*, which means noble. The Macquarries first appear in possession of Ulva and part of Mull, and, like the Mackinnons, " their situation forced them," says Skene, " to become dependent upon the MacDonalds," but later on Ulva was held under the house of Argyll.

John Macquarrie of Ulva is the first on record, dying about 1473. After the forfeiture of the Lord of the Isles they followed Maclean of Duart. When, in 1609, the Bishop of the Isles went to Iona as Commissioner for King James VI., among the chief men of the Isles who submitted themselves to him were Macquarrie of Ulva, Mackinnon of that Ilk, and ten others.

Lachlan Macquarrie (XVI.) of Ulva was obliged to dispose of his ancestral property, and in 1778, at the age of sixty-three, he entered the army.

When the old 74th Regiment, or Argyll Highlanders, was raised in 1777 by Colonel Campbell of Barbreck, Lachlan Macquarrie obtained a commission in it, and his name, under date 23rd December, 1777, appears among the officers of this regiment, which was disbanded in 1783 ; and after a long life, the last of the Macquarries of Ulva died in 1818, aged 103. He had several sons, some of whom distinguished themselves in India, where John Macquarrie of Ulva, Lieut. 114th Foot, predeceased his father ; and no one has yet come forward to establish in Lyon Court representation of the stem-family of the clan, though claimants are understood to exist. One claimant held the office of beadle in South Knapdale. Lachlan Macquarrie, the last of Ulva, was the laird of Ulva at the time of the visit of Dr. Johnson and Boswell of Auchinleck to that island in 1773. A history of some of the later chiefs, who went to India, has recently been compiled. Major-General Lachlan Macquarrie, Governor of New South Wales, 1809–21, was a cousin of the last laird of Ulva.

Breacan-feile, back view, with targe hung on shoulder.

84. MACQUARRIE

MACQUEEN

Badge :—Bocsa (Boxwood) or Lus nan cràimsheag, braoileag (Red Whortle).

THE Macqueens are stated to be of Norse origin from Sweyn, or Swyne, rendered in Gaelic " MacCuine " or " MacShuibhne." The Rev. Lachlan Shaw, referring to Corrybrough, describes it as " the property of Donald Macqueen, chief of that branch of Clan Chattan."

The Macqueens are known as Clan Revan, and the circumstances under which the Macqueens left the west coast and settled in Strathdearn are stated to be : Early in the 15th century Malcolm Beg Macintosh (10th of Macintosh) married Mora MacDonald of Moidart, and with the bride came, as was the custom, several of her kinsmen, who took up their abode near her new home. Among the followers were Reven-Mac-Mulmor MacAngus, of whom the clan Revan are descended, and Donald Mac-Gillandrish, of whom the clan Andrish. Roderick Dhu Revan Macqueen is said to have fought under Macintosh at the Battle of Harlaw, 1411.

Donald Macqueen of Corrybrough ; John Macqueen of Little Corrybrough ; and Sweyn Macqueen of Raigbeg, are parties to the Clan Chattan Bond of Union, 4th of April, 1609.

Donald Macqueen, 1st of Corrybrough, died about 1623, and is succeeded by his nephew Angus, one of the signatories to the Clan Chattan Bond of 1664. Donald, his son, succeeded him, and died in 1676, being succeeded by his son, Donald, who was a Commissioner of Supply for the County of Inverness, 1685–97. On the death of James, son of Donald, in 1762, Donald, son of James, succeeded. He was Sheriff-Substitute of Inverness, and died in 1792. His son, Captain Donald Macqueen, 7th of Corrybrough, died 1813, and was succeeded by his son Donald, Captain 2nd Madras Cavalry. He was succeeded by his brother, John Fraser Macqueen (English bar, 1838, Q.C. and Bencher, 1861). He died in 1881. After his death the succession to the chiefship, but not to the estate, opened to his only surviving brother, Lachlan, in the East India Company, who died in 1896. He was succeeded by his only son Donald, now resident in New Zealand. The chiefship and arms of Macqueen have, however, not yet been established in the Court of the Lord Lyon.

Among the leading cadets are the Macqueens of Pollochaig, Clune, and Strathnoon.

85. MACQUEEN

MACRAE

Slogan :—" Sgùr Urain " (A mountain in Kintail).

Badge :—Garbhag an t-sléibhe (Fir Club Moss).

IT is generally understood that the name Macrae—Gaelic *MacRath*—means " Son of Grace," and had, in all probability, an ecclesiastical origin. It occurs as a personal or Christian name in Ireland, and also in Scotland, from the 5th to the 13th century. It was common as a surname in Galloway, Ayrshire, and the south of Perthshire in the 15th and 16th centuries, and is still common, with various forms of spelling— M'Crae, M'Crea, M'Creath, etc. In Ireland it takes the form Magrath.

The highland home of the Clan Macrae, sometimes called " the Wild Macraes," was Kintail, in Ross-shire, where they are said to have migrated from the Lovat country about the middle of the 14th century, and the arms indicate that they originally came from Moray. They were related to the MacKenzie barons of Kintail, whose ablest and most loyal supporters they soon proved, and so became largely the means of raising the Barony of Kintail, afterwards the Earldom of Seaforth, to the high position it occupies in the annals of Scottish history. The Macraes were Chamberlains of Kintail for many generations, and frequently Vicars of the parish and Constables of Ellandonan Castle. The late Constable of Eilean-Donan Castle, Lieut.-Colonel John Macrae-Gilstrap of Balliemore, recently restored the ancient stronghold, one of the most picturesque in the highlands, and his son, Capt. John Macrae of Balliemore, is the present Constable.

Rev. Farquhar Macrae (1508–1662) was Vicar of Kintail for forty-four years. One of his sons, Rev. John Macrae of Dingwall (1614–1673), was progenitor of the Macraes of Conchra, a family that has been honourably represented in the British army for several generations.

Macrae of Inverinate claimed the chiefship of the clan, and Sir Colin Macrae, representative of that house, petitioned Lyon Court 1909, but the claim was opposed by descendants of Conchra, who alleged there was no chief of the Clan Macrae. The chiefship of this clan has not yet been settled, but that there is *no* " representer " of the first Macrae is an untenable proposition. The Rev. John A. Macrae is the present representer of Inverinate.

Eilean-Donan.

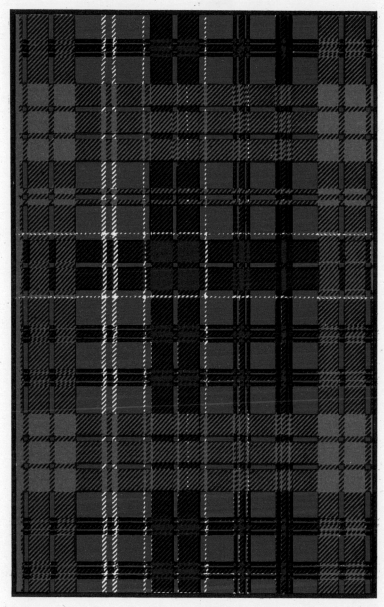

86. MACRAE

MATHESON

Slogan :—" Achadh-da-thearnaidh (" Field of the Two Declivities ").

THE chiefs of this clan from 1263 to 1400 run, according to a pedigree MS. of 1467, thus : Mathan, father of Kenneth, father of Murdoch, father of Duncan, father of Murdoch, father of Murdoch. This Murdoch might have been the Makmakan of Bower, the chief in 1427, who is named, however, in the traditions as Alexander, a name supported by Sir James Balfour's Alexander Macmurkine for the same personage. All the Matheson genealogies of the present day converge in Murdoch Buidhe (who flourished 1580-1602) ten generations back (in most cases) from the present day.

Murdoch Buidhe had two sons—Roderick of Fernaig and Dugall of Balmacara, Chamberlain of Lochalsh (1631). The former had an only son, John, who was father of John Mor of Fernaig who made money in cattle droving and became proprietor of Bennetsfield in the Black Isle in 1688. His son was Alexander, called 1st of Bennetsfield ; his son, John, fought at Culloden ; Colin succeeded his father, the Culloden hero, and had a large family. Dying in 1825, he was succeeded by his son, Captain John, or " Jack," the clan historian. John of Bennetsfield died without issue in 1843, leaving the estates embarrassed. His successors were his nephew and his nephew's son, who died in 1899, leaving the barren chiefship of the Clan Matheson to his cousin, Heylin Fraser Matheson, Housemaster of Eastbourne College (a son of Rev. Charles Matheson, son of Charles Mackenzie Matheson, third son of Colin of Bennetsfield), whose son, Colonel Bertram Matheson, claims the chiefship of Clan Matheson.

John Matheson, 1st of Attadal (1730), was great-grandson of Dougall of Balmacara ; his son and heir, Alexander Matheson, died in 1804. His son, John, had to part with the estates. He married Margaret, daughter of Captain Matheson of Shinness, head of the Sutherland branch. Alexander, their eldest son, entered into the India and China trade along with his uncle (Sir) James Matheson, and both amassed great fortunes. Alexander bought Lochalsh, the old family patrimony or *dùthus*. He was created Baronet in 1882. Sir Torquil, 5th Baronet, now represents this family.

Mathesons, traditionally a sept of the Lochalsh family, existed in Sutherland from 1492. The chief family was Shinness. In 1616 Sir Robert Gordon, to weaken the power of the Mackay septs, caused the Mathesons to elect as their chief " John Mack-ean-Mac-Konald-Wain, in Chinenes." Neil Matheson was chief of the Shinness family in Jacobite days ; from him descended the late Sir James Sutherland Matheson of the Lewes (1796-1887), famed for his wealth and philanthropy. His eldest brother, Duncan, was an advocate, whose eldest son, Donald, succeeded to the property of his uncle, Sir James.

Another branch which still holds an estate in the highlands is Matheson of Little Scatwell in Ross-shire.

87. MATHESON

MAXWELL

SIR JOHN MAXWELL, Chamberlain of Scotland, died without issue, 1241, and was succeeded by his brother, Sir Aymer, who, with other children, had two sons, named Herbert and John. Sir Herbert's descendant in the seventh degree, also named Herbert, was created Lord Maxwell, and, dying, left two sons, Robert, 2nd Lord, and Sir Edward; from the latter come the Maxwells of Monreith, created Baronets 1681, and now represented by Sir Herbert Eustace Maxwell, 7th Baronet of Monreith. Robert, 2nd Lord Maxwell, was succeeded by his son, John, 3rd Lord, who fell at Flodden, 1513; and he by his son, Robert, 4th Lord. This nobleman had two sons, Robert, 5th Lord, and Sir John, who became Lord Herries of Terregles, in right of his wife, Agnes, Lady Herries. Robert, 5th Lord Maxwell, was succeeded by his son, John, 6th Lord. He obtained the Earldom of Morton on the execution of the Regent, but was afterwards deprived of it. He was killed in an engagement with the Johnstons, 1593. His son, John, 7th Lord, killed Sir James Johnston of that Ilk, 1608, and was executed, 1613, being succeeded by his brother, Robert, 8th Lord, who was created Earl of Nithsdale. His son, Robert, 2nd Earl, dying unmarried, 1667, the Earldom reverted to his cousin, John, 4th Lord Herries, great-grandson of Sir John, 1st Lord Herries, mentioned above. John, 4th Lord and 3rd Earl, was succeeded by his son, Robert, 4th Earl, and he by his son, William, 5th Earl. This nobleman was out in 1715, but being taken prisoner at Preston, was found guilty of high treason, and sentenced to death. He escaped from the Tower by the devotion of his wife (Lady Winifred Herbert, daughter of the 1st Marquis of Powis), who, dressing her husband in female attire, remained in prison, allowing him to leave in her stead. The Earl died in Rome, 1744, leaving a son, William, who left an only daughter, Winifred, who married William Haggerston Constable. Their grandson, William Constable-Maxwell, proved his claim to the Lordship of Herries, 1858, but this peerage has now passed to the Duchess of Norfolk. Maxwell of Caruchan established in Lyon Court he was heir male of the Maxwells, but this line has since become dormant, and the chiefship is undetermined.

We now return to Sir John Maxwell, second son of Sir Aymer, mentioned at the beginning of this article. Sir John's great-grandson, Sir John of Pollok, had two sons, Sir John and Sir Robert. From the younger come the Maxwells, Baronets of Cardoness, and the Maxwells, Barons Farnham and Baronets of Calderwood. From the elder son come the Maxwells, Baronets of Pollok, whose direct male line ended in 1865, on the death of Sir John, 8th Baronet. He was succeeded by his sister, who married Archibald Stirling of Keir; and their grandson is now Sir John Maxwell Stirling-Maxwell of Pollok, K.T., 10th Baronet. The Maxwells, Baronets of Springkell, are a junior branch, deriving from William Maxwell of Kirkconnel whose son, Sir Patrick, was created a Baronet 1682. The 4th Baronet married the heiress of Heron of that Ilk. Sir Patrick Heron-Maxwell, 9th Baronet, now represents the Springkell branch.

88. MAXWELL

MENZIES

Slogan :—" Geal us Dearg a suas " (" Up with the White and Red ").

Badge :—Uinnseann (Ash) ; Menzies Heath.

IT is generally believed that this clan is descended from a Gaelic-speaking race, though the chiefs, *i.e.* the " stem family," are of Lowland origin. The clan seems to have been settled in Atholl from an early period. The name occurs in charters during the reign of William the Lion and the reign of Alexander II., for we find that about that time Robert de Meyners grants a charter of the lands of Culdares, in Fortingall, to Matthew de Moncrief. Sir Robert's son, Alexander, was possessor of the lands of Weem, Aberfeldy, and Fortingall in Atholl, Glendochart in Breadalbane, as well as Durisdeer in Nithsdale. From Alexander's eldest son descended Sir Robert de Mengues, Knight, whose lands were erected into the Barony of Menzies in 1487. His descendant, Alexander Menzies of Castle Menzies, was in 1665 created a Baronet of Nova Scotia. This dignity became extinct or dormant on the death of Sir Neil, 8th Baronet, in 1910, when his sister, Egidia Menzies of Menzies, became chieftainess of the clan.

A distinguished cadet family of the Menzieses was that of Pitfoddels, who branched off from the main stock in the 14th century. The branch is now extinct. Its last chieftain founded Blairs (R.C.) College.

In the Rising of " the '45 " the chief of the clan took no part, though the clan was " out " under Menzies of Shian.

To a Menzies Scotland is indebted for the introduction of the larch tree, which now flourishes all over the Highlands. The first larch saplings planted in Scotland were raised from Culdares, which house is now (since the death of Miss Menzies of Menzies) regarded as chief of the clan, its present representative being William Stuart-Menzies of Culdares and Arndilly, the lineal heir of Col. James Menzies, cousin of Sir Alexander, 1st Baronet of Menzies. He has, however, not yet matriculated his arms and supporters as the chief in Lyon Register, or assumed the name and title of " The Menzies of Menzies." Castle Menzies, a magnificent Scots baronial pile, now stands vacant but intact. The Clan Society, however, possesses the Old Kirk of Weem ; an important instance of a clan acquiring heritable property in the 20th century.

There is a Clan Menzies Society in Glasgow, whose headquarters are at Weem, in Perthshire, where it holds the Old Kirk of Weem.

89. MENZIES

MONTGOMERIE

MONTGOMERIE is an ancient Norman name derived from that fief in Normandy. Roger de Montgomery, called the Great, was father of another Roger, born about 1030. This second Roger was joint Governor of Normandy when William the Conqueror invaded England in 1066. He came to England the following year and was made Earl of Arundel. He died 1094.

The first of the family in Scotland was Robert de Montgomerie, who died about 1177, having probably come to Scotland with the first High Steward. The first of his successors who held a prominent position was John Montgomerie of Eaglesham who distinguished himself at Otterburn 1388. He married Elizabeth, daughter and heiress of Sir Hugh de Eglintoun. The grandson of this marriage, Sir Alexander, was created Lord Montgomerie before 1445. He had two sons (1) Alexander, (2) George, ancestor of the Montgomeries of Skelmorlie.

The elder son, Alexander, Master of Montgomerie, died in his father's lifetime, leaving Hugh, 2nd Lord, and Robert, from whom are said to descend the Earls of Mount Alexander in Ireland. Hugh, 2nd Lord Montgomerie, was created Earl of Eglinton in 1507. He was succeeded by his grandson Hugh, 2nd Earl, who, dying in 1546, left a son Hugh, 3rd Earl, a faithful adherent of Mary, Queen of Scots. He was father of the 4th Earl, and of a daughter, Margaret, who married Robert Seton, 1st Earl of Winton. Hugh, the 4th Earl, was shot 1586 in the course of a feud with the Cunninghams, and his son Hugh, the 5th Earl, died without issue in 1612. The Earldom of Eglinton then devolved on the Hon. Alexander Seton, third son of the above-mentioned Margaret Montgomerie, Countess of Winton, in terms of a Crown charter obtained by the 5th Earl in 1611 and confirmed by James VI. in 1615. On his succession Seton took the name and arms of Montgomerie and thus became chief of the family of Montgomerie according to the Scottish Law and custom of family succession, and by the Irish Montgomeries was, on that occasion, gifted a horse—really as "calp of *Cean-Cinnidh*." This earl was first a Covenanter but later became a devoted Royalist. Alexander, 10th Earl, a distinguished statesman, was shot by a poacher, 1769. His brother Archibald, 11th Earl, raised the 78th Highlanders. Archibald, 13th Earl, held the celebrated Eglinton Tournament, a magnificent display of chivalry, in 1839. Being heir male of the Setons he was created Earl of Winton 1859, but since he retained the name of Montgomerie alone he never became chief of his paternal line, and his son, Archibald William, 14th Earl, successfully vindicated, in Lyon Court 1860, his position as chief of the Montgomeries against an heir male claiming descent from Montgomerie of Laingshaw, who sprang from the third son of the 1st Earl. His descendant, Archibald, 17th Earl of Eglinton, is the present chief of the Montgomeries. His seats are at Eglinton. where the castle has been dismantled, and the old Castle of Skelmorlie, near Largs, which is the home of the Chief.

From Robert Montgomery, brother of the 1st Lord Montgomery, descended Sir James Montgomery of Stanhope, Lord Advocate, created a Baronet 1801. Sir Henry, 5th Baronet, now represents this line.

90. MONTGOMERIE

MORRISON

Slogan :—" Dun Eistein " (A fort in Lewis).

Badge :—Sgòd cladaich (Driftwood).

A S a Highland clan the Morrisons belong to Lewis and the adjoining mainland of North-West Scotland. The Morrisons of Perth and Lennox formed no clan, and the name in Gaelic is different. The latter is from Maurice, Gaelic *Moiris*.

The Clan Morrison derive their name from an adaptation of Gaelic *MacGille-mhoire* or *M'Gilmor, Gille-mhoire* meaning " Devotee of St. Mary." John Morisone, " indweller " of Lewis, writing about 1680, records that the first inhabitants of Lewis were men of three races—Mores, son of Kennanus Makurich, son of a king of Norway ; Iskair MacAulay, an Irishman (Issachar or Zachary MacAulay) ; and MacNicol, whose only daughter married Claudius, son of Olave, King of Norway. This, it will be seen, accounts for the three original clans of Lewis—MacLeods, MacAulays, and Morrisons. The MacLeods were undoubtedly of Norse origin. The English form Morrison goes as far back as the 16th century.

The first recorded Morrison is Hugh or Hucheon (Gaelic, *Uisdean*), the Brieve, contemporary of practically the last MacLeod of Lewis, Roderick MacLeod, chief from about 1532-1595. The Brieve held the hereditary office of deemster—judge or " law man," as the Norse called them. The Morrisons are still an important clan in the Hebrides and in the north-west mainland of Scotland.

Hugh Morrison of Islay married Sophia, daughter of the 2nd Earl Granville and a granddaughter of the late W. F. Campbell of Shawfield and Islay.

In North-Eastern Scotland Morison of Bognie is the principal family of the name and (though apparently unconnected with the West Coast Morrisons) the Bognie arms have latterly been associated with the tartan, but no family seems hitherto to have been accepted as chief of the clan. The 1st Laird of Bognie was Alexander, whose son, George, married Christian Urquhart, Viscountess of Frendraght. Duncan M. Morison of Bognie is the 11th and present Laird of Bognie.

Robert Craigmyle Morrison, M.P., was in 1945 created Lord Morrison, but has not yet matriculated arms in Lyon Register as a *duine-uasail* of Clan Morrison.

91. MORRISON

MUNRO

Slogan :—" Caisteal Fòlais 'n a theine " (" Castle Foulis ablaze ").

Badge :—Garbhag nan Gleann (Common Club Moss).

IN Gaelic the Munros are called Clan *Rothaich*. Their possessions were on the north side of the Firth of Cromarty, and the title of their chief is and was Munro of Foulis. According to Burke, Hugh Monro, first designated of Foulis, died in 1126. George Munro of Foulis is said to have got a charter from the Earl of Sutherland in the reign of Alexander II. (1214–49).

Robert Munro in 1309 got a charter from Robert I. for lands in Strathspey and the lands of Cupermakcultis. The Munroes held their lands of, and were followers of, the ancient Earls of Ross. The first chief evidenced by charter was Robert de Monro (1341–72).

Robert Munro of Foulis fell at Pinkie 1547. By his wife, Margaret Dunbar of Westfield, he left a son, Robert of Foulis, who died in 1588, having by his first wife had two sons, Robert and Hector, successively chiefs, and by his second wife a son, George of Obsdale, ancestor of the 3rd and subsequent Baronets.

Hector married, firstly, a daughter of Hugh, Lord Fraser of Lovat, and dying 1603, was succeeded by his son Robert, called the " Black Baron." He was Colonel of two Dutch regiments, one of Horse, the other of Foot, under Gustavus Adolphus, was wounded mortally by a musket ball in 1638, and was buried at Ulm. There were at that time in the Swedish army twenty-seven field-officers and eleven captains of the surname of Munro.

In 1632 the Munroes mustered 1000 strong at the funeral of Lord Lovat ; the Grants, 800 ; MacKenzies, 900 ; Rosses, 1000 ; and Frasers, 1000, all in arms.

The Black Baron, leaving no male issue and his daughter Margaret being married to Mackenzie of Scatwell, was succeeded by his brother, Sir Hector Munro, 1st Baronet, created 1634, who married Mary, daughter of Hugh Mackay of Farr. He died in 1635, and was succeeded by his only son, Sir Hector, who died unmarried in 1651, in his seventeenth year, when the title devolved upon his cousin Robert, who became the 3rd Baronet, and married Jean, eldest daughter of Sir Hector, the 1st Baronet. Sir Robert, who had seven sons, died in 1668, and was succeeded by his eldest, Sir John, who married a daughter of Mackenzie of Coul, and dying in 1696, was succeeded by his son, Sir Robert. Dying four years after, he was succeeded by his eldest son, Sir Robert, 6th Baronet, Hanoverian officer (37th Regiment), who fell at Falkirk. His son, Sir Harry, 7th Baronet, died at Edinburgh in 1781.

Sir Hector, 11th Baronet, Lord Lieutenant of Ross and Cromarty, died in 1935, when the baronetcy passed to a cousin ; but Foulis Castle, with the obligation to bear the name and arms, passed to his eldest daughter, Eva, Mrs Munro of Foulis (widow of Gascoigne of Muirton) in liferent as 32nd Lady of Foulis, Heretrix of the Clan Munro, whose son, Patrick Munro of Foulis, is 33rd Laird and Chief of the Clan. Their seat is Foulis Castle, Evanton, Ross-shire.

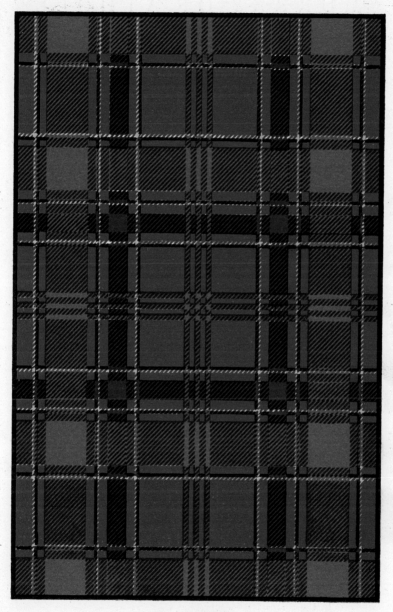

92. MUNRO

MURRAY OF ATHOLL

Badge :—Aitionn (Juniper) ; other Murray Badges are Broom and
Butcher's Broom.

FRESKIN, ancestor of the great family of Murray, was, there is every reason to believe, a Pictish noble of the old race of Moray. He probably represented a branch which supported the Scottish Kings, and thus supplanted the MacHeth line of *Ri Morev*, hence assuming the province name. He obtained from David I. a charter feudalising part of the old *duthus* of Moray and his castle of Duffus. His grandson, William, assumed the name " De Moravia." This William de Moravia had, besides his heir, Sir Walter, several other sons, from one of whom is descended the great House of Murray of Tullibardine.

From Walter Murray of Pettie and Boharm, derived the House of Murray of Bothwell, Chief of the Name of Murray, of whom was Sir Andrew Murray, the patriot, who fell at the Battle of Stirling Bridge. His son, Sir Andrew, was Regent of Scotland after the Battle of Dupplin.

The Murrays of Abercairney derive from Sir William Murray, 1st of Drumsagard, and claim descent from the House of Bothwell. Sir John, 2nd of Drumsagard, acquired Abercairney by marriage with a daughter of the Earl of Strathearn, and from his son Sir Alexander, 2nd of Abercairney, is descended the House of Abercairney, in Perthshire.

The Murrays of Atholl derive from Sir William, who acquired Tullibardine by marriage with Ada, daughter of the Steward of Strathearn, and Sir for David Murray, 7th of Tullibardine, the lands were erected into a feudal barony 1443. His son was Esquire to James II., Sheriff of Perth, and Keeper of Doune Castle. Sir William, 11th of Tullibardine, was Comptroller of Scotland and contributed to the escape of Mary Queen of Scots from Lochleven. Sir John, 12th Laird, was created Earl of Tullibardine, 1606. William, 2nd Earl, married Lady Dorothy Stewart, eldest daughter of John, 5th Earl of Atholl, and their son, John, was in 1629 confirmed as Earl of Atholl, whilst the Earldom of Tullibardine was diverted to his uncle, Sir Patrick of Redcastle. John, 2nd Earl of the Murray line, was created Marquess of Atholl 1676, and John, 2nd Marquess, Duke of Atholl 1703. His son William is celebrated as the Jacobite Marquess of Tullibardine, created Duke of Rannoch by the Chevalier, and by statute the dukedom was accordingly settled upon his younger brother, Lord James Murray of Garth. A younger brother, Lord George Murray, was Prince Charlie's celebrated supporter. The 2nd Duke of Atholl succeeded, in right of his mother, to the Sovereignty of the Isle of Man, ceded to the Crown 1765. The 8th Duke of Atholl originated the Scottish National War Memorial. His seat, Blair Castle, Perthshire, is a notable Highland stronghold. The Murray of Atholl tartan seems a version of that used by Murray of Pulrossie in the early 17th century, and thus evidence of the early use of tartan as a distinguishing clan garb. Other celebrated houses are the Murrays of Touchadam and Polmaise, and the Murrays of Balvaird and Stormont, of whom descended the celebrated Lord Chief Justice, the Earl of Mansfield. The seat of this line is at the ancient Royal Palace of Scone.

93. MURRAY

NICOLSON

Badge :—Trailing Azalea.

IN modern Gaelic the name of this clan takes the form " MacNeacail " ; while in old documents we have " M'Nicail." In Argyll the surname invariably takes the form MacNicol ; while in Skye and the North generally Nicolson is the approved designation. The Nicolsons held the lands of Scorrybreac, Skye, as principal tenants. " MacNicol of Portree," was, it is said, one of the sixteen men who formed the Council of the Lord of the Isles. Son succeeded father in the chiefship, and there is a local tradition to the effect that over one hundred chiefs of the clan were borne to their last resting-place in Snizort Churchyard from the old house of Scorrybreac. " On the 12th February 1813," it is recorded in the press of the day that " there died at Scorrybreac, in the Isle of Skye, in the eighty-seventh year of his age, Malcolm Nicolson, Esq., who, with his predecessors, lineally and without interruption, possessed that farm for many centuries back."

The last chief of Scorrybreac to reside in Skye was Norman Nicolson of Scorrybreac, who emigrated to New Zealand. He was a Gaelic bard of some repute. His line continues in Australia.

MacNicols are numerous in Argyll. The Rev. Donald MacNicol was minister of Lismore. He made a collection of Gaelic Ossianic poetry in 1755, and published in 1779 *Remarks on Dr Samuel Johnson's Journey to the Hebrides*, at which the great moralist " growled hideously."

Norman Nicolson, representative of the Highland Nicolsons of Scorrybreac, now in Australia, matriculated arms having a chevron between the heads, whereas the lowland Baronets of Lasswade received the undifferenced arms, and have been officially recognised under the chiefly designation Nicolson of that Ilk, and must accordingly be received as Chief of the Name. A baronetcy was conferred on this house in 1629, which is now enjoyed by Sir Arthur Nicolson, as 11th Baronet of that Ilk, whose seat is Grimista, Shetland.

Another branch, that of Sir George Nicolson of Cluny, a judge as Lord Kemnay, received a baronetcy in the person of his son, Sir Thomas, 1700. Sir William, 2nd Baronet, who married the widow of Thomas Burnett of Glenbervie, acquired that estate, which, on the death of the 3rd Baronet, passed in the female line to the present laird, Arthur Badenach Nicolson, 8th of Glenbervie.

94. NICOLSON

OGILVIE

Badge:—Sgitheach geal (Whitethorn, Hawthorn).

THIS clan derives its origin from Gilbert, third son of Gillebride, Earl of Angus. Gilbert assumed the name of his property, which was the Barony of Ogilvie in the parish of Glamis, Forfarshire, of which he had a charter from William the Lion about 1172.

Patrick de Ogilvie appears in the Ragman Roll, and from him descended a line of Ogilvies of that Ilk, which ultimately expired when the branch of Auchterhouse became the stem-family. The founder of this line was Sir Patrick Ogilvie of Wester Powrie, whose descendant, Sir Walter Ogilvie of Auchterhouse, Hereditary Sheriff of Angus, had two sons—(1) Alexander of Auchterhouse, ancestor of the House of Inchmartine; (2) Sir Walter of Lintrathan, Treasurer of Scotland, ancestor of the house of Airlie.

Sir John, 2nd of Lintrathan, had a charter of Airlie 1459, and his son, Sir James, was in 1491 elevated to the Peerage as Lord Ogilvie of Airlie. James, 8th Lord Ogilvie, was created Earl of Airlie by Charles I. in 1639, and, although not heir male, was acknowledged by the king as chief of the surname of Ogilvie, and so recorded in Lyon Register.

During all the troubles of the House of Stewart, the Ogilvies of Airlie stood loyally by the ancient monarchy. For this they suffered much. One of the tragic ballads of the period deals with the burning of " The Bonnie Hoose o' Airlie " by Argyll and the Covenanters. Several representatives of the family were attainted for the part they took in the Risings of 1715 and 1745. In 1778 a pardon was granted to Lord Ogilvie, in consideration of his extreme youth at the time of 1745 ; and in 1826 the Earldom of Airlie was restored to David as 6th Earl. The 9th and present Earl of Airlie is David Lyulph Gore Wolseley Ogilvie, K.C.V.O., M.C. The seats of the Airlie family are Cortachy Castle, on the river South Esk, and the Castle of Airlie.

The Ogilvies of Deskford and Findlater derive from Walter Ogilvie of Deskford, younger son of Sir Walter, 1st of Lintrathan. James, 2nd Lord Ogilvie of Deskford, was created Earl of Findlater, 1638, and in 1701, James, 4th Earl, who passed The Act of Union 1707, and repented it by 1713, was created Earl of Seafield. The Earldom of Findlater expired in 1801, but the latter has devolved on the Countess of Seafield. From Ogilvie of Dunlugas, cadet of Deskford, sprang George, the " wicked Lord Banff," of Forglen, " of very evill life," who, under a curse, was burnt to ashes in his castle of Inchdrewer ; only his shoe-buckles remained unconsumed.

95. OGILVIE

RAMSAY

SIMON DE RAMSAY lived in the Lothians in 1140, and William de Ramsay, probably his descendant, swore fealty to King Edward I. for his lands of Dalwolsy now Dalhousie in 1296. He afterwards joined King Robert Bruce. His son Alexander defended Dunbar against the English in 1338, and was later made Sheriff of Teviotdale. This appointment offended William Douglas, Knight of Liddesdale, and he took the first opportunity of capturing Ramsay, whom he imprisoned and starved to death in Hermitage Castle in 1342. His descendant, Sir Alexander Ramsay, had several sons. The second, Robert, was probably ancestor of the Ramsays of Cockpen and Whitehill ; the eldest son, Alexander, carried on the main line of the family. His great-grandson James was father of George, created Lord Ramsay of Melrose in 1618, which title he had changed to Lord Ramsay of Dalhousie in 1619. William, 2nd Lord Ramsay and son of the 1st Lord, was created Earl of Dalhousie in 1633. George, 8th Earl of Dalhousie, had seven sons—George, the eldest, became 9th Earl. William, the second son, succeeded to the estates of the Panmure family, and assumed the name and arms of the Maules. The 9th Earl died in 1838, and was succeeded by his son James, 10th Earl, who became Governor-General of India, and was created Marquis of Dalhousie in 1849. Dying without male issue in 1860, the Marquisate became extinct, but the Earldom reverted to his cousin. William Ramsay, or Maule, referred to above was created Baron Panmure in 1831, and died 1852. His son, Fox Maule, 2nd Baron, succeeded as 11th Earl of Dalhousie, but died without issue 1874. George, 12th Earl, was the son of the Hon. John Ramsay, younger brother of the above-mentioned 1st Baron Panmure. He died 1880, and his great-grandson, John Gilbert, is the 15th and present Earl and chief of the Ramsays.

A Sir John Ramsay, whose parentage is uncertain, was created Lord Bothwell about 1485. He was a favourite of King James III., and narrowly escaped being hanged at Lauder. In 1488 he was forfeited. His son, William, was father of Sir Gilbert Ramsay of Balmain, created a Baronet in 1625. The 7th Baronet died without issue, and the representation passed into female line to a cadet of the Burnetts of Leys, from whom derive a title created anew in 1808, which is now held by Sir Alexander, 6th Baronet.

The Rev. Andrew Ramsay, a younger brother of the 1st Baronet of Balmain, was grandfather of Sir Andrew Ramsay of Abbotshall, who was created a Baronet in 1669, but died without issue 1709.

The Ramsays of Bamff descend from Neis de Ramsay, Physician to Alexander II., who lived in 1232. His descendant was created a Baronet in 1666, whose representative is Sir James, 11th Baronet.

John Ramsay of Whitehill was created a Baronet in 1665, but the title expired on the death of the 5th Baronet in 1721.

The chief's principal seat is Dalhousie Castle, Midlothian, now used as a school, and Brechin Castle is the Earl's usual residence.

96. RAMSAY

ROBERTSON

(CLANN DONNACHAIDH)

Slogan :—Garg'n uair dhuisgear (Fierce when roused).

Badge :—Dlùth Fhraoch (Fine-leaved Heath) or An Raineach mhór (Bracken).

THE chiefs of Clan Robertson are descended from the Celtic mormaers of Atholl, through Conan de Glenerochie, a son of Henry, Earl of Atholl. They bore the name *de Atholia* until Duncan, 5th of Glenerochie, who led the clan in support of the Bruce at Bannockburn, founded the *Clan Donnachaidh*, for whose grandson, Robert *Riach*, the estates were erected into the Barony of Struan, 1451. His son took the name of Robertson, which became thereafter that of the family and clan.

In later centuries Clan Donnachaidh and its chiefs were noted for their intense loyalty to the Stewarts. During the Civil War a regiment was raised for Charles I. by the Tutor of Struan, and Alexander, 17th of Struan, celebrated as " The Poet Chief," first joined Viscount Dundee in support of James VII. in 1688, and consequently had his estates forfeited, but was pardoned 1703. He again was " out " in both 1715 and 1745, and died 1749. His sister Margaret Robertson, 18th of Struan and Chief of the clan, recovered the estates, which the government, however, seized from her cousin, the 19th Chief.

In ancient days the chiefs had castles in Rannoch and at Invervack, near Struan ; later, and up to about 1860, their principal residence was Dunalastair, or Mount Alexander, magnificently situated at the foot of, and in full view of, Schiehallion, in Rannoch. The burial places are at Struan and Dunalastair.

Miss Jean Rosine Robertson in 1910 succeeded her brother, Alasdair Stewart Robertson, 23rd of Struan, in the chiefship and in the estate of Rannoch Barracks, at the extreme west end of Loch Rannoch, on which is some of the finest fishing in the Highlands. The Barracks was originally built for the troops stationed there after " the '45." It was afterwards converted into a residence, but the estate has all been sold.

The oldest cadet family of Struan were the Robertsons of Lude ; others are the Robertsons of Inshes, Kindeace, Auchleeks, Kindrochit, Strathloch, Ladykirk, Faskally, Blairfettie, Killiehangy, and many other lairdships, chiefly in Atholl and the surrounding parts of Perthshire.

The chief of the clan is styled Struan-Robertson. The late Struan-Robertson next in succession to Miss Robertson of Struan (24th)—who entered religion—was George Duncan Robertson of Struan, 25th Chief, in whose favour the chief arms were matriculated in Lyon Court, 1936. He died 1949, and was succeeded by his eldest son, Langton Robertson of Struan, 26th Struan-Robertson, who resides at Kingston, Jamaica.

A Clan Donnachaidh Society was formed in Edinburgh in 1893.

97. ROBERTSON

ROSE

Badge :—Ròs Màiri Fhiadhaich (Wild Rosemary).

THE family of the chief of this clan, Rose of Kilravock, settled in the county of Nairn in the reign of David I. ; but their first designation appears to have been " of Geddes," in the county of Inverness, Hugh Rose appearing as a witness to the foundation charter of the Priory of Beauly by Sir John Bisset of Lovat in 1219.

His son and successor, also Hugh, acquired the barony of Kilravock by his marriage with Mary, daughter of Sir Andrew de Bosco, by Elizabeth, his wife (who was daughter and co-heiress of Sir John Bisset of Lovat). He was succeeded by his son, William, who had two sons—Andrew, the second, ancestor of Ross of Auchlossan in Mar, and Hugh, his successor, who, in a deed of agreement respecting the Prior of Urquhart and the Vicar of Dalcross, is styled " nobilis vir Hugo Rose, dominus de Kilravock." His son, Hugh, married Janet, daughter of Sir Robert Chisholm, Constable of the Castle of Urquhart, by whom he received a large accession of lands in Strathnairn, etc. The barony of Kilravock was erected by James III. for Hugh Rose of Kilravock in 1474.

Hugh, 16th Baron, entertained Prince Charles and the Duke of Cumberland on 14th and 15th April 1746. He was of Hanoverian sympathies. On the death of Hugh, 18th Baron, he was succeeded by his sister, Elizabeth, Baroness of Kilravock, and recorded as Representer of the Family, Chief of the Clan, who married Capt. Hugh Rose of Brea, and her son, Hugh, became 20th Baron and Chief by lineal descent.

The Barons of Kilravock intermarried with the first families in the North, and filled various situations of high trust and honour. The Castle is an old picturesque building, situated on the bank of the River Nairn. It was built by Hugh, 7th Baron, in 1460. It is still inhabited, and contains much old armour, portraits, and family relics. There is scarcely any family whose charter chest is more amply stored with documents, not only of private importance, but of great antiquarian interest.

The seat of the chief is still the Castle of Kilravock, which has been the residence of the Roses since 1460.

The 24th baron, Lieut.-Colonel Hugh Rose of Kilravock, C.M.G., died 1946, and (young Kilravock having fallen in action) was succeeded by his elder daughter, Anna Elizabeth Rose of Kilravock, 25th Baroness of Kilravock, and the present Chief of the Clan. The family has uninterruptedly occupied this picturesque castle since its erection in the 15th century, and along with which the chiefship has descended in an unbroken line.

98. ROSE

ROSS

Badge :—Aitionn (Juniper).

THIS clan is known to Highlanders as *Clann Aindreas*—Sons of Andrew. It is generally believed that the predecessor of the old Earls of Ross was the eldest son of *Gilleoin na h-Airde*, the ancestor of Anrias, who, again, was the progenitor of the O'Beolans or *Gillanrias*, old Celtic Earls of Ross. The first of the O'Beolan Earls of Ross was *Fearchar Mac-an-t-Sagairt* (Son of the Priest), hereditary Abbot of Applecross. For services rendered to Alexander II., Fearchar was knighted by the king in 1215, and by 1226 he was Earl of Ross. Since a Malcolm, Earl of Ross, existed in 1160 and two lines seem involved, it would appear the earldom really passed in the female line to the Abbot of Applecross. The 5th Earl of Ross (William) died in 1372, leaving an only daughter, Euphemia, who carried the earldom into the Clan Leslie. As the Leslies did not take the name of Ross the chiefship passed to Hugh of Rariches, the Earl's brother. Hugh founded the House of Ross of Balnagowan. At the beginning of the 18th century David Ross of Balnagowan was the last of his race in the direct line. He settled the estate on General Charles Ross, brother of Lord Ross of Hawkhead, a family which, however, was in nowise related to his own, but to whom, in virtue of the settlement and in accordance with the strictly *practical* Laws of Scottish heraldry, the Lord Lyon confirmed the chief arms of Ross. Upon the death, in 1711, of David, the last Ross of Balnagowan, the representation in blood of the O'Beolan Rosses devolved on the Munro Rosses of Pitcalnie. In 1745 the fighting force of the clan was 500 men.

Sir Charles Ross of Balnagowan, 9th Baronet, and by tailzie chief of the clan though not of "the blood," died without issue, 1942, since when the Chiefship has been dormant. Balnagowan Castle, in Ross-shire, is now occupied by his widow, Dorothy, Lady Ross of Balnagowan.

An obituary notice in August 1884 records the death of " Mr George Ross of Pitcalnie, in Ross-shire, and Arnot, in Kincardine, aged eighty-one. Deceased was the last representative of the ancient Earls of Ross, and was chief of the Clan Ross." He was succeeded by a grand-nephew, whose line, on failure of the name in the Balnagowan line, might inherit the chiefship, but Pitcalnie never held it *de jure* or *de facto*. Miss Williamson Ross is understood to be the present representative of the Pitcalnie line.

The surname Ross is from the county name *Ross*, so named from *ros*, the Gaelic for promontory.

99. ROSS

RUTHVEN

THOR, son of Sweyn, a Viking chief, was founder of the race of Ruthven which takes its name from the lands of Ruthven in Perthshire, and an early chief married the heiress of Cameron of Balgarno. Sir William Ruthven of that Ilk was created a peer as Lord Ruthven in 1487, and Patrick, 3rd Lord, is celebrated as the principal perpetrator of the murder of Rizzio, Mary Queen of Scots' Italian secretary. His son, the 4th Lord, was created Earl of Gowrie, 1581, but, having plotted to seize Stirling Castle, he was beheaded three years later, and though his son was restored to the family honours, John, 3rd Earl, became involved in the mysterious " Gowrie Conspiracy," when he and his brother were killed in Gowrie House during an alleged attempt on the person of James VI. and after a Parliamentary inquiry, their peerage was extinguished and the name and arms of Ruthven abolished, whilst the 5th August was appointed an annual day of public thanksgiving. The true explanation of these extraordinary proceedings is a dark secret which has never yet been explained. Dr Patrick Ruthven, the last Earl's brother, escaped to England, and assumed the title of Lord Ruthven, as did his son and heir, who lived until late in the 17th century, after which the direct line of succession became dormant, and the family is now represented by the descendants of the Hon. Alexander Ruthven of Freeland, fifth son of the 2nd Lord Ruthven. His grandson, Sir Thomas Ruthven of Freeland, was created a peer by Charles II., 1651. The dignity of Lord Ruthven of Freeland has, in accordance with the principles of Scots Law applicable, as laid down in the Court of Session, continued in his heirs female, having eventually passed to his daughter Jean, Baroness Ruthven, and afterwards to her niece Isobel, whose son James became 5th Lord Ruthven of Freeland, and Walter Patrick, 10th Lord Ruthven, is the present representative. He has had a distinguished military career, and was created a peer of the United Kingdom, as Lord Ruthven of Gowrie, in 1919. His brother, Sir Alexander, was created Lord Gowrie of Canberra on his appointment as Governor-General of Australia. In 1945 he was created Earl of Gowrie, thus reviving the ancient and historic title of his ancestors.

100. RUTHVEN

SCOTT

Slogan :—" A Bellendaine ! "   *Badge* :—Blaeberry.

UCHTREDUS filius Scoti lived in 1130. He was father of Richard, who is said to have had two sons—Richard, ancestor of the Scotts of Buccleuch, and Sir Michael, ancestor of the Scotts of Balweary. From Richard, the eldest son, descended Sir Richard, who married the heiress of Murthockstone, and died 1320, leaving a son, Michael, father of two sons, Robert and Walter of Synton. Robert's great-grandson was Sir Walter, who had two sons—Sir David of Branxholm and Alexander of Howpaisley. Sir David had two sons : (1) David, whose great-great-grandson, Sir Walter, was created Lord Scott of Buccleuch, 1600 ; and (2) Robert, ancestor of the Scotts of Scotstarvit. The 1st Lord Scott died in 1611, and was succeeded by his son, Walter, who was created Earl of Buccleuch, 1619. Francis, 2nd Earl, left two daughters successively Countesses of Buccleuch. Mary, the elder, married Walter Scott of Highchester—of the Harden line—who in her right became chief and was created Earl of Tarras for life. She died without issue when the peerage and chiefship passed to her sister, Anne, Countess of Buccleuch, who married James, Duke of Monmouth. On their marriage they were created Duke and Duchess of Buccleuch, 1673. The Duke was beheaded, but from them the present line of Buccleuch derives, as the titles of the Duchess were unaffected by her husband's rebellion and execution.

Sir Michael Scott of Balweary was great-grandfather of another Sir Michael, who was known as "the wizard." Sir William Scott, 7th Baronet of Ancrum, died in 1902, when the Baronetcy became extinct (or dormant).

Bellendean, near the head of the Borthwick Water in Roxburgh-shire, was the gathering-place of the Clan Scott in times of war ; for which purpose it was very convenient, being in the centre of the possessions of the chiefs of this name. "A Bellendaine ! " is accordingly cited in old ballad books as their gathering word or war cry, and as the slogan of the Clan Scott appears upon the standard of the "Bold Buccleuch," and is still displayed by his successor the present ducal chief.

Hugh Scott, 11th of Harden, succeeded in 1827 to the Lordship of Polwarth, and his successor, Walter George, is 9th Lord Polwarth and 14th Laird-Baron of Harden, and chief of the Synton branch of the clan.

The present chief of the Clan Scott is Walter, 8th Duke of Buccleuch, G.C.V.O., whose border seat is still the Castle of Branxholm, though the assumption and recording twenty years ago of arms as "Montagu-Douglas-Scott" has broken the hitherto continuous descent of the chief arms of Scott in a manner not realised by the late Duke when so doing.

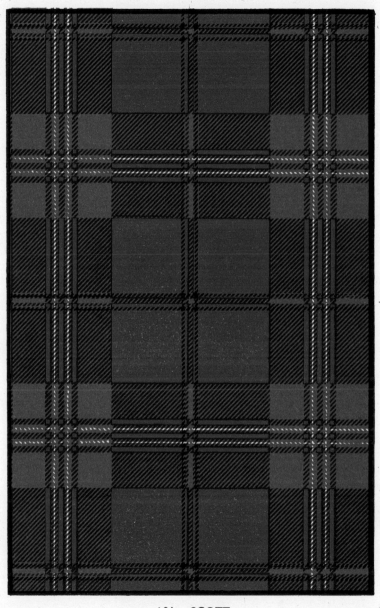

101. - SCOTT

SETON

Slogan :—" St. Bennet and set on ! "   *Badge* :—Yew.

THE noble House of Seton are stated to derive their name from the " sea-town " of Tranent, some miles east of Edinburgh, and about 1150 Alexander de Seton held the lands of Seton Winton and Winchburgh. Sir Alexander Seton of that Ilk engaged, with Sir Gilbert Hay and Sir Neil Campbell, in 1308, to defend the Bruce's rights, and subsequently signed the Barons' Letter asserting the independence of the kingdom in 1320. On the death of his grandson, Sir Alexander (probably fell at Durham 1346), Margaret, his sister, became Lady of Seton, and marrying Alan de Winton, their son William took his mother's name and became Lord of Seton and Tranent, and appears to have been raised to the peerage by James I. during his captivity. Others attribute the peerage creation to his great-grandson, Sir George, in 1445, " ane grit houshaulder all gevin to nobleness," who built the Chapel of Seton.

George, 5th Lord, and brother of one of the Queen's " Four Maries," completed the magnificent Palace of Seton. Mary, Queen of Scots, regarded him as her most faithful and devoted subject. He assisted her escape from Lochleven. His son, Robert, 6th Lord, was created Earl of Winton 1600.

George, 5th Earl, joined the Rising of 1715, and the peerage attainted. He settled at Rome, where he was a member of the Chevalier's Cabinet in 1740. Dying unmarried, 1749, the representation passed to Sir George Seton of Garleton, 3rd Baronet, descended from the 10th son of the 3rd Earl. He died unmarried 1769. The lineal representation of the Setons appears to have passed to his cousin John Seton, whose daughter, Mary Catherine, married John Broadbent, and their grandson, Thomas George Seton-Broadbent, eventually became heir of line of the House of Seton. Of the cadets, the most celebrated were the Earls of Dunfermline, deriving from Alexander, fourth son of the 5th Lord Seton, who became Chancellor of Scotland. Created Lord Fyvie in 1597, he was made Earl of Dunfermline in 1605, and completed Fyvie Castle. His grandson, James, 4th Earl, commanded a troop of horse under Viscount Dundee at Killiecrankie, 1689, so was forfeited as a Jacobite.

Sir Alexander Seton, younger brother of the Laird of Seton, married, in 1408, Elizabeth, daughter and heiress of Sir Adam Gordon of that Ilk. Of his sons, Alexander, the elder, became Earl of Huntly, whilst the second established the House of Seton of Meldrum, from whom descended Sir Alexander Seton, Bt., Lord Pitmedden, a celebrated judge. Alexander Seton, only son of the 1st Earl of Huntly, by his first wife, founded the House of Seton of Touch, Hereditary Armour-bearers to the King, represented by Sir Alexander Seton of Abercorn, 10th Baronet, *cr.* 1663, whilst by a second marriage, the Earl had his successor in the dignity, George, 2nd Earl of Huntly, who took the name of Gordon and carried on the chiefship of that clan.

John, second son of the 4th Lord, married Isobel Balfour, heiress of Carraldstoun, and founded the baronial House of Cariston, now represented by Sir Malcolm Seton, K.C.B., Deputy Under-Secretary of State for India.

102. SETON

SINCLAIR

Badge :—Conasg (Whin or Gorse) ; White Clover.

THIS clan claims descent from Woldernus, Count de St. Clair, in Normandy. Sir Henry St. Clair of Rosslyn supported The Bruce and signed the letter affirming Scots independence. His son was the " kind and true St. Clair " who fell in Spain beside Sir James Douglas and the Bruce's heart. Henry St. Clair, his great-grandson, became through his mother, heir of the Norse Jarls of Orkney, and was recognised as a scion of the Scandinavian blood-royal. He was Lord High Admiral of Scotland, and discovered Greenland. His grandson, William, 3rd and last Prince of Orkney, Chancellor of Scotland, founded the Collegiate Chapel of Roslin 1446, all the tracery of which springs from the celebrated " Prince's Pillar." Being descended from the ancient Earls of Caithness, he was created Earl of Caithness 1455. James III. compelled him to resign the island principality of Orkney. He settled the Earldom of Caithness upon his younger son. From his eldest son descended the Lords Sinclair of Ravenscraig, " chiefs of the blood " of Sinclair until their line failed in 1762 and 1784. Of the Caithness line William, 2nd Earl, fell at Flodden. John, 3rd Earl, was killed during an insurrection in Orkney. John, 4th Earl, was an adherent of Mary, Queen of Scots, and Chancellor of the jury which acquitted Bothwell of Darnley's murder. He died 1583, and had several sons, of whom the most celebrated was George Sinclair of Mey, Chancellor of Caithness. The eldest, John, Master of Caithness, was starved to death by his father in the grim rock-fast Castle of Girnigoe, but was ancestor of the 5th, 6th, and 7th Earls, and of the Sinclairs of Murkill and Ratter. Of these, Alexander, 9th Earl, was, at his death 1765, the last surviving peer who had sat in the Scots Parliament. John, 11th Earl, became Chief of the Clan Sinclair 1784, but dying unmarried 1789, the earldom and chiefship devolved on Sir James Sinclair, 7th Baronet of Mey, as 12th Earl. His grandson George, 15th Earl, died 1889, when James Augustus Sinclair, representative of Robert Sinclair of Durran, third son of Sir William, 1st Baronet of Mey, became 16th Earl and Chief of the Clan Sinclair. His grandson, James Roderick, is now 19th Earl of Caithness.

The Sinclairs of Roslin, Hereditary Gd. Master-masons of Scotland, descended from another son of the 1st Earl of Caithness, and eventually Roslin, the romantic fortress of "the lordly line of high St. Clair," devolved upon Sir James St. Clair-Erskine, 6th Baronet of Alva, 1789, who succeeded in 1805 as Earl of Rosslyn (a dignity conferred 1801 on Lord Chancellor Loughborough), now represented by Anthony, 6th Earl and Baron of Roslin. Sinclair of Herdmanston in 1677 became Lord Sinclair, and is now represented by Archibald, 16th Lord Sinclair.

The Baronets of Dunbeath and Ulbster are cadets of the Earls of Caithness. Sir John, 1st Baronet of Ulbster, is celebrated as founder of the Board of Agriculture and compiler of the Statistical Account of Scotland. Lord Pentland is a cadet of the Dunbeath branch.

103.   SINCLAIR

SKENE

THE founder of the Clan Skene is understood to have been a younger son of Robertson of Struan, and the first documentary evidence of the family is when the representative of the race, John and Patrick de Skene, submitted to Edward I. The lands of Skene were evidently already the property of the House, held allodially or in some connection with the Church or Order of St. John. The Barony of Skene is situated some eight miles west of Aberdeen, and the arms are evidently those of Struan-Robertson combined with the *skenes* or durks which allude to the name of the estate whence the name is derived. Indeed the original *skène*, or tenure symbol of the barony, is still in the family charter chest. The clan is known in Gaelic as *Siol Sgeine*, or *Clann Donnachaidh Mhàr*. The chief's arms are : Gules, three dirks or *skenes* supported by three wolves' heads ; Crest —an arm holding a garland ; Supporters—two Highlandmen (the Lord Lyon's warrant describes the dress in some detail and is of technical importance) ; Motto—" *Virtutis regia merces.*" At Skene House a carving of these arms is one of the earliest detailed representations of Highland dress.

In 1317 King Robert I., by charter, granted to his beloved and faithful Robert Skene the lands and loch of Skene. This was evidently the basis of the Crown tenure as a feudal fief.

The family of Skene of Skene became extinct in the direct line in 1827, when the estates of the family devolved on James, 4th Earl of Fife, nephew of the last Skene of Skene. The representation of Skene of Skene seems to have passed to the family of Skene of Hallyards, descended from Andrew of Auchorie, second son of James Skene, 12th Chief, who died in 1605. Since the Duff heirs of line dropped the name and arms, the chiefship of the Skenes seems now in the Laird of Hallyards ; the family of Prerau, in Austria, whose progenitor was Patrick, second son of Andrew Skene of Auchorie, being the next branch.

Among the notable Scotsmen of the 19th century, William Forbes Skene will hold a foremost place. Descended from the Skenes of Rubislaw he was born in Kincardineshire in 1809, and died in Edinburgh in 1893. He was the author of *Celtic Scotland* (3 Vols.), *The Highlanders of Scotland, The Four Ancient Books of Wales* (2 Vols.), and *Chronicles of the Picts and Scots*. In 1881 he was appointed Historiographer-Royal for Scotland. Sir John Skene of Hallyards, Lord Clerk Register under James VI., was a celebrated lawyer who edited the most important of the early collections of Scottish Acts of Parliament.

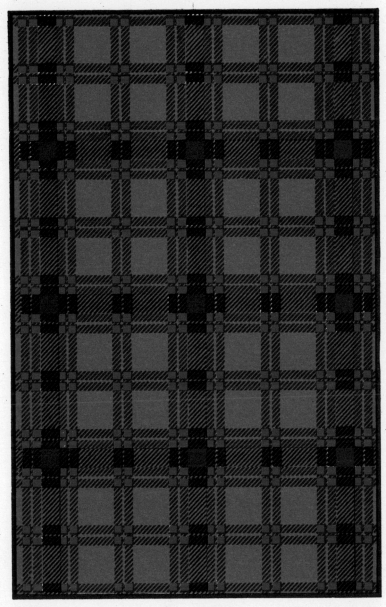

104. SKENE

ROYAL OR STEWART

Badge:—Darag (Oak) or Cluaran (Thistle).

THE Royal House of Stewart, whose traditional descent was of old traced to Banquo, Thane of Lochaber, has now been historically derived from a Breton (and therefore Celtic) noble, Alan, Seneschal of Dol, a scion of the illustrious Counts of Dol and Dinant. Alan the Seneschal, a crusader in 1097, died without issue, and his nephew, Fitz-Flaald, accompanied Henry I. to England and became Sheriff of Shropshire. His third son, Walter, became High Steward of Scotland in the reign of David I. and this was confirmed as an hereditary office by Malcolm IV., 1157. Walter, 6th High Steward, who commanded part of the Scottish army at Bannockburn, married Lady Marjory Bruce, by whom he had an only child, Robert II., eventually King of Scots. On the death of James V., the direct male line of the royal Stewarts failed, but the succession of the house was continued through Mary Queen of Scots' marriage with Henry, Lord Darnley, descended from Sir Alan Stewart, second son of Sir John Stewart of Bonkyl, a younger brother of James, 5th High Steward. James VI. was thus both heir male and heir of line of the House of Stewart, but it was as heir of line that he represented the House of Stewart descending through Lady Marjory Bruce, from the Royal House, and the long lines of our Celtic and Pictish kings. On the death of Prince Charles Edward and his brother, Prince Henry Benedict, the Cardinal Duke of York, the male line of the Royal Stuarts ended, and the Cardinal left his personal heirlooms, including The Coronation Ring and The Jewel of St. Andrew (still worn by His Majesty as Sovereign of the Order of the Thistle), and the " George " (*i.e.* the royal and chivalric jewels which at death are always handed to the sovereign) to George III., thus (in the absence of any *duthus* which he could settle) by Celtic custom nominating him tanist of the old Royal line. At the Scottish coronation the Sovereign was hailed as chief, and the *Ard Righ* (our King) is thus really our High Chief, and Scotsmen, in this sense, a grand clan of very wide dimensions. According to the principle of *tanistry*, this chiefship *of the Royal House* has accordingly passed through George III. and Queen Victoria to the present Royal House of Windsor, and King George VI. is thus Scotland's " Chief of Chiefs," Head of the Celto-Scottish Royal House. The chiefship of the Stewart Clan devolved upon the Earl of Galloway as nearest in blood bearing the name and arms of the House of Stewart. The plain arms of Stewart are in this case really the official arms of the High Steward, and accordingly merged with the Dukedom of Rothesay. The tartan here illustrated, worn by regimental pipers of the Scots Guards, and referred to by H.M. King George V. as " my personal Tartan," was known as the " Royal Tartan," and seems, historically, to be the official tartan of the Royal House of Scotland, rather than a Stewart tartan.

105. STEWART, ROYAL

STEWART, HUNTING

WHILST circumstances suggest that the Royal Stewart tartan is really the tartan of the Scottish Royal House, the green tartan known as Hunting Stewart, which has long been a favourite in Scotland, is that which may properly be regarded as the tartan of the Stewart Clan. Very likely the kings also used it on their own hunting expeditions, when the red sett might have been too conspicuous. Needless to say, the Stewart kings, and, indeed all branches of the Stewarts, were keen sportsmen, devoted to hawk and hound. They had innumerable hunting forests and hunting seats, but the best known to-day is Balmoral, in the Braes o' Mar. The Celtic kings had in early times a hunting seat at *Cean drochaid*, some miles farther up the river from Balmoral, where our King and Queen, still following old customs of our Celtic king-chiefs, spend the season of the "Autumn Hunting" (so picturesquely described by Taylor, the "Water Poet") amongst the Highland hills.

In this connection it may be stated that the first indisputable reference to Highland tartan occurs in the *Accounts of the Lord High Treasurer of Scotland* in August 1538. These accounts contain the following items :—

"Item, in the first for ij elnis ane quarter elne of variant *cullorit velvet* to be the Kingis grace ane *schort Heland coit*, price of the elne vj. lib. ; summa XIIJ. lib. Xs.

"Item, for iij. elnis of *Heland Tartane* to be *hoiss* to the Kingis grace, price of the elne IIIJs. IIJd. ; summa, XIIJs."

These articles formed part of the dress worn by James V. when hunting in the Highlands.

On the death of the Cardinal of York, and the heirs of line and tailzie *not having taken the name of Stewart*, the Stewart chiefship passed, according to principle, to the nearest heir male, George, 8th Earl of Galloway, as lineal descendant of Sir John Stewart of Bonkil, second son of Alexander, 4th Lord High Steward. Of this line, Alexander Stewart, 6th of Garlees, was elevated to the peerage as Lord Garlees in 1607, and Earl of Galloway 1623.

The *red* Stewart tartan appears to have been known originally as "the Royal Tartan," and has been described by H.M. King George V. as "my personal Tartan," and devolves with the Crown as *Ard Righ* and "Chief of Chiefs" —the Head of the whole Scottish "Clan" or family.

The hunting tartan is therefore regarded as that of the *Stewart Clan*, whereof Randolph, 12th Earl of Galloway, is now chief. His seat is Cumloden, Newton-Stewart, Galloway. There is a Stewart Society, of which the Earl is president.

106. STEWART, HUNTING

STEWART OF APPIN

Slogan :—" Creag an Sgairbh " (" The Cormorant's Rock "), on which is built Castle Stalker). *Badge* :—Darag (Oak) or Cluaran (Thistle).

THE Stewarts of Appin form the West Highland branch of the great Royal race of Stewart, and as such, have come to form a branch clan of considerable importance. They derive from Sir James Stewart of Pierston, fourth son of Sir John Stewart of Bonkyl, second son of the 4th High Steward. Sir James of Pierston was killed at Halidon Hill 1333, and his third son, Sir Robert Stewart of Innermeath, was father of two sons, Sir John of Innermeath and Sir Robert of Durrisdeer, who became ancestor of the Stewarts of Rosyth in Fife. The elder son, Sir John Stewart of Innermeath, had also inherited Durrisdeer, but exchanged it with his brother for the Lordship of Lorne. He himself had married Isobel, the younger daughter and co-heiress of John, Lord of Lorne, and their son, Robert Stewart, became Lord of Lorne and Innermeath. His elder son, another Sir John Stewart of Lorne, was murdered 1463, and by his second wife left a son, Dugald Stewart, 1st of Appin, who sought to recover the Lordship of Lorne from his uncle, Walter, Lord Innermeath, by force, but by a compromise he eventually received the lands of Appin. Duncan, 2nd of Appin, was Chamberlain of the Isles to James IV. and Allan Stewart, 3rd of Appin, established the clan by dividing his lands amongst his five sons : 1. Duncan, who became 4th of Appin. 2. John, ancestor of Strathgarry. 3. Dugald of Achnacone. 4. James of Fasnacloich. 5. Alexander of Invernahyle.

This is another instance of a branch-clan being apparently established by erecting five subsidiary families—*i.e.* a great *gilfine.*

Duncan, 7th of Appin, led his clan under Montrose at Inverlochy. Robert, 8th Chief, fought for the Chevalier at Sheriffmuir. Dugald, 9th of Appin, sold the estate in 1765, and was succeeded in the representation by his cousin, Duncan, 6th of Ardshiel and 10th of Appin, whose father, Charles, 5th of Ardshiel, had been an ardent Jacobite, and who led the Clan throughout the Rising of 1745. Ardshiel was sold by Charles, 8th Laird and 12th of Appin, but the title is maintained, and the present chief is Iain A. L. Stewart of Appin and Ardshiel, 15th Chief of Clan Stewart of Appin.

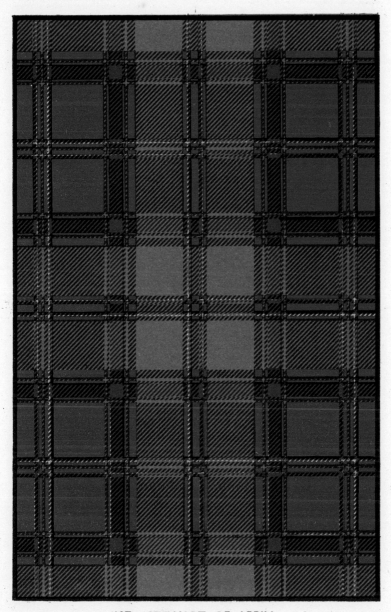

107. STEWART OF APPIN

T

STEWART OF ATHOLL

Badge :—Darag (Oak) or Cluaran (Thistle).

THIS tartan is not to be confused with the dark green tartan commonly known as Atholl tartan, which some have said is purely a district or local tartan used by Atholl men generally, particularly Stewarts and Robertsons, who formed the bulk of the population. It seems, however, in the nature of a Murray tartan and, if so, was used by them as members of Atholl " clan." The tartan here shown is stated to be that of the earlier (Stewart) Earls. Quite possibly it is really the tartan of the still older lines of Earls of Atholl. The ancient Earldom of Atholl was held by several of the Stewarts, notably Robert II., his son, Walter, and his ill-fated grandson, David, Duke of Rothesay. The title was ultimately conferred by James II. on his half-brother, Sir John Stewart of Balveny, son of Joan Beaufort, the widow of James I., by her second marriage to " The Black Knight of Lorn."

On the death of John Stewart, 5th Earl of Atholl, his elder daughter, Dorothea, wife of William, 2nd Earl of Tullibardine, became heiress, and, as Sir John Maclean of Duart explains, the Earl would have become chief of the Atholl branch of the Clan Stewart had he taken the name. He got a grant or confirmation of the Earldom of Atholl, but retained the name of Murray, since associated with the dignity.

The Atholl Stewarts were credited with a fighting strength of 1000 men, and reputed amongst the most disaffected to the Orange and Hanoverian successions. During the reign of William of Orange " 1500 Atholl men as reputed for arms as any in the kingdom " joined the Marquis of Tullibardine to take part with Viscount Dundee, but, on learning that Tullibardine designed to take the opposite side, they at once put themselves under the command of Stewart of Ballechin and set off to join Dundee's forces. In the subsequent battle of Killicrankie they took a leading share. At Culloden, the Atholl men and Camerons formed the right wing, and completely routed the Hanoverian regiments opposed to them.

The tartan here shown is believed to have been the distinctive tartan of these Atholl Stewarts. It is copied from a Highland dress worn by a Stewart from Atholl during " the '45," and still in the possession of a descendant.

Blair Castle.

108. STEWART OF ATHOLL

SUTHERLAND

Slogan :—" Ceann na Drochaide Bige " (Head of the little bridge)

Badge :—Calg-bhealaidh (Butcher's Broom), or Canach (Cotton Sedge).

THE Clan Sutherland derive their name from the Norse name *Sudrland*, Southland, the country being South of Caithness or *Galluidh, i.e.* " country of the promontory." The chiefs of the Clan Sutherland are descended from Freskin, ancestor of the Murrays. Hugh, son of William, son of Freskin, became—how, it is not known— lord of much land in Sutherland. His son, William, was created Earl of Sutherland about 1235. William, 3rd Earl, signed the Letter to the Pope 1320. Kenneth, 4th Earl, was one of the leaders of the Scottish Army at Halidon Hill 1333. William, 5th Earl, was father of Robert, 6th Earl, and Kenneth Sutherland of Drumoy, ancestor of the House of Forse. John, 8th Earl, became insane 1494, but had two legitimate children, John, 9th Earl, who suffered from his father's malady, and dying 1514 was succeeded by his sister Elisabeth, Countess of Sutherland, who married Adam Gordon, second son of the 2nd Earl of Huntly, who in her right became, in Scots Law, Earl of Sutherland. The Gordon earls did not take the name of Sutherland, and accordingly, as Sir Æneas Macpherson points out, remained cadets of the House of Huntly. George, 15th Earl, proposed to take the name of Sutherland, but was taken bound by the 1st Duke of Gordon to use the surname of Gordon only. William, 16th Earl, however, did so, and was duly recognised as chief of the Sutherland Clan. He supported George II. and was almost captured by the Jacobites. William, 17th Earl, left an only daughter Elisabeth, who, after a celebrated litigation, was in 1771 declared Countess of Sutherland. She married George Leveson-Gower, afterwards Marquis of Stafford and Duke of Sutherland in 1833. The Duke and his Duchess-Countess, were responsible for many improvements in the County of Sutherland, but the alterations, however well-intentioned, led to criticism which might perhaps have been obviated by more careful appreciation of Celtic sentiment. The Ducal line now bear the name Sutherland-Leveson-Gower, and George Granville, 5th Duke and 21st Earl of Sutherland, is in Gaelic styled *Morair Chat*. His seat is Dunrobin Castle. After the succession of the Countess in 1514, the male representation and rank of " chiefest cadet " fell to Sutherland of Forse, an estate which came to this branch in 1408 ; and in 1738 John, 13th of Forse, duly received the arms with the appropriate difference. His son, George, 14th of Forse, unsuccessfully claimed the Earldom of Sutherland in 1771. John W. Sutherland of Forse, who continued using arms as eldest cadet, died 1909. In 1928 the undifferenced Sutherland arms were awarded *pro indiviso* to his daughters by Lord Lyon Swinton, a form of " joint " matriculation negatived by the Court of Session in 1941. This conflicts with the awards of arms to the 16th Earl in 1718 and *en surtout* for the 2nd Duke in 1838. The arms with tressured augmentation being entitled to precedence, the Duke of Sutherland, representing the original heiress and holding the name, heritage and dignities of the race, seems (saving objections about the name "Leveson-Gower ") chief of the clan according to the old Law of Arms in Scotland.

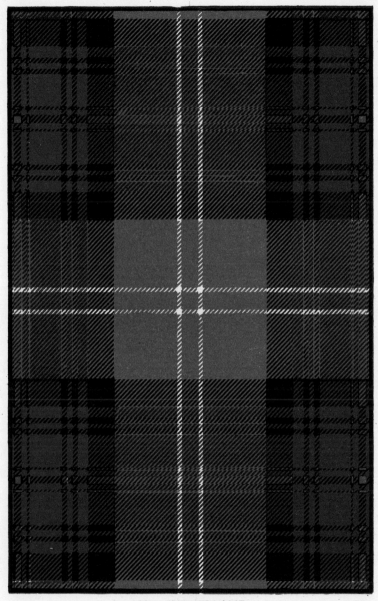

109. SUTHERLAND

URQUHART

Badge :—Lus-leth-an-t-Samhraidh (Wallflower, Gillyflower).

THE Urquharts of Cromarty were Hereditary Sheriffs of the old County of
Cromarty, much of which originally belonged
to them and whilst their genealogy has been
deduced from Adam, the descent of Urquhart
of Cromarty, the principal family of the clan,
commences as authentic history with William
Urquhart of Cromarty, Sheriff of the County
under Robert the Bruce. Alexander Urquhart, 7th Sheriff of Cromarty,
married Beatrix Innes of Auchintoul, and had two sons, of whom the
younger, John Urquhart, founded the House of Craigfintry. Walter,
the elder, was grandfather of Sir Thomas Urquhart of Cromarty,
knighted by James VI. His son, Sir Thomas Urquhart of Cromarty,
was the celebrated Cavalier who was one of the most quaint authors of
the 17th century, and is world-famous as the translator of *Rabelais*,
as well as many other curious works, including *The True Pedigree and
Lineal Descent of the Most Ancient and Honourable Family of Urquhart
since the Creation.* He was captured at Worcester, and dying unmarried
about 1660, was succeeded by his brother, Sir Alexander, at whose
death the representation passed to the line of Urquhart of Craigfintry,
in the person of John Urquhart of Craigston, great-grandson of the
celebrated Tutor of Cromarty. The direct succession of this line also
expired in 1741 upon the death of his grandson Colonel James Urquhart,
when the heirs female having deserted the " name," the chiefship
passed to the nearest heir male, William Urquhart of Meldrum, lineally
descended from Patrick Urquhart of Lethenty, second son of the Tutor
of Cromarty, being his eldest son by Elisabeth Seton, heiress of Meldrum.
He was by Lyon Court Decree 1741, adjudged chief of the name, and
from him descended Major Beauchamp Colclough Urquhart of Meldrum, who died from wounds received at Atbara 1898, since when the
name, arms, and chiefship of Urquhart have been dormant.

Meldrum House, in Aberdeenshire, has belonged uninterruptedly to
the descendants of the family of Meldrum of that Ilk, whose first
ancestor was Philip de Fedarg, living 1236. The Meldrums of Fyvie,
and the Meldrums of Cleish, in Kinross, to which belonged *Squyer
Meldrum* of Sir David Lyndesay's poem, were branches of the baronial
house of Meldrum of that Ilk.

110. URQUHART

WALLACE

THERE are various derivations given for the name Wallace; *e.g.* that it comes from the Latin form Wallensis or Walensis (cf. burg-ess from burg-ensis, and Francis). Wallensis is parallel to Anglo-Saxon Weallise or Welsh now. The surname Waleis or Galeis was common in England about 1300, when Henry Waleis was Lord Mayor of London. The English form is now Wallis Walays in 13th century), which means simply "Welsh-man." But in Scotland Walensis meant a Stratnclyde Briton, as we see from the old proclamations of Kings Malcolm and William to the people of the Glasgow Diocese (from Clyde to Solway), which is headed thus: "*Francis et Anglicis, Scotis et Galweiensibus et Walensibus*"; that is, "To Norman, French and English, Scots (coasts of Ayrshire, etc.), Galloway men and Britons (of Strathclyde)." The Scottish Wallace is, therefore, a native name meaning a Strathclyde Briton, and not, as is usually supposed, a Welshman coming in the train of the Norman French. The name arises naturally in the 13th century on the western borders—Ayrshire and Renfrew—of the old Welsh kingdom, which now marched with the coasts of these counties and Galloway. Richard Wallace of Richardston (Riccarton), 1165–73, is the founder of the race. His grandson, Adam Walays, 3rd of Riccarton, had two sons —Adam, 4th of Riccarton, Ayrshire; and Malcolm, who received the lands of Elderslie and Auchinbothie, Renfrewshire, and was the father of Scotland's great hero, Sir William Wallace of Elderslie, born 1274/6. He was captured in 1305, tried for treason, and hanged at Smithfield, London, 23 August 1305.

The Wallaces of Craigie, Ayrshire, are descended from the said Adam Wallace, 4th of Riccarton, uncle of Sir William Wallace. His descendant, Sir John Wallace of Riccarton, married Margaret, daughter and heiress of Sir John Lindsay of Craigie. His son, Adam Wallace, was designated of Craigie.

The second line of Wallaces of Ellerslie descend from the youngest son of the said Sir John Wallace of Riccarton, and in 1888 Captain Henry Ritchie Wallace established in Lyon Court his representation of the House of Wallace in Scotland. His son, Col. Hugh Robert Wallace of Busbie and Cloncaird, was succeeded in the chiefship by his sons Hugh, and Malcolm, last of Busbie, who died 1948, when the chiefship passed to his cousin (nephew of Henry Ritchie Wallace), Col. Patrick F. H. Wallace of that Ilk, now *The Wallace*, Chief of the Name, who resides at Corsee, Nairn.

III. WALLACE

WEMYSS

THE family of Wemyss is descended from a younger son of the Macduffs, the old Earls of Fife, who obtained from his father the lands of Wemyss, in Fife, about 1160. His descendant, Sir John Wemyss of Reres and Kincaldrum, living 1373, had three sons: David, his successor; Duncan, from whom descended the Wemyss of Reres; and Alexander, ancestor of Wemyss of Kilmany. The grandson of the eldest was Sir John Wemyss, whose fourth son, Thomas, was ancestor of Wemyss of Wintbank. The eldest son of Sir John was Sir David, who fell at Flodden 1513, leaving three sons: Sir David, James, and Robert of Caskyberry and Lathrisk. The eldest son, Sir David, was father of Sir John; James, ancestor of Wemyss of Caskyberry; and David, ancestor of Wemyss of Pitkennie. Sir John was father of Sir David; John, from whom descended Count Wemyss; and Gavin, ancestor of Wemyss of Wintbank. The eldest son, Sir David, had: (1) Sir John, father of Sir John, created a Baronet in 1625, Lord Wemyss of Elcho in 1628, and Earl of Wemyss, Lord Elcho and Methil in 1633; (2) Sir James, ancestor of Wemyss, Baronet of Bogie; (3) David, from whom descended Wemyss of Fingask; (4) Henry, ancestor of Wemyss of Foodie; (5) Patrick, from whom descended Wemyss of Rumgay and Craighall. The 2nd Earl died in 1679, leaving a daughter, Margaret, Countess of Wemyss, who married her kinsman, Sir James Wemyss of Caskyberry, who was created Lord Burntisland in 1672. Their son, David, became 4th Earl, and married the eldest daughter of the Duke of Queensberry. He was Captain-General of the Royal Archers in 1715, a position also held by his son, James, 5th Earl, who was officially recognised by Lyon Court as representative of the family and of the ancient Earls of Fife. His eldest son, Lord Elcho, was Colonel of Prince Charlie's Horse Guards and was attainted. The peerages were assumed by Francis, the second son, who succeeded to the estates and took the name and arms of Charteris of Amesfield under entail. His descendant, Francis David Charteris, is now 10th Earl of Wemyss. The Wemyss estates, along with the arms and chiefship of the race, devolved on the 5th Earl's third son as James Wemyss of Wemyss, to whose great-great-great-grandson, Captain Michael Wemyss of Wemyss, the undifferenced arms of the family were confirmed by Lyon Court in 1910, as nearest heir of line and tailzie bearing the name of Wemyss. He is accordingly the present chief. His seat is Wemyss Castle, in Fife.

112. WEMYSS

INDEX

Abbots, hereditary, 4
Aberdeen, plaids, 6
Alteration, 19, 42, 44, 57
Address, forms of, 63–65
Alloa, 3.
Anstis, Garter, 42
Archers, Royal, 10, 11, 13
Ardmillan, Lord, 18, 21
Argyll, Council of, 67
Armorial Bearings, 58
  relative to Chiefship, 22, 25, 28 n. 2, 26, 29, 35, 42, 47, 58
  relative to Clan, 24, 26, 27, 35, 60
  privileges of Clansmen, 57, 60, 69, 70
  grant of, 29, 60
  settlements of, 40, 44

Badges, cap, 27, 32, 60
  plaid, 6.
Banbury, Earl of, 54
Baron, relative to chiefship, 30
  official Rod, 30
  precedence, 42
  Courts, 16
  Supporters, 59
Baronetcy, 31, 50
Bellendaine Standard, 28
Bell's Lectures, 27
Bogus chiefs, 32
Brentano, F. Funk ; definition of feudalism, 15, 50

Campbell of Ashomel, 55
  of Craignish, 54
  of Dunstaffnage, 21
  of Innerneil, 34, 35
  tartan, 7
Cap, Chieftain's, 32, 33
Captain, 38
Cawdor, 45
Ceann Cath, distinct from chief, 50
Chief, 26
  of clan and family synonymous, 26, 36, 44, 50
  Mackenzie's definition, 26
  admits clansmen, 57
  gives certificates of descent, 57
  " Highland," 20
  Inauguration of, 29, 30
  Titles of, 51
  Gilfine, 33
Chiefship, a dignity, 29, 42, 50, 54
  Esquire, 29
  in Royal Prerogative, 51
  delegated to King of Arms,
  determination of, 43, 49
  determined ministerially or judicially, 36, 50–54
  declaration of, test, 51
  for publication and use, 24, 45n7, 53
  related to arms, 27, 28, 33, 50
  successive, 35
  patriarchal nature, 35
  descendable to females, 46, 47
  a heritable not elective subject, 43, 44, 50
Chieftain, 31

Chieftain 31—recorded in Lyon Court, 32
  representer, 33
  of gatherings, 33
  cap, 33, 34
  of district, 32, 54, 56
  origin, 32, 47
Chymmis, 26
Clan, definition of, 3, 25
  nature of, 18, 24
  feudalised heritable subject, 25, 36
  honourable corporation, 36, 43
  Recognised by Imperial Parliament, 21
  same as family, 24, 26, 41, 50
  Council, 16, 55, 67
  Allan, 39
  Chattan, 45
    chiefship declaration, 23, 51
  Chisholm, 34, 35
  Grant, 35
  Ronald, 38, 43
Clearances, 17, 26
Colonsay, Lord, 20
Commendation, 32
Commander of the Clan, 50
Community, Honourable, 24
Companies, Clan, 18
Coulton, G. S., 13
Council, Clan, 16, 55, 67
Court of Session, no jurisdiction in designations or pedigrees, 22, 54
Cowley, Countess, 31
Craig, Sir Thomas, 30, 38
Crests, women may inherit, 60
Cunningham, Aubrey, 14, 16
Cunningham *v.* Cunningham, 33, 41
Crown Superior of Chief, 25

Dallaway, J., 31
Death Duties, inimical to clanship, 66
Declaration of Chiefship, 23, 51
  of Pedigree, 35
Dearbhfine, 36
  like " Royal Family," 37
Designations, 51, 61–63
Determination of Chiefship, 44, 50
  Burkes, 41
  Clan Chattan, 51, 210
  O'Neil, 29
  by Lyon, 50
  Ministerial Act, 51
Dickinson, W. C., 30
Dignity, 29, 42, 45, 50, 54
Donald, Clan, 47, 51, 174
Duin-vassal, armigerous Clan Society a corporate, 55
Dunedin, Lord, 21 n. 1, 22 n. 2, 28 n. 2, 50

Edinburgh; tartan used in, 12
  Lord Provost, 21
Elected Chief becomes hereditary, 43
Election, competent only in limited circumstances, 44
  by landed men, 44
Elgin, highland city, 6
Erskine, Sir Alexr., Declaration by, 50
Esquire, related to chief, 29, 42

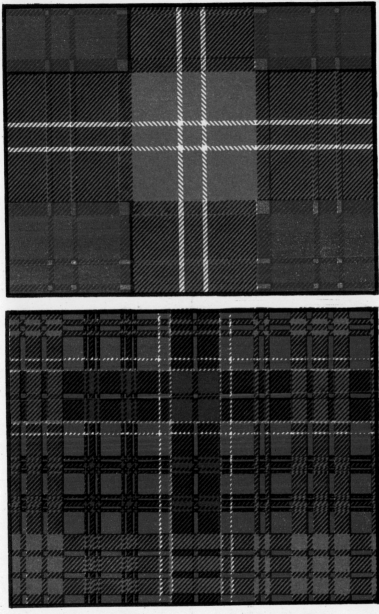

113. LENNOX   114. HUNTLY

115. JACOBITE   116. STRATHEARN